Messengers of Hope

The Walk-in Phenomenon

Books by Carol E. Parrish-Harra

Messengers of Hope

The Walk-in Phenomenon

by
Carol E. Parrish-Harra

SPARROW HAWK PRESS
TAHLEQUAH, OKLAHOMA

Library of Congress Cataloging-in-Publication Data
Parrish-Harra, Carol E.
Messengers of Hope—The Walk-in Phenomenon
     An autobiography including a walk-in experience, guidance, ageless
     wisdom, spiritual teachings, prophecies, astrological data, community
     building and living.

ISBN 0-87613-079-1: $19.95
1. Spirituality, 2. Walk-ins, 3. Ancient wisdom teachings, 4. Babaji,
5. Sai Baba.

Editor: Mary Beth Marvin
New cover and book design: Mary Beth Marvin and Michelle Miller Killian

Library of Congress Catalog Card No. 0-945027-19-2

Rev. Carol E. Parrish-Harra, Ph.D.
Academic Dean, Sancta Sophia Seminary
Light of Christ Community Church
11 Summit Ridge Drive
Tahlequah, Oklahoma 74464

Dedicated to those
who have eyes to see
and ears to hear

Editor's Note. An asterisk indicates terms that may be new to some readers, terms which will be found in *The New Dictionary of Spiritual Thought* by this author (Sparrow Hawk Press, 1994), a companion volume of over 1,100 (now being expanded to over 2,000) words, concepts, and symbols helpful to this work. Its definitions relate to spiritual sciences, esoteric Christianity, astrology, Agni Yoga, metaphysics, ageless wisdom teachings, and more. Available from Sparrow Hawk Press.
lccc@sanctasophia.org   www.sanctasophia.org

Contents

List of Illustrations

Foreword
by Kenneth Ring, Ph.D.

When the author of this book called me to request that I contribute a foreword, I was initially very flattered to be asked. But when she went on to inform me that her book dealt with her life as a "walk-in," shudders of second thoughts quickly arose in my mind and I began to wonder whether I should retract my consent before it was too late.

I was familiar with Ruth Montgomery's concept of a walk-in from reading her book, *Strangers Among Us*: supposedly a highly developed spiritual entity who, usually during a spiritual or near-death crisis, enters into and takes over the functioning of a human being who no longer wishes to live. As a scientist, I found it too *outre* to give it much credence. I also knew that Carol Parrish-Harra had been specifically identified as a walk-in by Ruth Montgomery in her later book, *Threshold to Tomorrow*. Though I have to admit, I found many of Mrs. Montgomery's case histories in that book to be utterly fascinating, I still had difficulty swallowing her walk-in interpretation of her material. I didn't even like the term she chose; it smacked, I thought, of tabloid journalism. I am just a snob about such things, I suppose. Nevertheless, I had to concede, whatever the explanation of the phenomenon Ruth Montgomery had identified, she was certainly onto *something*.

The reason I felt so secure in that judgment was, frankly, because of my own recent work in near-death studies. At the time Carol called me, I had finished about two-thirds of my book, *Heading Toward Omega: Near-Death Experiences and Human Evolution,* which deals chiefly with the transformation in the lives of near-death survivors following their near-death experiences (NDEs) and with the larger, collective meaning of those transformations for humanity as a whole. And in many of Ruth Montgomery's cases that involved near-death crises, she was finding precisely the same kind of dramatic life changes in her subjects as I had with my own near-death survivors. Indeed, several of the people she identified as walk-ins provided even stronger and more compelling evidence of extraordinary transformations than some of my own best examples! So while I found myself dubious about her interpretation, I was decidedly envious of her case history material. In any case, parallels between her findings and mine simply were too plain to be denied.

So I capitulated and told Carol, "Yes."

It wasn't only because of my inability to dismiss the relevance of Ruth Montgomery's findings from my mind that I accepted Carol's invitation. It was also—and primarily, I think—that I could in no way dismiss *Carol.*

Although she and I have only met once—and then briefly at a conference—we have been corresponding for some years. I first heard from Carol in 1980 when she wrote to describe her 1958 near-death experience—an event, as this book now makes clear, that was the turning point in her life. I was deeply moved by reading her powerful account of this experience and wrote to her to express my appreciation for her beautiful narrative. As we corresponded, I grew familiar with Carol's work and life. With great interest and admiration, I followed her developing career, albeit at a distance. Even in those early days of our friendship, it was already clear to me that Carol was a woman whose all-too-evident gifts—intellectual, psychic, and spiritual—were bound to lead her to a position of national prominence in New Age circles. And her recent accomplishments as a writer, lecturer, and minister have certainly established her reputation at that level beyond any question. Yet, it is in this book that Carol reveals for the first time the *basis* of her remarkable gifts which are responsible for her influential role in the

New Age Movement. When I read her story—the story of her life *since* her near-death experience—I knew that, despite my wavering, it was, after all, right for me to write this foreword. It was Carol herself who had finally dissolved all doubts.

Not only is this an important book for reasons I will shortly make clear, it is a deeply courageous one. Carol's story is of course unique but it fits a *pattern* I have observed in quite a number of near-death survivors I know. Most have been reluctant to speak too freely of some of the inner changes they feel were triggered by their own NDEs. The fear of disbelief, ridicule, or even scorn is still a sensitive issue for many near-death survivors, and it is a factor that tends to make them reticent to speak out about the deeper implications of their experience. Carol Parrish-Harra, however, has now come along to speak for the many who have been silent. And the spiritual growth process she describes and the conclusions to which it has led her will, I'm sure, serve as familiar points of references for many others who have been thrust through an NDE or some other spiritual experience into an entirely new mode of being.

Carol has come to a deep understanding of the meaning of her own experience through a process of personal maturation which has led her to reflect upon its broader significance for all humanity. Through my own work with hundreds of near-death survivors, I have been forced to grapple with precisely the same issues that Carol has had to confront and have *independently reached a conclusion that is virtually identical to hers*. Carol's comes out of the matrix of her own life; mine derives from my research data, but on this matter we speak as though with a common voice.

I will not spoil your reading by divulging here any of Carol's own views nor the way in which they are disclosed here. I will only say that her story is packed with spiritual events and personages that will keep you deeply absorbed as her personal odyssey unfolds. Neither will I comment upon the strictly metaphysical portions of her book except to say that those who hunger for metaphysical truths will find much to chew on here. You will have to make up your own mind of course whether Carol is indeed a walk-in or has perhaps simply come into her own authentic being to which her pre-NDE life had not granted expression.

Actually, Carol prefers the term "messenger" to that of walk-in—and so do I. To me, it is in fact Carol's messages that constitute the ultimate, pre-eminent value of her book. I am personally convinced, moreover, that it is not only her message but *the common message of the people* with whom I have been working these past six years. As such, it is not just an important message; it is an absolutely *urgent* one which we can no longer afford to disregard. If we hear this information *and heed it,* the future of our life on this planet may be saved from a grim fate so many fear. The fact that Carol speaks for many—eight million adult Americans are now estimated to have had a near-death experience—forces us to consider her words most carefully. Because she shows us how and why we may, indeed must, foster the development of a loving and caring human species on Earth, she is truly a messenger of hope. It is up to all of us to contribute to the realization of the vision Carol has shown us to be within our power.

January 27, 1983
Storrs, Connecticut

Acknowledgments

Certainly the first version of *Messengers* never would have been written without Ruth Montgomery urging me to tell my story. Her friendship continues to bless me. To my dear friend, Rusty Petters, who figured it out, and to my husband, Charles Harra, who has the courage to participate in my life, my eternal love and gratitude.

This volume expands upon the mission I feel I was given during my near-death experience, updating the story of the unfolding work since 1983. I wish to acknowledge the efforts made by the villagers who have joined us—some for short periods, others for years—for they also have caught the vision and contributed so much to the Great Work: especially Lucille and H. J. Perry, Grace Bradley, Betty Carper, Sally Brown, Marjorie Stuth, Charles and Doris Pass. Each of these has spent years anchoring the church, the school, and the village, greeting guests and trying to help others understand what we are all about. My gratitude to the newer stabilizers who take up the work as some of us age: Peggy Stephens, Linda Oliver, Diana Cheek, Bonita Plymale. To others who know I await their arrival, please hurry.

To Liz Nelson, founder of Walk-ins for Evolution (WE), for doing her part, to Ed Hager and his wife Mary, who stabilize many in ways never known by most, to messengers who are daring to plant seeds everywhere—together we give and receive, and we do make a difference.

I hasten to express my appreciation to my ever-faithful editor, Mary Beth Marvin, who catches inconsistencies and joins me in my love of writing and to Michelle Miller Killian for her hours of careful detail to artistic design and for sharing her creative talent with all of us.

May we each fulfill our part in the Great Work!

Introduction

In the first *Messengers of Hope*, 1983, I attempted to describe who I once was and the change to the woman I am now. In the interval, I was engaged in a painful process difficult to explain. Knowing the original Carol "died" and a new being arrived for a special task was lonely, confusing, and frightening. Today, years later, I continue to share this experience, fully aware some question and others scoff. At times, writing about those extraordinary years was very painful. However, I share because the time has come to do so. My thoughts are addressed to those who have *the eyes with which to see and the ears with which to hear.*

"To awaken" is a term commonly used in religious, esoteric, and spiritual teachings. My own religious, esoteric education has made clear the concept expressed by that term: we "wake up" to the fact of God, to the knowledge that we are more than our bodies, emotions, and mind. Ultimately, as *expansion of *consciousness occurs, we integrate these aspects into a wholeness, a harmonious, smoothly operating personality into which spiritual inspiration flows. With this story, I will suggest another dimension, another connotation to "waking up."

A rare phenomenon was addressed in ancient teachings which challenges modern religious thought. In Hebrews 13.2 we read, "Be not forgetful to entertain strangers; for thereby some have entertained angels unawares."

Other lesser-known writings speak of the *hierarchy (or elder brothers of humanity) who guides the Earth from spiritual dimensions by communication with *adepts living on the Earth. Adepts are awakened beings who have mastered the process of integrating personality to provide vehicles through which soul awareness can flow undistorted. These teachings speak of the *"externalization of the hierarchy." This means that from time to time, when humanity's needs are great, some of the elder brothers (adepts) enter physical bodies in order to be of special service to humanity.

In *Strangers Among Us* Ruth Montgomery presented these ideas to the public, coining the word "walk-in" to identify souls coming in to serve humanity in specific ways. Walk-ins enter the body of certain unhappy people—people wishing to die—who give their consent and cooperation at a spiritual level. The departing one is rendering a service to humanity. The new soul who has chosen to enter into the body is prepared to render service as well.

Some readers will remember such a story dramatically told by Lobsang Rampa in a series of books published since 1960 wherein recurring themes stand out. His work supports the thought that Eastern and Western spiritual paths have traits unique to each respective tradition. Yet there consistently remains the reference in each to an agreement between certain beings in which one gives up his/her body to another. In my story of exchange I attempt to share the trauma involved, the reason for such beings coming in, and a plea to humanity to listen.

This change of body inhabitants is believed to be happening more often today. Spiritual wisdom teaches, the universe functions with perfect economy of energy, nothing is wasted. The exchange of which I write may be seen as an application of this law. If we believe all things work together for the good of all, we may imagine the wisdom of incoming souls assuming a body already created by another. The process gains importance at certain historical periods, especially when the incoming soul has a unique mission pertinent to a specific time, such as in the needful era of the third millennium.

Personally I find "walk-in" sensational, not a term I would have chosen, but I trust in its directness. It has gotten the attention of many. I prefer the term "messenger" because I think it acknowledges the reason for such an exchange. I challenge you to ponder the implications laid before you.

In 1982 when Ruth made my name public, I had waited twenty-four years before speaking, and for a good reason; I sought to build the necessary credibility, demonstrating my sincerity and honesty through my daily expression. It is my personal integrity I place before you on these pages. I tell my story, asking for compassion for all those who "wake up" to the multidimensional life, especially for messengers who need encouragement and support.

Many change their names in order to capture more of their personal soul vibration. The first time I was called "Carol Parrish," I knew this was a strong name for public work. Previously, it was as if my personality was not robust enough. Later I will choose the name Carol E. Parrish-Harra. No, the "E" is not a typo—it is a change I prefer.

For years I used Carol W. Parrish-Harra, the "W" because it is my only 5 and I cannot give it up. My birth name was Carol Elizabeth Williams, so the "W" was accurate. Then it was pointed out to me that "E" is a 5 and my real initial too. With two numerologists giving me new ideas and inspiration, I realized "W" brings energies that manifest in extreme highs and lows and "E" would help me move more easily from level to level, somewhat like a ladder. This could make a difference in a life as hectic as mine, especially since I already have a near sun-moon opposition.

I like the name Carol Elizabeth, but it is too long. When combined with Parrish-Harra, a book cover would have little room for a title. Wanting to claim the benefits of the rich variety of letters Elizabeth contains, I decided to use Carol E. Parrish-Harra. I will not change Carol (I have always liked my name) because it is a 22; I value Parrish because it is a 44. I keep Harra because I rejoice in having Charles in my life. So, I reaffirm my lovely birth name. "Elizabeth" has waited patiently for reclamation. In due time, all the influence will be integrated. I am giving up nothing as I continue to grow and change.

God, my Mother and my Father,
Sometimes you hide your face from me
Behind the fog of your clouds.
Sometimes I cannot see because of the darkness.
Then I must find within myself
The Light to show me the Way.
Though clouds come and go,
The sun always shines.
I think it is my challenge to know the sun
beyond the clouds.
Shining in peace, even while it storms.
I seem to find you here, too, within my heart.
Dear God, you are truly everywhere.

November 12, 1981

The Exchange

A secret, once told, is readily known. A mystery revealed may be difficult to comprehend. Once unveiled, it may remain a mystery until, through a gradual inner process, its significance becomes perceivable.

In 1958, at age 23, a great and awesome mystery engaged me in a life process which was to become both bewildering and beautiful, both astonishing and agonizing. Herman Melville wrote that in every person "reside certain wondrous occult properties . . . which by some happy but rare accident . . . may chance to be called forth." This summons occurred during childbirth, when I awoke from anesthesia to a life more unconventional than could be imagined.

Enlightened beings, who, after successfully completing numerous incarnations, have attained sufficient awareness of the meaning of life can forego the time-consuming process of birth and childhood, returning directly to adult bodies.

A Walk-in is a high-minded entity who is permitted to take over the body of another human being who wishes to depart. Since a Walk-in must never enter a body without the permission of its owner this is not to be confused with those well-publicized cases (such as were described in *The Three Faces of Eve, The Exorcist,* et al.) in which multiple egos or evil spirits are

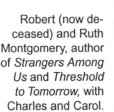

Robert (now deceased) and Ruth Montgomery, author of *Strangers Among Us* and *Threshold to Tomorrow,* with Charles and Carol.

vying for possession of an inhabited body. The motivation for a Walk-in is humanitarian. He returns to physical being in order to help others help themselves, planting seed-concepts that will grow and flourish for the benefit of mankind.[1]

In *Strangers Among Us*, Ruth Montgomery continues her explanation, stating that the personality originally created by the one choosing to leave is intact for the incoming soul, i.e., the body, emotional makeup, intellect, and memory. S/he must now use this already developed form and impress its inherited personality with new vitality, ultimately exchanging old thought and feeling patterns with its own. This conversion is slow and partially responsible for the trauma experienced by the incoming one. Imagine, as well, the puzzling difference felt by those around this changing personality through this transition!

The greatest challenge during this critical period for the walk-in (for clarity I will continue to use this word coined by Ruth Montgomery) is to remember her/his mission, the reason for accepting this role. In addition to formidable humanitarian tasks, a further obligation is usually to complete some responsibilities incurred by the outgoing soul.

Reading Ruth's words, my first reaction is shock; it does not seem constructive to publicize this concept I thought so very hidden. At the same time, here is confirmation of my entry. Questions begin to swirl in my mind: *How will messengers (walk-ins) get people to listen to their wisdom if people think they are so strange?*

Probably there is no better time for such a change to occur than during what today is called the *near-death experience, or NDE, generally a result of a serious illness or accident. Carol—the original builder and creator of the physical, emotional, and mental form—departs in this manner and donates the *vehicle to an incoming soul.

The near-death experience in 1958 totally changes the life of the Carol personality and provides a whole new assurance about the continuity of life. Now I *know* there is a great deal more than earthly life; I have experienced a part of the other, and I remember it. I wish to share with you this secret of mine, a mystery which slowly unfolds.

During the birth of a child, young Carol gets into difficulty when she is given sodium pentothal, a relatively harmless drug for most people. An allergic reaction occurs. When the lungs collapse, the spiritual body separates from the physical and moves to a place of observation near the ceiling. She looks down upon the physical body, not immediately knowing who it is. Watching the hurried efforts of the doctors and nurses, young Carol sees the baby born and realizes she is the woman giving birth. The new infant is a little girl. Hovering near the ceiling like a bobbing balloon, she sees a silvery umbilical cord connecting her to the top of the head of the physical person on the delivery table. It is incredible—impossible to understand!

Suddenly, in a brief moment of a fast, whirling motion, she finds herself rushing toward what seems to be vast space. Her physical self on the table is no longer in view. She is in a cool, peaceful place, with lovely stars, and she feels a dear, sweet serenity. Relief envelops her. The knowledge that she is leaving behind a life of pain, sadness, and impossible tasks helps sweep her rapidly into the embrace of the heavens.

The Carol I am now stands for a brief moment behind young Carol who is before a Being with a magnificent presence—not an exact form, rather a radiation of soft, penetrating light. The voice of a Presence holds the deepest tenderness one could ever imagine: "Look." She peers into an area suddenly enclosed by a large golden frame. A bright falling star moves from an upper corner and continues slowly, gently, across the framed space. As it gets to the lower corner, its light goes out. The voice tenderly says, "Death makes no difference in the pattern. If you are, you always will be." For a critical, rapturous moment, we, as two entities, pause; then she passes into the care of those who receive departing ones. I stand in the light.

In the Bliss

As this loving, powerful Being speaks now to me, my mind is flooded with vast truths far beyond ordinary ability to explain. I understand life and death, and any fear I had as an incoming soul ends instantly. A completeness is contained in the realization that I am being strengthened in order to retain and to share these life-enriching principles, in time.

I experience this Presence for what seems to be endless time. The *Light Being—pure, commanding, all-expansive—is without form as it directs great waves of awareness into my mind. As I respond to the revelations, I know them as Truth. I have a complete trust and comprehension of the profound words I absorb in this moment of preparation.

Whole concepts register within me—waves of thought, ideas vastly greater than young Carol has ever heard. Without effort I absorb clear thoughts in total wholeness. In that Presence, I realize consciousness is life, that human beings are designed to live through much. The living consciousness, veiled by personality, continues forever. I know the purpose of life does not depend on an individual; life has its own purpose. Serenity permeates my being.

An intensity of feeling rushes through me, as if the light that surrounds that Being is cleansing my whole nature, permeating every cell. Absorbing the energy, I sense what I can only describe as bliss. That is such a little word, but the feeling is ecstatic. Love whirls about me, enters my chest, and flows through me. I am immersed in love and awareness for an indescribable time.

In the bright light of this Presence, my courage swells. The wonder of life and the secrets of the universe fill me—revelations I know I will recall at a future appropriate time. I feel buoyant and strong, prepared to allow life to lift and guide me.

This intense rush of energy penetrates every part of my being. As I absorb the pulsating love, bliss becomes my nature. I am whirled downward and outward. The feelings are dynamic, rolling, magnificent, expanding. Time rushes about in great swirls, and there is no place to catch hold. Suddenly, darkness; the heaviness of the physical body makes itself felt. I let myself rest in that darkness—tender, caring darkness like a womb—enfolded in the memory of great love.

Part of me regains physical consciousness; another part holds back, still floating somewhere, trying to hold on to the love, peace, and safety of the minutes just past.

Medical hands turning my body pull me from the inner world of peace. For a brief instant, I remain poised between two worlds, not quite committed to the outer. To my innermost being, I question, *Do I really dare to do this?* The echoing answer is, *Yes!* And it is done.

Excitedly I open my eyes to look into the future; I embrace a new life in the physical body. As the new Carol, I will be able to share, to grow, and to serve. As I open my eyes, relief shows on every face. I tell them, "It was wonderful, beautiful. I am fine!"

"Young lady, you gave us quite a scare!" the doctor scolds. Words rush from my mouth—"I am not who you think I am!"—about the bright light, about how I understood life, about the power and the clarity I experienced. Patting me, the doctor said, "Forget it. People often hallucinate under medication. It does not mean anything. Rest now. You've had quite a time. Just forget it."

As I look from face to face, each set of eyes closes to the words and beauty I try to share. My eyes fill with tears. No one will or can believe. No one even wants to hear what has happened, what wonderful things I have to tell. Tears roll down my cheeks as I turn my face to the wall. I wonder how I will ever do what I am to do if no one will listen.

I close my eyes, trying to recapture that feeling of true peace, the last I will feel for many years. Part of me begins to realize I have a lot to do before I can share my precious experience, much to bear before I can make myself understood. I escape into sleep.

Fighting to Remember

As I sleep for the next few hours following the NDE, my husband is again called to the hospital; they believe I am dying. It is the next day before I grasp the physical world or feel any attachment to it. Later, when I speak of the experience to my husband, my words are prophetic, although I do not know how much so at the time. "Every-thing is different. I am not like I used to be. I know much more now; things are different. I am not the same. I cannot go on as I used to be!"

Home from the hospital with infant Susan, the hours rush by as I care for our children—the new baby, our sixth. With only one child in school, there is too much work for the luxury of time to ponder the experience. A transcendent awareness that such beauty, love, and com-passion exist is always in my consciousness, but it seems out of reach. Not until years later do I appreciate this transition period, when, as an incoming soul, I struggle to reshape the former Carol's personality and complete some of her responsibilities.

My world demands unceasing physical exertion, and I can hardly stagger through each day. The only time I dare stop is to nurse Susan and rock her a bit. Even then, Mary Beth, barely thirteen months, wants to be rocked too. If I do that, what about three-year-old Michael? If not for five-year-old Brenda, I could never have met the challenges waiting for me each day. Her love for the little ones helps me im-mensely. Her tender care of Susan, so tiny and new, allows me time to rock Mary Beth so she will not grow to resent this baby sister.

The exhaustion is not new. Even before the pregnancy, young Carol was reaching the end of her rope. Three months before the NDE, she learned her husband was having an affair with one of her close friends. It became so serious, the two left their families to be together. Al-though both reconsidered and returned home to their mates, the pain of this experience was the last straw. Carol now wanted to die. Believ-ing her seemingly endless efforts were useless and that she would never be able to manage, she had no hope. She and Bill were completely unhappy.

Feeling trapped, she considered taking her life. She discussed prac-ticing birth control, but her husband ridiculed the thought. Question-ing her faith and selfishness, he challenged, "What kind of woman are you?" It is she who had convinced him to convert to Catholicism, who had wanted him to be baptized, and who had him agree to have their children raised in that faith. Calling her "cheap and selfish" and accusing her of daring to "chicken out" of her commitment, his sharp words stung as he yelled, "You had better do some talking to God!" Shaken by such anger, bewildered and exhausted, young Carol agreed to do as he said and made the effort, though often in bed at night she laid awake fervently wishing to be dead.

Now, with the memory of that previous Carol still intact, remembering the struggle of the preceding months, my feeling nature seems disconnected, unable to function. I can find no words to communicate that the most comforting moments of this life came when it appeared to everyone that Carol was dying. How can I explain that?

When I experience dark moments of confusion, I question: *Did this happen because I wanted so much to die? Was my mind so unkind as to tease me by showing me all that beauty, then taking it away? Perhaps I was not worthy of the heaven I was shown, that sublime place of indescribable comfort, love, and peace.* Then other memories, my own, would cover me.

I was so strong in that heaven-place, where I comprehended everything that mattered. I even knew what I was to accomplish! It was completely clear to me that everything has a purpose; things which appear useless or accidental are, in fact, of genuine consequence. I understood life and death had different connotations in that space, a significance beyond traditional perceptions. I knew it was unnecessary to feel anxiety. In the warmth of that total love, Carol had been shown the children and told that all would work out.

As time passes, I realize "It" is teaching me

Even with this exquisite memory, however, it is difficult to cope with myriad daily claims to my energy. As I struggle to retrieve the rhythm of family duties, curious detachment seems to take over. It seems I scarcely know my husband, my children, my parents. My ever-present question: *Will I ever love them again as before?* My incessant internal questioning produces no answers.

Following the NDE, all emotions seem less focused. I know I love the six children, yet daily predicaments appear less critical. I feel no one could believe such feelings. It seems I love any child I see as much as I love my own. I love other people with the same emotion I have for my parents. I am not less protective of my family; I just feel involved with everyone else as well!

I struggle to deny some of these powerful feelings that rush into me because they are so frightening. At other times, I am strangely distant, observing a painful or emotionally charged situation from an impersonal curiosity. In these situations, often the question I ask or the response I make seems out of place. I realize I seem aloof to others at these moments; at other times I get so immersed in feelings of love, I have to struggle to separate myself. Observing these emotional shifts, I watch as personal, possessive feelings give way to an objective, general acceptance.

The shift toward more peace increases as I begin to believe in my own individuality, gradually judging myself less harshly. As I allow and embrace my own feelings, an inner trust emerges. I ponder and find comfort in the pool of inner knowledge. This growing sense of security is a buffer from the painful past of the former Carol, with whose memories I still live.

As I continue the task of clearing the energy of the previous Carol's personality, Bill and I quarrel more often; I become increasingly withdrawn, angry, and silent. Pouting because I cannot put my pain and detachment into words, unable to explain how hurt and tired and lonely I am, I survive by retreating into silence, doing what I must to get through each day. Occasionally, memories from the first Carol's personality cause me to wish to be done with it all.

Even though we attempt to make the marriage work, Bill plainly wants to be free. However, I make it clear that I "talked to God" as he commanded and I will never give him a divorce. He loves the children, but he wants a wife willing to go out with him to drink and laugh and enjoy his interests. I am not the right person, and it is obvious our marriage was a mistake. We do not speak of our incompatibility. Somehow the situation seems out of our hands.

Alone

Young Carol's view of life was quite different from Bill's which was more macho, less a homebody. Although he was proud of having a large family, he was little involved with child rearing, typical for the 1950s and '60s. Carol was a naive and unsophisticated young woman, always struggling for parental acceptance. This came only when her house was neat and her children were clean and good, or when she was outshining other young mothers her parents knew. She worked hard to hear her mother say, "Carol outdoes me. I do not know how she does it all. Her house is so clean, and with all those kids." During this transition, those compliments are still part of what keeps me going, struggling harder on days when there is no escape into silence. It should not be difficult to imagine that with all these pressures, plus the inner inexplicable experiences I was having, most of my energy is expended in meeting the daily challenge of maintaining my sanity.

Powerful psychic experiences begin to occur after the NDE, making me even lonelier, even though they are propelling me toward some improbable, remote future. However, as the personality adapts to the walk-in influence, attitudes and emotions become easier to express.

Moments of touching in to inner events increase, causing me to appreciate young Carol's childhood and grandparents. Daddy Parrot, her grandfather, emigrated from England as a young man and had a perception never voiced. He would tell her, "You can do anything, be anything. Just do it." He was one who knew she was not lying when she "saw" things others did not. Remembering his wise advice sustained Carol and now me, as I undergo this confusing adapting process. He had taught, "It is okay to 'see' what you see. Just do not tell everything you know, and it will be easier." He was right!

Grandmother, a gracious and social woman crippled with rheumatoid arthritis, encouraged the shy, sensitive child in her own way. She told her, "You come from a long line of strong women. Shape up."

The gift of unconditional love given by these grandparents allowed young Carol to tell them about those things she felt and saw but kept secret from others. In this trying transitional time, I appreciate their recognition that young Carol was psychically sensitive.

A few months after Susan's birth, another profound psychic occurrence takes place at Mass. As communion time approaches, the bells ring. This is my favorite moment: The priest holds the Host high in the air. I strike my breast: *Dear God, how I love thee, how I love Jesus, how I adore thee!* Suddenly, the ceiling seems to open up! A rich, dazzling love explodes within me. As my eyes fasten on the Host, it shatters into light—colors leaping, dancing, rays flashing from wall to wall.

The church is filled with breathtaking brilliance, proclaiming the power of the Mass and the Host, beyond doubt.

I cannot move; my body and eyes are rigidly fixed. Unable to slide back onto my seat, people have to climb over me to go to communion. I remain kneeling, transfixed, ecstasy flowing through my body and my mind. I have no idea where the brilliance is coming from, nor do I know what is happening to me. I can only be with this power, kneeling there until the service is over.

Afterward, the priest comes to see if I am all right. He tells me to get up and go home. I try to talk, but only tears come. That convinces him I should leave immediately and without talking. Obviously he does not know what has happened to me. Subsequently, when I try to talk with him about the experience, his response to my questions intimidates me. He really does not understand. I wonder, *Am I too crazy or ignorant to be heard?* It is unbelievably difficult. I suspect my husband and priest are right: I had better get a grip on myself or I will end up in a hospital.

New experiences continue to present fresh challenges. One day, while praying, I feel a wave of energy move through me. My physical body becomes rigid in response. A soft sound is coming from my lips, almost a hum, and then I feel an *out-of-body, rushing bliss. It seems to soar, then burns down and settles in my head. My forehead pulsates with energy. Though detached, I am somehow experiencing it at the same time. The back of my head becomes involved, and another circuit of energy explodes. The top of my head seems energized, and these three points whirl with activity, swelling and rushing with vitality. As they continue to expand, suddenly my whole head seems afire with a whirling energy. The three centers become one, as the energy settles into a small, steady glow deep inside my head—a soft radiance. Soon, additional inner knowing and more security settle into my life. I would later come to know this as a *kundalini experience.

A Different Love

After the NDE, my vitality is low and family duties take every ounce of strength. Months pass and the loneliness grows, but I soon discover a way to sit in the quiet and reconnect with the love I had experienced. Having no concept or technique, I just become quiet, sit still, and remember. In my mind I recreate that presence of light, and I ask the liquid essence again to love me. I bask in that indescribable love that seems to heal my broken life magically. Gradually I develop a habit of resting in the Presence once or twice a week, asking it to love me, and I love it in return.

Sometimes, sitting in our yard watching the children, I feel this love so powerfully, my chest floods with ardor. Recalling the living love that flowed to me from the Light Being in those quiet times, I am curious, for it now seems to cause me to feel deeply about people around me, a different caring than the sentimental emotion young Carol had felt.

One day Aunt Lee, our neighbor, comes across the street to tell me about her sister who is critically ill. As she cries, the energy in my body seems to pull me to her. I reach out and hold her, wanting to stop her pain more than anything in the world. I am unembarrassed at my tenderness, though this reaction is totally atypical. The shy, young Carol had not been in the habit of responding so openly to another. Somehow I realize this new experience is related to the Light Being. Always too busy, Carol had let the rest of the world take care of itself, certain its troubles were not hers to fix: "I have enough to do, thank you." But, after the experience in the delivery room, the new Carol truly cherishes others, wanting to do something about everything! But none of this makes sense. I cannot solve my own problems or even finish my own work, so how can I help others? It becomes a relief to sit quietly with my own thoughts to soothe me.

I often feel out of place. It seems to make others uncomfortable to hear my unusual feelings and thoughts. I find no one with whom I can talk about the light in my head, the intensity of the feelings evoked by beauty or my knowledge of the presence of God.

Time does heal, thank goodness. I gradually learn not to voice my questions. As an incoming soul rebuilding a personality, I struggle with many obligations, trying to preserve my impressions of rushing forward into this full and challenging life, promising so readily over my shoulder, "Yes, yes, I can do this!" In those moments, I rejoice to have reentered physical life, eager to strive to meet the opportunities of a bright new era. I know a time of greatness is fast approaching Earth, and I am preparing. I know why and how. My greatest challenge now is to remember all this, so I tell myself daily, "It will work out!"

Listening

The bright light of love that I recreate and savor almost daily seems my only contact with the great beyond until one day, two or three years later, it begins again to provide the familiar tide of thoughts. Ideas and concepts once more begin to fill my mind, comforting and encouraging me.

Knowing these ideas are mine to share, I ponder how in the world I will ever be able to do so. The concepts, profound and uplifting to me, are hard to convey; I have no words for giving them to another. As time passes, I realize "It" is teaching me; I do not know how to say so. My only concept is that God loves me and is guiding me in some way.

As I awake early one morning, about 5 or 6, I recall a powerful dream: I am walking in a place I know as the moors. Wearing a long dark green velvet cape tied at the neck, it catches on the brush at the side of the path. I am watching my step carefully to avoid the boggy places. I reach up to pull the ties of the cape away from my throat and walk a short way; the cape tangles on the brush and chokes me again. After repeating this several times, I try to pull the ties loose again in order to breathe. When I just jerk the ties to untie them, the cape slides loosely to the ground. I walk forward, free and uninhibited, and I don't look back.

Immediately, I know my marriage is the long dark cape choking me. I resonate to the awareness—heavy, hard, sad, restrictive. I know this. Excited by the dream, I quickly take my shower, dress, and then call my husband who lives elsewhere. He is at work and answers my call. He has asked for a divorce several times, and I have always said, "No, never." Now I tell him, "I am ready. Go ahead, get a divorce," only to hear, "I'm thinking about moving back in. There is no reason I can't. We've never done anything legal. I'll come by Saturday and we can talk about this."

I am stunned. I know my life is better, my children more settled since their father moved out. I cannot—will not—let this happen. Numbly, I go to the office. From there I call an attorney friend, make an appointment, and that woman who said, "Never," begins divorce proceedings.

Thus I embark on one of the most painful but transformative experiences of my life. As a sincere Catholic mother, I believed there is little worse than divorce. I have a daughter in the convent. Will she hate me? My children are in a Catholic school. I go to Mass every Sunday and love the Church. It comforts me. Now I am breaking a cardinal rule, but also I know it is the right thing for me.

As I learn to reflect upon what I know deep within, I review the vast understanding I want to share. Just as the seed of a flower contains the wisdom of how to bloom and how to create, I realize I contain knowledge on many levels of existence. I know the insights needed are indelibly etched into my memory. Stepping into the light, its bountiful energy swirling through my consciousness, was the most important moment of all.

In the presence of the Light Being I realized the physical body I entered will have to be strengthened and rebuilt. Young Carol's memory and sensitive intuitive nature will serve me well, and her previously intimidated personality will yield to new influence. The old devotional temperament will become better balanced. Her heavy dedication to duty—"even if it kills me"—will always be a factor, but greater awareness will encourage new objectivity. In *esoteric terms: the potent *Ray 6[2] emotional influence will become a more tempered Ray 2.[3] The ability to see both sides of an issue will be cultivated. Heavy programming of absolutes of right and wrong, as well as feelings of inadequacy, will be reworked as new energy impresses the vehicle.

As the next few years pass, I notice the steady change, as do others. I become a more courageous person; life seems more desirable to me. *Something* is happening. I feel better and gain energy. Occasionally, at the very perimeter of my mind, I *know* my life is important. I sense pieces of knowledge and guidance bringing these experiences into focus. Fighting to remember *that something I am to do*, I know I have a specific reason to be alive, and I will surely discover a way to fulfill that reason someday.

2

When the Student Is Ready

Part of my attention is always focused inward as my busy, productive life passes. Life unfolds with more harmony. *Synchronicities are more frequent, and the right books just seem to appear. Support comes from many sources. As *meditation patterns become established, insights calm my restlessness.

My relationship with Bill remains awkward—from polite to volatile. He experiences acute guilt over the danger to my physical safety. He loves the children but cannot fathom his wife. He wants to be free, yet neither of us sees a way out. We avoid speaking of our incompatibility.

The pain of previous years is etched into the relationship. While attempts to forgive and forget are made, no new bond grows. Heavy responsibilities and acute awareness of commitment will linger for years. When the new baby is baptized, a young mother stands alone, while an unhappy father stays home, confused by the struggle of life.

For a few years, Bill makes occasional efforts to relate to a wife who seems to be existing in some world of feelings and ideas too strange and complicated to follow. Once content to stay home, as the years pass, she becomes a career woman. So often pregnant, now she speaks of education and success. The shift becomes increasingly complex to a family in which intense ambition and powerful goals for women are discouraged. Confidence grows as hidden talents emerge, heartening my faith in this new inner nature.

Between 1958 and '68, the struggle to discover myself often finds me kneeling in the confessional—crying, pleading for direction, angry. I believe the priest must have answers but will not rescue me. Devouring *Imitation of Christ*[1] until I can quote it to myself, I try to stop the perceptive insights that come, seemingly so illogical. I have no one to whom to turn for direction, but I know I am to become acceptable, capable, and strong.

Entering an attitude of quiet receptivity one day, spontaneous joy floods my being. A picture is clearly shown in my mind: a small ball of shadows expands, opening like a fan of peacock feathers. As I watch within, it soon fades away, but I feel a vague sense of remembrance, or recognition. I return many times to that pleasant inner quiet before the sign reappears. As months pass, this symbol strikes a chord of wonder in me. It seems a priceless, precious gift, but I do not know its meaning.

The royal bird.

Between the near-death experience in November 1958 and '65, I give birth to four more children. The first, a son, delivered prematurely on November 6, 1959, is a tiny human form just not ready to live. When we lose him, I experience an incredible feeling of surprise, then failure. I thought everything was fine. My spirits had been high, even less confused. To my relief, I had been developing more positive feelings about life in general.

My grief, not acute but rather vague, creeps upon me at unlikely moments. I have a problem facing it squarely and feel miserably inadequate. With five daughters and one son, my desire for a boy is intense. I feel I have failed our older son by not giving him a much-desired brother.

In October 1960, I deliver a beautiful baby girl. I experience no concern for the sex of this baby, only a burning desire for a healthy child to compensate for the failure. Two years later, November 1962, the son, and brother, arrives. Severe hemorrhaging follows a remarkably speedy delivery with little pain. Amazingly, this proves to be the next important step in my awakening process.

As the doctor advises me to have surgery to prevent the risk of future children, I remember a promise: *I am to have one more child, a girl*. I cannot allow the surgery, for I recall my agreement with the Light Being. It is vague, but I *know*; I am confident. It does not matter that the doctor and others think me stubborn and foolish. I will give birth to another girl! This shocking recall generates another round of wondering. The only framework I have for such an obligation is that *I have promised God*, I cannot break my vow. Medical emergencies will surface again, and surgery will be all right only when my commitment is complete.

When a lovely, lively baby girl arrives on April 6, 1965, as "prearranged," feelings of success flood me. Having fulfilled my commitment, my heart sings with joy! As my sense of security grows, I listen even more to the wee small voice within. It speaks to me through a widening stream of dialogue which reveals both personal insights to me and to others regarding the world around me.

Practical Information

In 1962, I grow increasingly concerned about a particular look Mary Beth has from time to time for a few seconds. I try to determine her problem for a few months. She is five, usually animated and active, yet at times, with no other noticeable change of expression, the light leaves her eyes for a split second. I point this out to both her father and grandmother.

When we visit the family pediatrician, he finds nothing. Later, watching her play tether ball, I glance up at just the right moment to see the dull instant of no light pass over her face. Her timing is thrown off, and the ball smacks into her face. I cry aloud, "What is that?" and hear an instant response, "Epilepsy." No one else is near. Who has answered? As I wash her face and dry her tears, my heart beats rapidly. What if it is epilepsy?

As soon as I can put her back to play with the other children, I call the doctor and ask him point blank, "Could Mary Beth have epilepsy?" He tries to calm me, "Do not worry, Carol, our examination does not indicate epilepsy." Again I press, "How would you test her if you thought she did?" She would have an EEG at St. Petersburg Children's Hospital, he explains. "You do not need to do that. Your imagination is running away with you because of your concern." But I must understand Mary Beth's health situation, and I must know if I can trust the inner voice that answered my impulsive cry. "Please test her!" I plead. Finally, to pamper me, he agrees. I have taken a giant step, following the advice of my inner guidance.

When Mary Beth has the EEG and petit mal is diagnosed, the astonished doctor questions how I could have known. "I just knew," I say. But now we have a closer bond. With medication, the condition is soon under control. Now I realize a lesson of great import: *That voice can and will yield information I can get nowhere else.* Mary Beth continues medication for five years with little further difficulty.

My devotional nature celebrates the joy of weekly Mass. My fervor increases when I join the Night Adoration Society of the Sacred Heart of Jesus. Slipping from bed to light a candle to pray and chant awakens my desire to know hidden mysteries. I realize a flow of energy often builds in my chest and with it comes a power to comprehend matters not limited to daily life. A *just knowing* grows more frequent and significant.

In the midst of my Night Adoration, sometimes a pounding force rushes up through me. My body sways, my shoulders stiffen and slightly arch, and my mind floats in that loving bliss. Later, I awaken lying on the floor, cheeks wet with tears. Sometimes I open my mouth and sweet songs flow. Again a voice tells me things about myself or about life and its purpose.

The confessional resounds with my tears and despair, but it is no use. No one cares. Father gives me absolution and feels he has done his best. He probably has.

Then the door, so barred to outside relief, opens to an increased sense of achievement. Desperate to help feed my family, employment is necessary. When I find I am capable, my self-esteem grows and in time provides the catalyst for separation and divorce. Common sense now compensates for lack of educated skills, and I soon achieve a faculty for meeting challenges.

The years pass, and the once harried mother, lonely and worn, gives way to a busier woman, proficient and strengthening daily. I study night courses continuously. I learn to budget time and money. As I discover talent and drive, I become increasingly positive and receive praise at work.

Years of struggle end as Bill and I decide to let go. Fighting fear and guilt, we each experience a sense of defeat and remorse. But with new confidence and freedom, I grow truer to myself. With time to spend quietly, philosophically, to become secure with my own changes, the conflict within dissipates into an unusual ideology.

Two years or so after Bill's death in a small plane crash in 1980 (we had finally divorced in 1967), I receive a touching, most revealing message through the mediumship of Rev. Marilyn Rossner of Montreal. In 1983, I get a phone call from the home of Allan Otto in Minneapolis, where Marilyn was visiting.

An entity had interrupted her readings during her busy day of appointments, and she told him to wait until her rest about 6 p.m. She settled down, but she had forgotten the incident when he appeared, identifying himself as "Bill, and I belong to Carol" with a rapid image of me. At the time, Marilyn knew me only as the wife of Charles Harra. She recognized the image, but knew no more. Bill showed her a plane crash, the way he had died, and asked her to tell me he loved me and that he was sorry it had been so hard.

Marilyn's message was powerful, for she knew neither him nor of his death. It seems he had awakened on the spirit side and realized how challenging our years had been. I am grateful we had resolved many of our issues before his death and that the sensitive young man confused and pained by alcohol was recovering. Later I realized he was what today is known as an adult child of an alcoholic parent and had lived out that painful, dysfunctional behavior to a T.

Unexpected Relief

No events are more significant to awakening to my inner nature and to my various levels of self than meetings in St. Petersburg with the Rev. Leroy Zemke and Mrs. Ann Manser (now deceased). Later, it will be

Ann as a teacher who readily triggers my "knowing" and introduces me to basic wisdom teachings. It begins when I am invited to a discussion group in Clearwater, Florida. I slip into the lovely suburban home just as a handsome young man, Rev. Zemke, writes his topic on the blackboard: *"Astral Travel." I think, "Oh no, a travelogue."

Soon on the edge of my seat, I am listening to a description of a phenomenon I know so well. At the break, I push through the group to question Rev. Zemke. Emotion floods me as I utter, "Sir, I think you have saved my mind."

Rev. Zemke is pastor of a *metaphysical church I soon visit. A converted little theater with larger-than-life paintings on the walls and a flowered carpet on the stage accords an unusual atmosphere. I find a seat in the very back. The evening program begins with singing and a short lecture. The highlight, a demonstration of psychic impressions, catches me by surprise. I have never seen such a thing.

When Rev. Zemke steps into the audience, I am amazed. Speaking into a microphone, he asks me to say my name. After my response, he describes my office and a personal situation. Then he thoroughly overwhelms me by saying, "Someday, young lady, you will stand in this spot and do this very thing. You are a natural psychic and do not know how to use your gift." He moves on to attune to another person. I rush out of there, heart pounding. Wanting answers to relieve my loneliness, moods, memories, and confusions, I know I am at the brink of discovery.

On my next visit to the church, a Saturday afternoon social, an elderly lady I will come to know as Ann Manser approaches me with a mysterious remark, "Where have you been? I have been waiting for you."

Ann becomes my guide through esoteric literature. A former Catholic, she helps me deal with the pain and loss I feel as I draw away from traditional religion and enter a new life of mystical awareness. She encourages my life of prayer, meditation, and a regular time for contemplation. With her vast knowledge of inner space, energies, and symbology, she answers my questions and my needs. I safely share my memories, my dreams, my visions. She tests my intuition, my psychic impressions, and my *inner-plane experiences. She leads me in exercises, reads my diary, and encourages me to believe in ideas as broad as those in science fiction. These ideas make sense to me and answer questions I have pondered for years to no avail.

Ann responds to my scariest impressions with wisdom. With her, recall of other lives seems less shocking. This refined, elegant lady commands logic and respect. She combines the sincerity of a true spiritual teacher and the skill of a superb writer.

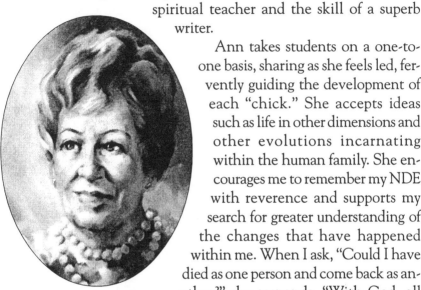

Ann Manser

Ann takes students on a one-to-one basis, sharing as she feels led, fervently guiding the development of each "chick." She accepts ideas such as life in other dimensions and other evolutions incarnating within the human family. She encourages me to remember my NDE with reverence and supports my search for greater understanding of the changes that have happened within me. When I ask, "Could I have died as one person and come back as another?" she responds, "With God, all things are possible." And, "If you have these things to do, Carol, you had better get to work."

In 1969, one rarely hears such terms as *aurascope*—reading the aura—which is what Ann calls her interpretation of the soul colors in the auric pattern of one to whom she attunes. Ann is often hard to fathom. Critical of sloppy work, eager to question and challenge, she encourages me to acknowledge I am here with a duty. She stresses that a superior air reeks of ego and blocks the flow of intuitive knowledge. I believe Ann sees it as her personal duty to knock any excess wind out of her students' sails at each opportunity, which is rather frequently!

I truly learn I am bright and indisputably capable—not a bad thing to find out at age thirty-three after ten children and a painful divorce. My illusions of perfect mother–perfect homemaker shatter.

Ann introduces me to the planet Sirius as a real force in a committed spiritual family relationship. The little-understood concept of a spiritual family (*evolution) incarnating for group service becomes personal. In the aurascope, then in teaching, she identifies Sirius as my true home, validating more of my inner knowing. I feel I am truly on the spiritual *path, and she agrees I have a reason for being. Ann encourages a life of preparation with the guiding thought, *When the student is ready, the teacher appears.* Ann is my answer to agonized prayers.

Many esoteric writings refer to humanity being guided by great ones from Sirius. "Sirius is the star of initiation . . . earth's hierarchy is under the spiritual direction of the Hierarchy of Sirius."[2] The advanced soul who entered has been revealed to have a certain relationship with Sirius; it is confirmed by the exchange occurring in Scorpio, the channel for Sirius energy.

The How of the Walk-in

Walk-ins are incarnating souls who take a short-cut into physical life, instead of the usual route, fetus to adult. A walk-in soul literally and figuratively "walks in" to a ready-built human body. Desiring to die, the occupant offers its body as a gift to an incoming soul, saving the time and energy required in the usual maturing process.

The outgoing soul continues living and learning in the spirit world, just as we all do when we leave the physical dimension. A similar situation arises when a person is in a coma for an extended time; in that case the physical body continues to live even as the consciousness focuses on the nonphysical plane. Let us give this more thought. If a person is unconscious for a long period, months or more, what is that soul doing? I believe the soul busies itself in the inner world, just as we do each night behind the *veil of sleep.

We have a consciousness thread (*antahkarana), life thread (*sutratma), and creative thread,[3] and we are to understand the purpose of each. The life thread brings the energy of spirit and matter together, charging the physical body with life force. The consciousness thread, the connection with the soul, expresses as the lower part of the mental unit and the higher as awareness, *High Self, or what one has learned from past-life experiences. Built by personality, the third thread, an extension of the life thread, aligns the *chakras and energies and expands as our thoughts grow more noble. This profound linking is the work spiritual aspirants do by contemplation, creative thinking, and being on the path. The ever-expanding use of higher energies stepped down prompts the personality to prepare for *soul infusion.

Relating this to physical life, *what is going on in a comatose state?* The body is without physical consciousness. Still occupying the body, the soul keeps it charged through the life thread. The consciousness is active on nonphysical planes. As long as the consciousness thread remains intact, the patient may awaken and return to full functioning. Often s/he recounts being at another place or accurately describes happenings in this reality later, even though in a coma. Some recall meeting another they have known, such as a deceased relative, or an occurrence during the coma it seems they could not have known.

However, in the case of a second soul being given the physical mechanism, the consciousness thread itself is changed. The original creator releases the consciousness thread; with help from the *Lords of Karma, the incoming soul is attached to it and through it to the physical vehicle. The new force flows gently into the old personality mechanism. As a result of new soul energy, the creative thread gradually alters and adjusts to the new forces. If opportunities are favorable, rapid changes may occur.

Many questions remain. *Is there still a tie to the departing soul?* I saw the previous soul pass into spirit in the usual way—what we call death. Then the incoming soul brought in the energy to change and recharge the life. Physical, emotional, and mental vehicles provide the incoming soul with the energy of the outgoing soul, while the incoming soul must gradually convert body and personality frequencies to its vibrations. It is this period, I believe, wherein the new inhabitant faces great confusion and conflict.

Think about this. As we wear a pair of leather gloves for a time, they adjust to the size and shape of our hands; then we give the gloves to another whose hands are a bit longer or wider. At first, the gloves may not fit well, but as they are worn and give a little, the new owner is increasingly comfortable in them. So it goes with one personality gifted to another.

How interested is the outgoing soul in how the old personality fares under the direction of the new inhabitant? Just as we differ here, I believe souls continue to differ on the spirit side, determined by level of development, reasons for leaving, and so on. Delighted to go on, I believe most outgoing souls do little looking back.

Many walk-ins reveal limited interest in the past. Perhaps higher ones impart a wisdom to minimize this. Certainly we see grounds for grief, concern, and interference. The departing soul will be rewarded for rendering this service to those guiding humanity. The optimism of the incoming soul will release into the personality (life, consciousness, and creative threads) some energy to flow through the *aka cord to the departed one, rather like a bonus for the service.

In the spirit world the outgoing soul is invited to tend to opportunities for comfort, enrichment, learning, and healing, as is any freed soul. Training differs according to the evolution of the soul. If much earthly pain and negativity have been felt, as with the majority of those who "walk out," special attention to healing is needed. Similarly, walk-ins here on Earth need support and confidence, for many have had hard experiences. Those who have such a daunting time, yet now serve a useful purpose, need tenderness from those who can understand such phenomena.

Believing planet Earth and humanity presently face a time of great testing, certain souls desire to impress those they can reach with a special message. By accepting a ready-made, grown body, even if unhealthy or imperfect, messengers make themselves heard much sooner.

Agreeing to complete some unfinished tasks for the departing soul, when they come into the physical plane, walk-ins may fulfill responsibilities to aging parents, children, or a mate. Since most people have ties which are abruptly severed by death, the walk-in tries to honor those obligations if possible, repairing and transforming the life it inherits.

Just as turning on a light in a darkened room creates a different picture, exchanging souls naturally alters personality. The incoming soul is challenged by the newness of the situation. Due to needed healing or correction in most cases, it may be months or years before s/he realizes what truly happened. This veil benefits the incoming soul, who is coping with quite enough. Only an aware few detect striking changes, generally neither the public nor the extended family. If spiritual succor is available, esoteric philosophy softens the trauma and provides welcome support.

Human relationships are the testiest yet most precious learning tools, so the greatest responsibilities are to those with interlocking ties to the personality. If these can be elevated to spiritual ties, loving in a higher, holier sense, they adjust and remain rich. If they are personality level, self-centered ties built on power, ownership, or manipulation, they may grow apart as the new nature takes over.

Like attracts like is a rule on the nonphysical plane, and when a life is to function from a certain level of reality, it loosens ties to other levels. This accounts for the dissolution of many marriages after a walk-in enters the picture. If one's life energy is devoted intensely in a given direction, unless the mate can share that enthusiasm, the relationship moves toward dissolution. Birds of a feather do flock together, so like-minded companions are such comfort.

With many challenges facing the walk-in, the incoming one rejoices if the departing personality has psychic sensitivity in its basic make-up. The exchange is less difficult when personality can be easily impressed with the spiritual knowing of the incoming soul. While all walk-ins have not necessarily acquired sentient or psychic vehicles, it stands to reason that a delicately tuned mechanism is helpful. We realize the better the connection between levels of consciousness or vehicles, the clearer the soul expresses—thus the benefit of a sensitive personality. Further, the new soul may be able to generate rapid changes to *chakra energy centers. In many cases, more and more breakthroughs occur as the intense new soul orchestrates the opportunities at hand.

Lest the word *psychic* is misunderstood, let us recall that *psyche* means "of the soul." We extend the definition of *sensitivity to phenomena* to mean sensitivity to "soul pictures, impressions, thoughts, or intuition." Now we understand the joy of a soul blessed with an easy-to-impress basic mechanism.

"Walking in" to a healthy physical body is desirable, naturally. However, as a brush with death allows the exchange in many cases, most walk-ins must strengthen or rebuild the vehicle they receive. Walk-ins have the further responsibility of impressing their new vehicle with their personal spiritual energies. The first seven to nine years prove critical. Lives must be rearranged to expedite the reason for entry. Finding encouragement and support becomes a challenge. Since virtually no one dares tell the story, these years may be devastatingly lonely. This pain often causes the new soul to search for contact with the higher world.

For nearly forty years, I have been studying the transformation process. More and more, I find myself thinking of walk-ins as a vanguard of the anticipated *"externalization of the *Hierarchy." People around the world familiar with *Theosophical Society materials, the writings of H. P. *Blavatsky, Alice *Bailey, and others, recognize the probability of helpful entities from higher dimensions. This externalization assists the era shift from Piscean to Aquarian. Many state that followers (disciples) of the *Christ will come to Earth to take their positions, ready to serve. I choose to think we are observing this today as *world servers take their places.

The externalization of the Hierarchy is manifesting in preliminary ways. Walk-ins coming to Earth bring previous spiritual development to serve humanity's imminent crisis. The Hierarchy is evidenced as well through the emerging high consciousness of many embodied individuals. People busy with everyday living are rapidly sensing their spiritual nature; through intuition and the bombardment of new ideas, they awaken to deeper thought, to ethical and spiritual matters.

Self-examination stirs memories long hidden behind conscious mind. As minds search, examine, and stretch, truths previously obscure find acceptance. The logic of *reincarnation has become more acceptable in the West in recent years. Increased knowledge and new dimensions in the natural sciences facilitate our grasp of concepts advocated by mystics for centuries.

The idea of souls coming to assist humanity should be hopeful and rewarding, even if it seems hard to imagine. Movies such as *E.T.*, *Close Encounters of the Third Kind*, *Ghost*, *Contact*, and others plant seeds which support theories relating to walk-ins. *Contact* contained scenes quite comparable to an NDE, skepticism of earlier years, and the struggles of one who does break through. While most walk-ins may lack the charm of an E.T., all are trying to present new ways of life, greater inspiration, and love. Their challenging stories teach us much about expanding consciousness.

Walk-ins need compassion as they strive for necessary balance to fulfill their missions. Every day, as puzzle pieces fall into place, they discover more of who they truly are—the end of one struggle, the onset of another! These servants of humanity are different; they have something to say or to give to others, in their own way, from their own resources. The spiritual nature previously hidden behind conscious mind and from the public must now plant its seed, paint its picture, or speak its word. Who will receive these treasures?

The Doors Fly Open

The detachment I experienced upon returning home from the hospital gradually subsides. In time, a new intensity expands. I am virtually never lukewarm emotionally. When I care, I really care! These feelings increase if someone is in pain. As my concern reaches the one suffering, I become very uncomfortable. The sensation is so strong, I feel swollen, usually in the chest area. Sometimes my back arches slightly, compelling me to sit very straight to be comfortable. I ache to touch the person and often feel at one with her or him. As I fulfill these impulses, I overcome my prior hesitancy. Soon it becomes natural for me to reach out, to touch, and to hug.

Even as I work in the business world, I find myself preparing for ministry under Ann's tutelage. With her direction, my long-held glimpses of speaking, teaching, and doing form constructive patterns. She encourages my preparation for ministry, and by May 1971 spirit guidance prompts me to realize the time for ordination has come. I have no rational explanation of how I reached that decision. I had fulfilled the requirements of the Spiritual Center at St. Petersburg, where the Reverends Elmer and Thelma Fischer are directors and copastors. One evening, they encourage me to become ordained; three times, I reply, "There is no way."

Driving home to Dunedin that night, I cry and explain to God why I cannot be ordained. Combined with mixed emotions, the hour-plus ride is exhausting. Finally at home, I fall into a troubled sleep. I awake early the next day, open my eyes, and say clearly and out loud, "I am going to be ordained."

July 3, 1971, becomes the wondrous day. My grieving parents—Catholic and so proud of my large family—now put their home on the market and leave Clearwater. It takes years of loving for them to accept this.

These occurrences of love and inspiration lead me naturally into a healing ministry. When the power of spiritual impulses is revealed through a physical healing, it seems the time has come for a more public work.

The Temple of the Living God invites a particular minister to teach a course in healing. Now a minister on staff, I join the class, though uncomfortable with the subject. I am intimidated by the intense feelings stirring within me.

The healing course becomes very important to me. My seventeen-year-old daughter is critically ill in the hospital. The third week we meet, I am anxious for the class to end so I can go to the hospital. As the Lord would have it, the air conditioning man comes that day to install a new system in the church, so the group meets at my house, which delays me. When the meeting ends, the minister asks the group to join in a healing prayer for my daughter. As we pray, I feel the energy focus and I am aware of the group's sincerity as they work with her. I leave immediately for the hospital.

My daughter has been critical for two days with hepatitis. When I arrive, she is receiving injections for nausea. She looks up and says, "Mother, make me well." I reply, "Honey, only God can heal you."

She looks straight at me, "Then why are you taking that healing course?" At that moment, it becomes very real. All I can say is, "Honey, close your eyes, and I will work with you." I go to the head of the bed and place my hands over her, trying to remember diagrams and positions and sequences. Truthfully, I can only say I am sincere. I do not really know a technique. I work over her entire body, down to her feet. When I finish, she has fallen asleep. I sit down and sincerely pray she will be better. Time passes; I must go home to take care of my other children. From home I call the hospital at eight o'clock and am told, "She has slept ever since you were here." Leaving her in their care, I go to bed.

About 6 A.M. the next morning, the phone rings and the voice on the other end says, "Mother, I am well." I ask without thought, "Who is this?" I am stunned. I jump into my clothes and go to the hospital. As I rush in, the doctor confidently standing by her bed declares, "Isn't it wonderful the way teenagers bounce back!"

I do not know what to think. I am amazed. When I talk to the minister who has been teaching our course, he says, "Well, that is what is supposed to happen!" Now I earnestly want to study *and understand* healing. When Rev. Zemke asks me to teach a healing class soon after this, I am ready to share experiences that are happening around me.

Suffice it to say, since that time, healing has seemed such a natural way to show our love and caring. Later, I am blessed to study Reiki with Mrs. Takata Hayowa, who brought that ancient technique to the U.S.

Healing energy is quite similar to the peace and love I felt in the presence of the Light Being during the NDE. Many find they experience a loss of the sense of time while working with healing, as their awareness is focused in this free-flowing, bountiful love.

Even words can be a healing resource, like defining LOVE as *Lots Of Vital Energy. Words such as peace, calm, energy, at-one-with, and caring resonate. Add your favorite. The healing flow brings what we need and delivers that *agape love the world so desperately needs. I hesitate to use the word *love* because of the sentimentality it can insinuate. My personal inner opening for healing is triggered as I think and feel, "I care."

3
Discipleship 101

Since the NDE, I have struggled consistently through the years with my personality. A private, sensitive person, young Carol placed great emphasis upon children, home, and personal interests. She thought, "If it does not happen in my yard, it is not my concern." So involved with raising children, whom she loved dearly, she had little to do with others. With time and energy demanded at home, little reserve remained for outside interests. A homebody, she rarely left the house except for errands, barely noticing the world at large. Her nose was to the grindstone, as was her heart.

Shortly after the NDE, emotional patterns of the new Carol change. The quieter, less self-centered personality now cares about the entire world. Earlier detachment is replaced by a new fervor, an unconditional love for all children, both of this household and of the neighborhood. It matters that children around the world are starving, that strangers are suffering. As the window of the world opens, involvement follows, and confusing changes disturb the status quo of family life.

The intensity of caring of which the walk-in is capable rarely is centered at a personal level. Later, you will see, Ann Manser describes this quality in the aurascope of the incoming soul. Even when a matter concerns another, I seem to have to aid, comfort, and relieve when possible.

Unconditional, impersonal love is rarely understood or even considered desirable in a family setting where personal love is often demonstrated through possessiveness. Gaps in the marriage widen. Intense feelings about some issues and great freedom in others create too much confusion to be acceptable.

Another dilemma surfaces when awareness acquired behind the calm of meditation unfolds. Recollections occur—of people, scenes, and times I do not know consciously but recognize. When I discover a book on reincarnation and examine the common sense of this philosophy, pieces of puzzling memories seem to drop into place and order comes to the mosaic of an emerging life.

Years later, a noted hypnotist comes to see me. Interested in psychism, particularly in sensitive children, he questions me about a number of areas and asks if I have ever been frightened by or had a bad psychic experience.

I share with him a memory of an experience of young Carol's at about age fifteen. While living in boarding school, one night she awakened to see a beautiful lady in the room. With a Catholic background, stories of Lourdes and Fatima flooded her mind. Scared to death and believing Our Lady only appeared to saints, she closed her eyes and covered her head with blankets.

Now, after the soul exchange, we explore this experience under hypnosis. I do not know what will happen, but my curiosity is so great, I agree to the experiment. It has since helped me better appreciate the makeup of personality and its tools, particularly in walk-in context.

Led back in time, memories sharpen as I experience two and three years before. Time adjusts—back to age thirty, to twenty-five, then to age twenty-three. My memory and emotions shift as I move into the life of the other Carol and am carried even further. Emotions were more turbulent and fearful. I return to the vision of the beautiful lady. Until this moment, I had not recalled she had spoken. Yet, as I am questioned, "Did she speak? Did she say who she was?" I remember a gentle, sweet voice, "I am Theresa, and I want to help you. Your life is hard. Offer yourself to me, and I will help you. There is a bond of love between us. I will come to you when you call."

In young Carol's stunned mind, this registered only at an unconscious level. Later, when Carol was nineteen, she took "Theresa" as her confirmation name. Though she bore six daughters and a favorite name was Theresa, she never gave it to any of her daughters. It was too intimate to share.

I wonder about this experience as I contemplate the many pieces of the walk-in puzzle. I, the present Carol, have a great love of *Saint Teresa of Avila, her strength and courage. As a mystic, she is more admired as time goes by. Some years ago, in discussing past lives with Leroy Zemke, I shared such feelings. He suggested I may have known St. Teresa or she may have influenced one or more of my lives. I believe this may be a connecting thread between young Carol and me.

*Inner-plane experiences teach me a great deal (events happening at another level are remembered here, usually occurring behind the veil of sleep—like a dream but feeling entirely different). One time, finding myself in another dimension, I am crossing a campus with others on a pleasant afternoon. I am walking with a man I do not know in my physical life, yet in the experience I feel I know him well. It seems he has vouched for and is sponsoring me in an important matter. We are walking behind a young man I know as one of my students in daily life. The man ahead of us is carrying a pillow with a sword resting upon it. We proceed to an elegant building, like a cathedral, up the steps, and into the great hall.

The long, imposing room is lovely. At the far end we move up more steps to stand before a man in regal robes, obviously the authority. Ceremoniously he takes the sword off the pillow and says, "Who vouches for this woman?" The man by my side presents me. The wise one says, "Turn and look." As I look through the walls, it is as if they are glass, yet from the outside you cannot see in. Many people are going about their business. Then the dignitary turns and says, "All those who have assisted this one, take a step forward, and all those she has aided, take a step forward." At his command, many move forward knowingly, while others, active in their own pursuits, advance unconsciously. He tenderly says to me, "Remember how interlocked we all are. No one gives to another without helping oneself, though it is not always known in the mind." Next, I am kneeling, and he blesses me.

Some weeks later while lecturing in Atlanta, I receive a special gift. I am a guest in a lady's home, and she has invited me and others for dinner. The door bell rings, and I go to the door. One of the gentlemen standing there says, "Carol, do you know me?" I gasp, "You are the man who was with me . . . there, aren't you?" He takes my hands, kneels in the entry hall, and prays. Later, he says, "So seldom when we know each other on other levels can we bring that down here and recognize each other." We laugh and hug each other, much to the stunned looks of the bystanders. We share our story and have an evening to get acquainted on the physical. I have never seen him again. Only once I called him in an emergency, and he told me, "Remember, Carol, the spiritual path is a jealous mistress. If you give yourself to it, you can have little else." A powerful truth, yet as we give ourselves first to God, everything else will be given unto us.

Rev. Torkom Saraydarian

Another significant event came in much the same fashion. I was taught to call referencing other dimensions "inner-plane experiences." I am in what I believe is either Germany or Switzerland. I am on the front row in a lovely room with a grand piano, a superb chandelier, and several rows of splendid upholstered chairs, the latter facing two grand windows through which one views two magnificent mountains. A short, handsome, dark-haired gentleman enters the room, and I know he is a great man, a great teacher. I am thrilled to be there and to be able to hear him.

About five years after first receiving the words *Agni Yoga in my meditation, I fly to California to meet Torkom *Saraydarian. He is in a large room, and although it is different from the room in my inner-plane experience, I recall that room. This one has similar large windows, and I look out as I walk over to take his outstretched hands. Behind Rev. Saraydarian are two prominent mountains. He says, "It is nice to be with you again. I met you in Germany, did I not?" I sputter, "I have never been to Germany." Smilingly he says, "Now we both know better than that, do we not?"

One must realize the great goal of meditation is to develop the *antahkarana and to gain conscious knowledge of what is going on at each level of one's nature. If, in fact, we are beings both spiritual and physical, both soul and personality, then we acknowledge that just as personality lives the everyday, mundane life, the soul lives a high and increasingly sensitive life. The time comes when, from the physical/material level, we invite the soul, the spiritual self, to blend with our experience here. Prior to this, vast separations exist between our physical nature and our inner reality. Then spiritual hunger signals readiness, and the quest ensues.

We become aware that behind the veil of sleep, as well as beyond our everyday consciousness, our nonphysical level freely continues its higher-plane activity. Many stories tell of Eastern *Masters and Western saints who have practiced bilocation. Acquaint yourself with the story of *Padre Pio, recently made a saint by the Catholic Church. He experienced a court case in Italy in the twentieth century centered around the issue of bilocation. Phenomena filled his life and confused many. Such phenomena attract considerable attention as a way of proving, if we choose that term, that life exists on more than the physical with which we are most familiar. Meditation is the bridge to the higher world, and as we develop spiritual attributes, many other kinds of awareness may come as well.

Being a Student

Private study with Ann is supplemented by classes with other teachers. Eastern philosophy expands my knowledge of the differences and similarities of Christianity, Hinduism, and Buddhism. Rev. McBride Panton of St. Petersburg guides me through Vedanta, Upanishads, and the Bhagavad Gita. At Ann's suggestion my horizons broaden again with classes at the Spiritual Center for training and ordaining ministers. I have no thought of entering the ministry. I simply seek food for my insatiable spiritual hunger.

At the Spiritual Center directed by Revs. Elmer and Thelma Fischer, their program, with an excellent reputation and staff, includes weekly public worship services. Rev. Irene Palmer becomes my instructor and polishes my skills. A Capricorn, Irene is practical and down-to-Earth, and her effect upon my public work continues today. I often recall her words of wisdom as I try to help students refine and clarify impressions.

Ann stretches me, answers my big questions, and provides clues to the overall picture of life and soul. Irene gives me many basic how-to's, an essential foundation comparable to kindergarten and grammar school. Gradually the two merge. I begin to lecture at the Spiritual Center, a metaphysical version of a small Bible college; I learn to pray spontaneously in public and to give psychic messages. The Temple of the Living God and the Spiritual Center in St. Pete nourish me while I live in Dunedin with my family of small children who are quite unaware of the unfolding in their mother's life.

Now, my heart goes out to my parents who watched and wondered what was happening to their daughter. They wanted me to continue to be their nice Catholic daughter—not to make a big deal of what they did not understand. They know I am struggling and searching. Those years strained them, yet they saw an unhappy young woman become more joyful, free, and content.

These are wonder-filled times. My life is busy, happy. My inner nature rejoices in the bliss I discover in my periods of quiet. Listening patiently to the guidance from within, I learn the meaning of *witness consciousness* as I observe my struggle and folly. I realize that one Carol, a personality, is awakening to her potential, and a wiser level is moving into play when the occasion is right. This latter Carol feels free to believe in idealism and high principles often hard to achieve in everyday life. This one understands life's challenges from an impersonal level, knowing her vision holds ideas that cannot yet be shared; time must pass for the path to clear. As she becomes more prepared for the service for which she has entered, striving for her soul purpose, the two levels of her nature grow more integrated.

The outer personality is going through a metamorphosis that defines values and peels away unnecessary duties. Moving personal experiences lead me to depart the business world for a position dedicated to assist others in their spiritual search—ordination! In 1971, the human potential movement is growing, and I find myself offering insights and supporting others as interest in sensitivity gains momentum.

Believing myself to be one who is committed to working with humanity for as long as it takes, I harbor no feelings of "hurry up and get finished." Many express grief at being in physical form, as had young Carol. Spiritual students often long to "get off the wheel," to be free from physical life. Others, especially if less philosophical in nature, dislike the idea of reincarnation because they dread being "recycled," they say. Others find hope in reincarnation because they find no satisfaction in traditional Western answers.

Living here on Mother Earth, I believe we should realize we have a wondrous opportunity through physical life and we are part of a greater *Plan. We either respond or not. A basic question all major religions seek to answer is: *Is there an advantage in creating a positive attitude toward life when so often life holds quite difficult or tragic experiences?* Some religions respond by suggesting that rhythms and cycles hold answers, that cause and effect contribute to the greater picture. In fact, this is the most common thought. The Christian Scriptures can be read to support both theories.

Familiar verses of Ecclesiastes 3 help us grasp the concept of cycles. "To everything there is a season, and a time for every purpose under the sun . . . a time to reap and a time to sow . . . a time of war and a time of peace."

Galatians 6.7, "For whatever you sow, that shall you reap," and Ecclesiastes 11.1, "Cast your bread upon the waters, for you shall find it after many days," support our understanding of cause and effect.

Choosing between good and evil is considered a major reason life is given us. We are challenged to live well as full partners in a higher Plan. To hate life, to dislike participating in its lessons, devalues the experience of life given by the Creator. We may be thrown into conflict with our self-preservation instinct and can only feed inexplicable pain and distress while undermining our bodies, as well as our emotional and mental health. We must realize hating others or ourselves is self-destructive. If we believe there is purpose, we will see our opportunities to demonstrate and witness. Spiritual aspirants are encouraged to serve God, one another, and the world.

Often in esoteric circles, those really grieving or unhappy with human life are seen as foreigners to the system, i.e., wanderers, aliens, space beings. If this is so, and I believe there is some truth to this, these people often live out of sync with the times, so attuned to whatever *was* that a great deal of waste occurs for them in the here and now.

A Reason to Be

If we believe we are here for a collective reason, as well as for an individual purpose, we will realize life more deeply. If we studied human beings with the insight used in sensing other forms of nature, we would see that humanity is learning how to use power, how to create, and how to live in peace with all of creation. If we believe some souls are committed to working with humanity through its vicissitudes, we comprehend Jesus' comment in Matthew 28.20, "Lo, I am with you always, even unto the end of the age."

When each of us fulfills our part in the greater purpose of human life, leaving the world a better place than when we found it, we bless both the world and our individual lives. If we believe the human *group mind unfolds its potential as each of us grows, we may acquire the incentive to try. Should we believe humanity shapes the destiny of planet Earth, we determine how we wish humanity to live, refusing or accepting personal involvement.

Great thinkers have dealt with the philosophical insights of this challenge since earliest times. Collective wisdom—often called ancient—has been passed from generation to generation. Perhaps we sum this up by realizing the wonder we experience when touched by one who has truly made a meaningful contribution. Mother Teresa, Martin Luther King, Jr., and Mahatma Gandhi in far different yet similar ways selected a goal and did it.

When we have the vision to see how we can contribute and then make the effort, often we receive the necessary supportive energy and see the merit of our actions. Spiritual teachings reveal that life's major opportunities are not found in other dimensions. The use of physical bodies in health and strength, the use of spiritual, creative energy in the form of sexuality, and the use of energy as money give us plenty of challenge on the Earth plane—plus time itself, which is not known in higher realities.

In this dimension we work with the resources of the world of dense form. Our body and basic nature create our tool box of strengths and weaknesses, traits and skills. Our sexual nature adds spice through the power of attraction and repulsion. We learn rules of higher dimensions. The concept of positive and negative power as electric and magnetic, even if not clear, impels us. Certainly discernment is demanded if we are to express our sexual nature positively and constructively.

Collective energy can be power or force or money—all quite similar ideas. When we build influence, we say we have power; when we save our income, we have currency—money. Regulating the flow of income and outgo requires wisdom and will, for we may either selfishly waste and indulge or fearfully horde for tomorrow. As we regulate the flow, we create and regenerate. This is a divine attribute *made in the image and likeness* of the Creator. We weave our life and what we desire as we consciously become a cocreator with life. As these awarenesses become our reality, joy flows more fully and our sense of belonging increases. Unhappiness often comes from resisting creativity. Even a party is not much fun if we do not wish to go!

Listening patiently to the guidance from within, I learn the meaning of *witness consciousness* as I observe my struggle and folly.

In the 1970s, expansion of consciousness became "in"; parapsychology became a popular pursuit, as an air of sophistication surrounded metaphysical terminology. While many people became armchair Buddhists, under it all pulsated an honest-to-goodness search, sincere and hopeful. Students filled classrooms as meditation approaches were taught by devotees of one path and another. The allure of things rumored and wished for was broadly spoken.

Students of both science and art learned to meditate, and most had at least one experience unexplainable by logic. A personal experience of insight or revelation or meaningful fancy helped many reach their subconscious in some acceptable way and expand their lives. Fast on the heels of experiential techniques came biofeedback to preserve the new progress in a technical manner with which our dial-and-gauge society is most comfortable. Through Silva Mind Control,™ thousands discovered information previously thought unknowable. Other courses gave precious new tools for healing prayers and psychic attunements; *dowsing became more than "water witching."

Just as there seemed no limit to the acceptance of new ideas, the tide began to turn: *ESP became unremarkable, disciplines became dull. But the most ancient principles—idealism, nobility, purity—survived the clutter. Steadfast through the phases of expansion, ancient truths endure as fads recede.

Expanded experience in the 1960s and '70s had its impact in the '80s as a new basic belief. Once-uncommon words came to be more traditional. What real difference does it make to say "spiritual energy is sweeping the Earth" or to say "the action of the holy spirit"? Now ready and strengthened by personal experiences, the sincere searchers of those three decades integrate scriptural messages with daily life. Challenged to put reality into practice on the physical plane, the bottom line is, can we alter the rapidly degenerating quality of life into a vision of love, acceptance, and sister-brotherhood? Can we create a world of peace and sharing? Do we really believe the lion and lamb are to lie down together? The inner voice says, *Reveal thyself. If you love me, follow.*

Can you see the Christ within yourself and life? This is the challenge, for until you do, the Christ-Within cannot awaken. If I say, imagine the brightest light-being you can, what occurs within? Do you see it? If I say to you, image the most beautiful woman and you give time for it to emerge, you will see a creation of great beauty, a lovely woman with the graciousness of love and light about her. If I say, create the strongest, most handsome man you can image, a picture will come to mind. Even if you begin with a thought of another living being, if held in the brightest love, it will alter and improve.

From where do these images come? They rise from the resources of your consciousness because they exist within you. So it is with the hard-to-create Light Being. The exercise to create the Being of Light forces you to reach to that level of self where that awareness arises. You call it into action. When you reach to find the loveliest woman or the exemplar of masculinity, you are sifting through yourself and finding that consciousness, even as once upon a time you pulled your personality into being.

Message Carol received June 16, 1979

As we sow seeds in the third millennium, we deepen our awareness in numerous ways of interlocking ties throughout the world. Modern media keep us informed of earthquakes, weather changes, food shortages, and hostilities nation to nation. We are being forced to know we are One with All, whether we want to know it or not. Now is the moment for which many messengers have awaited. The question becomes, have they been able to hold on to their reason for being here, or has the dense material plane and its selfishness captured them?

4

Sharing the Aurascope

aving been accepted by Ann Manser, seer and the first teacher of esoteric material I encounter, I become a dedicated seeker. I often say my goal was just "to know everything and to be perfect." Ann struggles, as I do, with love of the Church and feelings of growing beyond it. Her respectful approach serves me as I try to hold to the past with one hand and reach for the world beyond with the other.

As stated earlier, Ann did a specific type of soul analysis which she called aurascope. The aura is the color recording of life that is perceivable about each person, animal, plant—every living thing. This vibration records our thoughts, emotions, and soul patterns, as well as incoming and outgoing energies. The pattern and interpretation of the soul colors Ann finds in the aura speak to her about the evolution and objective of each. I am eager to learn what such a study will tell me about myself and my purpose.

In June 1969, Ann does my aurascope. The material is quite lengthy, so I am choosing the most pertinent for purposes of this book. The aurascope begins with an explanation of the uniqueness of each aura.

In each aura is some quality, shade, tone, or pattern unlike any other aura, thus each aura becomes a precise signature of the personality it surrounds.

Colors of your aura are a clear and wide medium shade of blue; a very dark shade of blue; another medium shade of blue that has a pronounced rattling sound in it; a medium shade of blue that is a most joyous, surging color; a regular singing blue; a dark and troubled blue that heaves in long rollers like the ocean; a light pink; a deep violet shade; one bright orange; one strange shade of orange-pink; a cream color with little straight pins of rose color in the cream. This gives you eleven colors and brings your present living and that of the past six years under the vibration of this number in which the soul and intellect of an individual receive understanding and wisdom from the Spirit of God, the aura of God which fills all space, the Holy Ghost.

Reading these words the first time, I recall the struggles of 1963 to '69, and I feel, "Yes, this applies." I have had so many painful experiences, often seeking God's help. I have been so alone with my awareness and vision of what I am to do, struggling to hold my home life together for the benefit of children, husband, and myself. I long to find solutions to the chaos about me. Step by step, the help gradually comes. The unexplainable events seem to be from the Holy Spirit. The paper continues.

This Hebrew number and letter, Lamed, teaches that our difficulties are self-induced, thus do we become our own judge and hangman. How long you will stay under the influence of the number Eleven depends upon how rapidly you unfold in your studies of the wisdom teachings. You may move out of it into a higher number within the next five years . . . or you may stay longer.

Looking back, I can see how wonderfully my life moved between 1969 and 1974. I truly believe a door opened in 1974, and I flew free. It was in late 1972 and early 1973, in fact, that I began a first spiritual community in St. Petersburg, revealing a whole new vista to me.

Your aura as a field of color is bright and sparkling like a spring morning after a rain. In fact, your aura reminds me of a rainshower just past, glittering and shimmering as if colored drops of water were hanging all through it. It trembles all the time, not in fear, not for any special reason except that it is your nature to be vibrant and alert, ready to move forward, ready to please, to improve in any way possible. All your colors have a commonality, a joyous uplifting vibration deep within each color. No matter what happens to your outward life, this joyousness, this bliss consciousness of your true being, remains intact. You can always go to your center of being and obtain help when troubled. This is going to God, of course. Your inner center is God, your contact with and understanding of God—part of your pattern, your framework, this heart center of God within your personality.

My life has presented many experiences that demonstrate the truth of Ann's perception. Since my wonderful experience of the Presence, I have not known the kind of despair young Carol had. I believe the new me can reach a level the earlier Carol could not. Exciting new ideas are introduced:

This proclaims you as an old soul—if nothing else does! In fact, you belong to the oldest spiritual family incarnating upon Earth at this time. I might mention that, as members of this ancient family from another planet incarnate, they are only fragments, that is, the incarnated part is only a fragment of the whole personality (soul). It is like taking a book off a shelf of books to study for a certain reason; you do not need the whole shelf of books, you need just the one for this time. So you choose just the one part of your personality—a spirit-economy, you might call this, to be used in this one life at this one time. The rest of the personality is accessible as you learn how to approach it, how to raise your consciousness to contact it. When the time is right, you will be able to do it.

This idea forms the basis of my perception of High Self and the *Christ-Within and helps me see that individuals may be focused at one level while much more awaits discovery. We come to recognize the precious moments when we receive guidance and are not too quick to presume valued information comes from an outside source, guide, or wise one. It may be one's own Self awakening!

The Great Central Sun of your planet is Sirius. That is where you come from and to where you will return eventually, your own spiritual home. As each one of us who is incarnating works with one attribute of the whole family, we can get overloaded on one thing, but thus we continue to purify and spiritualize that one aspect of the whole group.

My heart sings as she tells me of ties to a spiritual family.

The perfume of your aura is a violet fragrance, not violets, but an essence of all violet flowers mixed together—a fresh and lovely fragrance, again like flowers that have just been washed in a spring shower. It would not surprise me to know that you weep easily and often—all these glowing rain drops in your aura!

As I read this, I think of many people for and with whom I have cried. How easily the moisture comes to my eyes—often tears of happiness and joy. It seems my cup runneth over. The aurascope continues to explain the meaning of each color. As an artist, Ann naturally places much importance on shades and variations of color, and their meaning to life.

Your first blue, a clear medium shade, extends to a wide area around you . . . a field color used for about everything you do. It is exceedingly active, bright and observant, very pleasant in meeting the public in a business way. This color is composed, reasonable, calm at all times, even if other colors kick up a row within you. You overlay this color, covering your whole personality with it, until you choose to remove its protective covering. This blue is efficient, trustworthy, faithful, both to you and to any other person to whom you feel an obligation. First and most important, this is a business color.

Your second blue is dark, wholly an intuitive color. This dark blue guides the first blue a great deal in all you do. You glance into this dark blue, as into a mirror, before you work with the first blue, and in this dark blue you receive directives for the moment and for your next move. For inner guidance you depend very much on this dark second blue; it has never and will never let you down by betraying your trust in any way.

Ann later tells me this indigo color is the color of the psyche, a color hard to identify on the physical but powerful in the inner world. She teaches me how to use a bowl of water to ignite the inner eye. Later, I buy a crystal ball and play with it. The water, the crystal, a mirror can be used to *skry (a form of divination) if we have this inner blue with which to work. We perceive with this indigo or soul color as the higher reflects its message downward.

The third blue, Ann says, is
interesting due to the sound it emits. Any medium shade of blue is a mental quality used in everyday life—in habit, routines, daily duties,

problems. This blue sounds like teeth clicking together in a chill. The sound is audible to my objective senses! This is a kind of static nervousness you have fallen into by having too much to do, too much responsibility, being rushed for time. . . Actually you do have enough time. This blue has gotten into a habit of tension. You carry a heavy load of responsibility by choice . . . you chose just before you came into it. You have your life well ordered and going as you previously had planned. So try to drop this tension. Rationalize about it. . . . Let it ride along as it is supposed to. It will.

The third blue is a color of orderliness, precision, perfection, and a lot of things in your life . . . want you to think about these . . . perhaps you are putting too narrow a view upon all three. Your whole plan of life is orderly, precise; because you are following your spiritual direction, your plan is going exactly as it should. Isn't that a type of perfection?

The fourth blue, a joyous spiritual color which bubbles over into your everyday hours of living, literally sings as it moves along. An acquisitive color, it spiritually knows you have not demonstrated in your life a great deal of the knowledge and wisdom you have, and it longs for this to come about. As it longs, it stays in this beautiful bliss consciousness, this awareness of what is available and what will one day be yours. . . . this is a mild state of *samadhi, the heights of which all Children of the Path desire to attain above all else . . . lovely color.

These words certainly ring true. As illogical as it may seem, my life has been happy from some inner source.

Your fifth and last blue is dark, stormy, surging—heaving in great waves through your aura, at times darkening the whole field of color with its force and its troubled appearance. This is your place of stress and resistance in your personality, the repository within you where all of the troubles and stresses of your whole spiritual family are placed, along with your own stress and strain. This is for you to overcome, to lift, to sublimate. If something is there for you to work with, it is as if someone came along and said, "Here, take this, too. It is more of the same. You can clear it as easily as you can clear your own . . ." so you have both to work on, and when you do, you help the whole family advance in evolution. Each member of the family has this communal thing to deal with, both in the good . . . and in the adverse. When understood, it can be-

come a most beautiful sharing, a kind of vicarious atonement, the highest place of brotherly love.

I have come to know this deep rolling wave of emotion as my Pisces part and feel it surge and dive into the deep sorrowful place. Somehow the painful depth of where that goes in its suffering and martyrdom identifies with my Piscean ascendant and the Piscean age we have just come through. With all this blue, no wonder it has been a favorite color for so many years of my life. Later my favorite color will become violet, a strong second earlier.

Light pink is a vibrant color . . . smiling, gracious, and attractive, with acceptable manners and mannerisms. It takes a very long time to get a pink in the aura . . . many lives of discipline, training in social behavior, training in ethics, in thinking of other people's comfort and well-being . . . after a long time this color and its attending qualities go inward . . . that individual becomes magnetic, naturally attractive, attentive and gracious. People with this shade of pink are pretty, beautiful, attractive; if they are actually not, then they appear so, which is the same thing! Attained light within shines through the physical form.

Violet is a shade of beauty awareness, often of longing and nostalgic feelings about what one does not have and cannot seem to attain . . . a color of vision and idealism. Your violet, dark and rich, shows a measure of contentment. Spiritually, mentally, and perhaps emotionally, you have attained beauty in your life. There is considerable healing in this color—not healing as a conscious attribute, but a natural healing force, an intrinsic quality. . . . You will never do more with this color than now; it is as it should be for this life. In your next life, you will use this violet in a much more important way. It will then be one of your most important colors in that life's work, coming into full force as a healing and creative color.

As I continue to grow and ponder the universe, I wonder about the healing work of the future and feel intrigued by Ann's suggestion. Remember, we take all our colors, including those gained in this life, into the next.

Orange is a color that comes easily before an audience, the color of the public speaker, an actor, an entertainer, an emcee—of the one to many. There is self-assurance in this orange, a kind of forgetfulness of self, and unself-consciousness. A committee color, a mediator, an ar-bitrator, it never gets thrown off base . . . never loses its centerpoint of thought. It can give a kidding and take the same, without giving or taking offense. A friendly color, quite certain that everyone likes it and you . . . and of course, that is the response!

If I feel terribly shy or vulnerable before a lecture, I visualize this color flowing to and around me until I sense its flow. I experience the comfort it gives, and I am ready to do my thing. I think the color awakens the performer Leo in my chart. Or it may be because it works with the lower chakra centers, where our sense of security resides.

Orange-pink, an unusual color . . . cannot be described because it cannot be pigmented . . . more of a psychic shade than a material . . . does not belong to our spectrum of color at all. This color comes from the Sirius spectrum and therefore does not mean what it would if we mixed orange and pink together. Here it becomes a mental prerequisite, a place in your mind where you do not think like anyone else at all. This ties in with your particular stress place and how you react to it. This inclusive color operates in gathering together like vibrations. You cannot use it for yourself alone but for yourself as you relate to others and as they respond to you. When other living beings require something special, you seldom try to figure out why they need what they do; you just take it for granted that what they require is the thing for them; that what they desire or want is the right thing for them to have (if you can obtain it for them). This is a wonderful selfless reaction. You do not like to be questioned as to why you want some certain thing when you do. Let it suffice that you do want it, you grant the same privilege to others . . . without imposing your will on them . . . one of the major reasons you have been given this community-stress thing to handle as regards your spiritual family. It never occurs to you to say, "Well, what is he worried about THAT for?" That he is worrying is all you need know to come to the rescue if you can.

Cream is a color of sensitivity in an aura . . . your cream is not given to getting your feelings hurt, not that kind of sensitivity . . . this sensitivity goes to an intuitive understanding in relationships with other living beings. Through this color you can immediately put yourself in the place of another and see why he acts and reacts as he does . . . through this cream, you see the action behind the result.

I have felt that both the orange-pink and the cream are the vibrations I use in making spiritual attunements that have to with personality traits and spiritual reasons for certain things to be dealt with, karmic patterns working out, or past-life influences responsible for events in a life. The color study is drawing to a close.

Rose-colored, straight little pins with heads and sharp points are in the cream. A color superimposed upon a basic color has only to do with that color. It is not related to other colors in the aura. So your little sharp pins have to do with what the cream color exposes to you about other living beings, what your sensitivity relates to you about them and their actions and reflexes.

Rose is the color of love. Pins are sharp and penetrating. They can hurt . . . when they are stuck into something, a situation, a problem that comes to your attention, but even if you inflict pain with the pins, they eventually do good to the one upon whom you have used them because they are motivated by love; always love; nothing else . . . kindness, compassion, love . . . backed by your deep intuitive understanding and sensitivity.

I cringe when I think of this "sticking pink pins into others." At times, I realize I do this. I feel it is very important that those who love us tell us the truth; yet so often they will not. We may think we are protecting those we love by believing them to be different than they really are. As we become clearer about who they really are and still love them, we become happier and so will they. If we can stand to hear the truth, even if delivered with a pin, and still love others, we will be a better and more balanced person, giving and receiving the support we need. I say this as an Aquarian who can take criticism only in small doses. My guidance has been to speak the truth in kindness, and I struggle to do so.

The aurascope taught me much about my personal nature. I have withheld some information, but the teaching material is here as we learn the first clues to identity with Sirius. Later, astrological details will refer to Sirius.

The challenge of walk-ins, the would-be messengers, is to recall they have come into this dimension to deliver a message. Even while they stretch to deal with the powerful information they carry, can they be of any earthly good? Many can.

Teachers—Inner and Outer

nn's ideas were taught on an oral, one-to-one basis. To preserve them, she spent years writing the *Shustah material,[1] her legacy. Her perspective of ancient wisdom was primarily Christian kabalist. Her writings include sixty-six lessons on ageless teachings and sixty-six lessons on the *Kabalah. Since color was her favorite medium, the work teems with theories of life as vibration as revealed through color.

The prospect of being a soul incarnating from the Sirius family, a free-soul evolution, presented a means to objectively accept portions of myself and my experiences. It is heady stuff! Ann thoroughly explored the evolutions. Her perspective: many streams of life, "families," incarnate in our solar system. Earth being a slowly vibrating planet, contact with other families excites and inspires the human kingdom. She made these ideas—basic to most *gnostic thought— real to her students in her unique, colorful way.

Pythagoras taught that unless we study mathematics or a physical science, we should not have access to wisdom teachings. He may have had something! I often think, how fortunate I had to work each day; evenings were filled with raising my children. Those years of lofty fantasies and dreams of devas, spacial beings, and messengers from Sirius were balanced with dinner to be cooked and laundry done. Today, when I see heavy work patterns and family demands in the lives of impatient, fervent aspirants, I know it is a blessing. If both the stretching of reality and the grounding in earthly effort prevail, in time a great soul may stand revealed. We recall the guidance to "chop wood and carry water."

Ann graphically describes two major spiritual paths. Using the kabalistic Tree of Life, she says that, like most spiritual teachers, I am on the arrow path, while humanity, as a group consciousness, is on the lightning path. Let me show you:

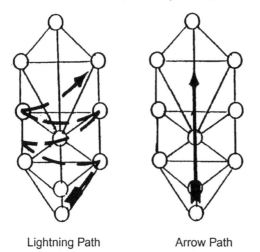

Lightning Path   Arrow Path

On the lightning path we are pulled to and fro by the world's polarities and always striving for balance. We go to the midpoint, pass it, may go to an extreme, check ourselves or are checked by life situations, then we swing back toward the midpoint, much like a pendulum or the *middle-road path.

A teacher, usually fervent and impatient, chooses the arrow path—highly disciplined, straight toward God. These souls try everything, often a great deal that is unwise; they usually suggest the opposite to their students, to learn through the teacher's experience, not to try everything. This "taking the gates of heaven by storm" type is powerful and fervent, as is the energy. The dedicated life is focused into a tight pattern—the reason this person can rapidly penetrate the secrets of the universe.

We recall here the kabalistic warning from the Talmud. Kabalah teachers taught: Four people enter the studies—the first one dies; the second wanders around and loses reason; the third misuses the knowledge and is turned back; the fourth proceeds in peace and reaches *enlightenment.

Because of their fervor, students of the arrow path may be in greater danger. The lightning (zigzag) path brings a natural balance; moving between polarities, from one extreme to the other, means a more gradual process toward high consciousness with greater stability. On the arrow path, fanaticism, imbalance, and *karma may easily be created and greatly delay one. The warning is really to say, "The path of a dedicated seeker and knower is fraught with danger." A teacher is a kind of protector for the student, but the student must accept guidance or a teacher can be of little help.

As this bombardment of data enters my life from the outside, doors continue to open. My personal life remains full, and my business life reaches exciting heights. I discover confidence and strength as I learn to "hold my own" in challenging areas. Recognition encourages me. My perceptive skills are a benefit in the market place. As promotions come, my income advances. In lectures as a personnel manager, I apply knowledge acquired from spiritual studies. I love it!

My inner life in the late 1960s is equally exciting. I struggle to find a daily quiet time in a never-quiet household. As a night person, hard to stir in the morning, I elect a late-hour discipline time. My day begins at 5:30 A.M., but no matter what else, I am home, quiet, and ready for my meditation at 11 P.M. Ann, then Irene, prescribes exercises and techniques for me. I record the impressions I receive in journals and dream diaries, listening for the wee small voice as it grows clearer. The uncontrollable waves of emotion and energy of earlier years steadily decrease. I say affirmations and learn to talk myself down when I feel I am losing hold.

Noticing how sensitive my body is to certain foods and spices, I watch my diet. Neither alcohol nor meat has played much part in my thrifty life. My necessarily simple existence has served me well; perhaps I have been protected. Just past thirty, single, and getting attention as never before, I contend with questions of sexuality. After all, I had married two days after high school graduation at age sixteen.

Ann, Irene, and Leroy listen while I talk. I gain some insight to my passionate nature that seeks spiritual satisfaction. Ideas of celibacy fascinate me in a society bombarded with sensual advertising.

The unrest of women everywhere engrosses me. The women's movement inspires and calls, presenting ways to explore and to share ideas and opportunities. I am touched by the patience of the founder of the Temple, Rev. Laurane Stroud, as she relates her spiritual unfoldment of fifty years ago when, so isolated, no one in Alabama believed her experiences. While inspired by the endurance of women waiting "their turn," I am impatient and want to do what I came in for—now!

I see the stability women have, but I choose to break out. I do not have Laurane's kind of time. I am turned off by the anger of early feminists, yet I know a new time has come. I do not identify with extremists, but I certainly do with moderates. I have suffered job discrimination and low wages while I train men for positions above me. I hear, "Men have to make more money than women because they are primary bread winners," yet I have eight children at home to support. Strong feelings rise as I deplore the inequity of the system. My parents do not want me to upset the applecart: "These things move slowly."

In time, I no longer separate spiritual concepts and guidelines of life from my career. Everything merges into a challenge to make the world a better place for me, my children, other women, and yes, men. I feel equality for souls, that a spiritual concept cannot be true unless it applies to all. I find wisdom in and respect for every religion. I am comforted by the mysticism of Eastern teachings when I suffer from the analytical edification of the West. I am angered by the only-way attitude of Christianity. If I wait for the Church to help me, I may lose my sanity. I try to subdue the anger, but after my divorce and loss of the Catholic support system, which stood by me through abuse but not divorce, my indignation rises. Close friends evaporate with the scandal, although they knew for years my husband was both abusive and unfaithful. It is a crazy culture that fosters dishonesty, or so I saw it.

I hunger for freedom; I dislike pat answers. I want to know what Truth really is. I want to know it all and now. Eastern teachings engage my mind in searching inquiry, and though they often give me more questions, the *koans give me peace. When I discover, "If one way is right, the other way is not necessarily wrong," a powerful breakthrough eases my guilt at not being like everyone else. I begin to leave behind "right or wrong" to find a new platform of comprehension. I can be right, and others can also be right. Hurrah! I can just be me.

Now I accept this impersonality as a way of being objective and true to insights I might lose if I identify more closely—empathy rather than sympathy. Then one evening, Rev. Zemke takes me aside to talk to me about someone at the church calling me aloof. My feelings are so hurt. I recall saying, "How can I be seen as aloof when I care so much?" He explains the positives and negatives of detachment and how it causes some not to feel loved enough. I have much to learn about expressing love more openly.

Acutely sensitive and intense, my personality struggles to stabilize. I must love others without over-reacting and be more objective about my weaknesses. I intensify my purification work, eager to achieve what I had held within so long.

The years 1970 to '73 challenge my strong ego in power struggles with others and seem to intensify my other weaknesses. With the aid of my inner teacher and Ann, I see my character flaws more clearly, then confront them one by one. It is not a talking process but down-to-Earth work on weak areas. Culling them as I can, I learn not to expect shortcuts. I cry, I pray, I apologize; mostly I become more honest with myself. With each bitter struggle, I learn to shift to my inner guide and seek understanding.

The now-familiar sign of the unfolding peacock comes to me again and again with wisdom. Tender words of the inner voice give me hope that my spiritual fortitude will last and I will love enough to do what I have come to do. When my ego becomes demanding, I experiment and find I can play most of the psychic games, i.e., past-life contacting, channeling, aura reading, psychometry, and so on. I am tempted to the utmost. It is a long time before I can really give myself to the mission at hand. I bargain with God, giving in as little as possible, but gradually I am ready. Finally, I know that from now on, wherever it leads, I will follow my guidance. Resistance dissipates; I change my lifestyle and claim my inner allegiance, but not until a most dramatic occurrence I am finally ready to share.

The Visitation

The years of preparation are filled with work, family, and study. Wonderful experiences pepper my life, weaving inner and outer aspects together. Soon it is Ordination, July 3, 1971, St. Petersburg, Florida, where I step into the role for which I have prepared myself with the most able assistance of a heritage of strong, dedicated spiritual workers. Now I feel indisputably upon my spiritual path. Having left my business employment, I am associated with a local metaphysical church now and just beginning to teach spiritual classes and do private counseling.

A remarkable story about an inner experience is often met with such incredulity that many keep silent, shielding precious moments from misinterpreting minds. One such experience occurred to me early in 1972. So remarkable and potent, rarely have I shared this pearl beyond price until now.

My rather rambling house has a large bedroom which can be entered by either of two doors. One night, alone and a bit uncomfortable—all the children are away—the last thing I do before going to bed is lock those doors. I read, as is my custom, and finally turn out the light. In this rarely silent, empty house, I fall asleep, only to awaken, conscious of a presence in the room. Incredibly, I feel unafraid of this strangely familiar presence. Sitting on the bed next to mine a tall, striking gentleman in an elegant robe of the Orient and turban of aqua blue silk peers at me most seriously.

El Morya

Everything within me recognizes him. I have no name to give him, but I KNOW he is not a stranger. I sit up and push myself back against the pillow. The scent of roses fills the room, though none are present.

"I am El Morya," the gentleman announces, "the one who comes to you with the sign of the peacock. I come to tell you many things. Take your pencil and pad, and write down what I say. Otherwise, in the morning you will think this is all a dream." Reaching for pad and pen I keep beside the telephone, I write. The message is profuse. My fingers race to capture his words. His calm voice goes on and on, giving me information I did not realize I had been anticipating. As I write, I question little, just obediently record pages of material pertaining to my purpose in life.

You are here for the purpose of God, others, and the Plan. You do not belong to your family or to yourself. Your home is to be a place of honesty and integrity. Your soul cannot live and do its work in deceit.

Your life is meant to be hard, because it has a purpose, and much is to be done before it is over. Someday you will look back and see how it has been five lives in one.

Your restlessness regarding religion is because religion is mostly empty form. Your work is to revitalize the form into a container that has spiritual meaning.

As a woman, you are asked to go where women rarely go and to practice bravery and courage. You are not to harbor anger or hatred. Move forward through the lives you live without looking back. This will challenge you.

You are of the first ray on loan to ray two for a holy purpose. Healing is needed for the world. Aid all persons in a healing ministry.

The children are not for your happiness. They are tests for you, as well as being loved ones. They care little for you or your work. Your influence will matter little to them. Do not seek pleasure here.

The world is your home, and you will weep many tears for it. You are to love the unlovable and try to awaken them to their purpose in life. The love of which I speak is not emotional, but a rich, inex-

haustible supply of sustaining energy that flows into life again and again, but not everyone understands this.

You are with me in another place [inner-plane life], so you know me here. You will work with me later. Now I am awakening you to minor things so you will be ready when the time comes.

Whether I come again is not important, I have come once. It is begun. If you wait for me to come before you believe, I will not. If you do what I ask you, I do not need to come again.

My greeting to you, "Rejoice." Whether in pain or pleasure, in death or life, always rejoice. Rejoice that you have eyes and ears, that you have pain and joy. Rejoice that you are in your place doing that for which you entered.

Carriers of the dispensation are few. Again and again, you will be blessed and strengthened by being in the presence of the spiritually great. This will cause joy, even sickness if you are out of synchronization with their rhythm.

You are to carry a harsh message, a message people will hate at times, and many will misunderstand you. Does this stop one from being of God? Angels treading among men must remember they are angels and not beg men to understand them. Do not cry out against those to whom you have come.

Your children provide for you an understanding of the weaknesses of the world. You need them. There must be heart ties to the human family. Your students will reflect to you your strength. If you encourage, they will encourage you. If you doubt yourself, they will doubt you.

Resist not being a woman. DO NOT fear to break through the walls of restriction, for this is part of what you are to do. Many strong and enlightened teachers from the past are taking bodies as women now to help bring in an equal age. Spirit can work equally well in either. Do not become a bitter woman, for this is worst of all.

My name, whispered daily in your ear, comes to help you grow wise and strong. For this you have come into this body.

I do not remember the end of the visit. As I awaken the next morning, I immediately recall my impressive, exciting "dream." I remain quiet, trying to summon the details. When I recall as much as I can, still in awe of the power of such dreaming, I swing my feet off the bed, and there on the floor rests the legal pad covered with writing.

I reach for it quickly, hands shaking, and read the dictated notes, some of which I have shared with you. The enveloping feeling of rich love and the perfume of roses build again as I recall the visitor with the piercing eyes who looked right into my soul.

The visit was real! He was here in my room!!! Was it a physical manifestation or a vision? How can I know? Who is he? I recognized him, but has anyone else ever seen him?

His clothes were so elegant, his manner so refined. His patience with me contrasted to his piercing eyes—both tender and fierce. He had called me an affectionate name, something like "child." Later I come to know the word *chela and to learn many more things about him.

This visit throws my life into high gear. I seek advice from Ann, Leroy, and others. Everyone points me to the material of the *Theosophical Society and *Blavatsky, and more doors open. Leroy and others fill in the gaps of my understanding. I read everything I can find, especially about the Masters. Now it is not just a term. Before, it was a rank, a level of development, a goal, as in Masters of the Far East. Now it is a person—precisely, Master Morya.

About this same time, early 1970s, I locate *The Finding of the Third Eye* by Vera Stanley Alder of London. What a wonderful book! I tell my friend, Grace Bradley, "This is the book I won't have to write." I need this so much; now to locate the author. I write the publisher, Rider and Company, London, asking them to forward my letter but receive no response.

When David Spangler of Findhorn fame visits St. Pete, I discover he knows her well; he encourages me to write again. In a few months, her response arrives, and a treasured ten-year relationship with my second teacher begins. I quickly acquire every book she has written. (She handed me her last, *From the Mundane to the Magnificent*, in person as it arrived from her publisher.) Combined with Ann's training, they give me the best of both worlds, and I love teaching from them. Her personal letters are discourses on the future and questions I am to answer.

Unforeseen Romance

St. Pete is my home base as my horizons broaden, teaching in Cocoa, Orlando, Sarasota, Gainesville. My great delight is sharing my inner realities to an awakening society. My limited personal life changes when unexpected but not unpredicted romance enters my life. In the late 1960s, psychically awakened people begin asking me, "Does the name Charles mean anything to you?" At first, I respond in the negative. When it happens several more times, I realize Carol is the feminine of Charles, and I begin responding yes. Perhaps they are perceiving the masculine aspect of my strong personality.

One morning in meditation, I receive a message that a man will come into my life to help me with my mission and he will say, "Let me tell you about my peacock." This, of course, has great meaning for me. The peacock signaled direction for me, as a symbol representing my inner teacher. I paid attention.

The peacock itself carries great significance in both Eastern and Western wisdom traditions. In the East it is the sign of the Master, one who has evolved to high consciousness and sees through many "eyes"; in the mystical Christian tradition it represents the Phoenix or all-seeing eye of God. Even today, the beautiful Wells Cathedral in England has a large cross with a fully feathered, long-tailed peacock sitting on the arm, representing the Christ ever renewing life.

Since I have no idea I will remarry—in fact, protest when the subject arises—I do not believe this to be a marriage partner but one with whom I would share the development of a center or school after we somehow discover we are both guided by the same inner teacher or Master. The peacock, so symbolic, would also be his inner signal, and thus we would come together for the greater good.

Mr. Harra and his mother come to Lake Junaluska, North Carolina, to the SFF annual retreat, where all of us attend Marcus Bach's morning lecture. As I take my seat toward the middle of audience, I notice a gentleman toward the front with a flowing aura about him. A woman sits with him. I wonder if this is a workshop leader.

After the lecture, I come face to face with this gentleman, the lady at his side. He hesitates, to allow me to step into the aisle, and asks, "Aren't you Carol Parrish from St. Petersburg?" As I nod, he continues, "I am Charlie Harra of Sarasota, and this is my mother, Shirley Harra of Tampa." I respond, "I saw a lovely light around you in chapel," to which his intrigued mother replies, "And what does that mean?" I answer, "It means he is a very fine person." And she agrees, "Indeed he is."

This synchronistic meeting bears fruit a couple of months later when I get a call from Charlie Harra. He is in Sarasota and tells me his mother has fallen and broken two vertebrae a few days before. At her age, the injury is taking its toll. Suffering greatly, she leaves the hospital with restricted activity and heavy doses of pain medication prescribed. The prognosis is serious. Charles and a friend bring me to Tampa for a spiritual healing for his mom. Using an energy transfusion method, I work with her and then am taken home.

A month or so later, the Sarasota chapter of SFF invites me to be their guest speaker the next month on the subject of spiritual healing. When the evening comes, as I enter the hall, chairperson Gloria Albritton tells me, "Charles Harra is introducing you tonight."

In his introduction I hear for the first time an update on his mother's condition. Charles had timed the treatment: twelve minutes, after which his mother slept quite deeply most of the day. The next morning, she chose not to take pain medication and went with her daughter on a fifty-mile drive. She returned to her regular lifestyle and to her apartment (where she continued to live alone until her ninety-seventh birthday).

Days later, her orthopedic surgeon, who had read her x-rays and was a neighbor, came over to ask what had happened to his patient since she had not come back for follow-up. In addition to her back feeling better, she explained, her mind seemed clearer. Mother Harra said she felt younger after the healing.

This lecture triggers sufficient interest in spiritual healing to spawn an eight-week class, meeting all day every Saturday. Mr. Harra organizes the enrollment. These day-long sessions create an atmosphere for blossoming friendships. Another class follows:

this time a weekly spiritual science study group, again in Sarasota, and again Mr. Harra participates.

Imagine my surprise when, after class one night, my dear friend, Grace Bradley, and I accept an invitation for coffee, and while chatting, Charles Harra off-handedly says, "Let me tell you about my peacock." My undivided attention focuses on every word. I am stunned. This gentleman is uttering those meaningful words! My mind reels as he describes his real, live pet peacock. Now my image of what this would mean begins to crumble. I am numb as I stand up; Grace and I go to the car. As we drive home to St. Petersburg, I am barely able to talk. My mind races to find meaning to this development, but it will take a year or two for these pieces to create this new chapter in my life.

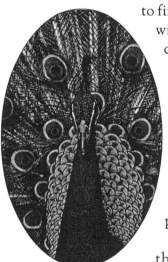

"Let me tell you about my peacock."

Although I had told others of these meaningful words in the past, I cannot share them with this man. I watch and wonder. With family, studies, teaching, and work commanding all of my attention, my social life is nil. I love being free to do what I know is mine to do. I have no clue how this puzzle might be resolved.

Charles Harra had been involved in the studies, attending seminars and classes since his Air Force service. As a pilot in England during World War II, phenomenal experiences had stirred his inner nature, and he had sought out the Silver Birch writings.[2] While flying missions and later working in base operations, his spiritual psyche began to declare itself.

A couple of months later, tiredness begets magic. Frustrated and exhausted from proofing a new catalog of classes—at this time I am president of the Florida Humanistic Institute—Grace asks me what I would really like to do. I tell her I would love to go out on a boat and rest. I have a small catamaran I enjoy from time to time but not as often as I would like. Grace says, "Why don't you call that man in Sarasota who's offered to take you on his boat?" What a great idea. Indeed, I call Mr. Harra (as I still often refer to him) and ask if this would be possible. This call triggered a friendship that even today continues to touch so many lives—not just my own.

Charles becomes a regular in my group life. The community in St. Pete knows him as a quiet, helpful member, as well as a person with great know-how. Our friendship grows, and I realize I had better be careful; I cannot let anything into my life that might distract me from my work.

Charles' forty-foot twin-engine cruiser is his release from his work and soon becomes mine as well. We enjoy long talks and philosophical discussions as I laugh and rest between the hectic home-life with my children and a demanding schedule of classes. I love my unfolding life.

Am I falling in love? I cannot see how I can leave my wondrous opportunities. I constantly hold in heart and mind, "I must not forget the commission I received in the Light." Pushing aside feelings for this sincere man, I work harder.

One day on the boat at the Venice Yacht Club on Florida's gulf coast, we almost speak of love. As I glance up, a rich pink color surrounds Charles and floods my heart. "Charles, your aura is all pink." He responds, "Yours is too." I think, "I want to marry this man." Tears fill my eyes as he touches me gently, and we withdraw into our own thoughts. It is months before words carry us closer. I know Charles has other ladies in his life, and for me it is all or nothing. We talk openly and seriously. I have no expectations as I leave for a circuit of lecturing.

Charles is a highly eligible bachelor. He had been married years before and has a twenty-year-old daughter. As business manager for New College—now an honors college for University of South Florida—he enjoys an active social life. This chatty, handsome Gemini, with a lovely yacht to boot, squires lovely ladies about regularly. His sparkle and quick sense of humor charm us all.

As I prepare to return from my tour of several weeks, my secretary, Phyllis Zinns, tells me Charles has called and wants me to return his call. When I do, he persuades me to change my ticket and fly to Sarasota, rather than Tampa, for the weekend. When I see him waiting for me, I realize I need to guard my heart. A rich smile and warm embrace welcome me. An SFF retreat is this weekend, and I am not working, just present to recuperate.

That evening, a gentleman shares some messages. As we sit on a couch across from him, he says to Charles, "I see you and your wife going to London. There is something important for the two of you there. You will be very happy." We are not married, so I am not sure what he means. However, within months of our marriage, we find ourselves making our first trip to visit Vera Stanley Alder and rejoicing in a significant new friendship and spiritual ties.

Our lives shift into high gear. As I prepare for my sermon one fine Sunday morning in autumn 1975, a knock comes at my door. It is Charles, who rarely comes to St. Pete in the morning. He comes in saying this will take only a minute. Seated on the small couch, he takes my hands and asks me to marry him. And I utter, "Yes, yes, I will." We stand; a quick kiss and he rushes out, saying he'll see me after church. Within minutes I am conducting the church service, all the while thinking, "Carol, you have just changed your life." I am wonderfully, magically in love with this man with all of my being. He later tells me that while looking into my beautiful blue eyes, the color shifted to a dark brown. He said he felt intuitively that when he proposed to me, El Morya accepted.

As a Gemini and Aquarian, we talk about everything—especially my commitment to my mission, his appreciation of my efforts, and how he would support them. Now I can tell him about the "peacock prophecy." Secret plans begin for a small, beautiful wedding at a community outside Gainesville which Charles and I have frequented. I call Mickey Singer, the leader, to share my good news and ask him to perform the ceremony at the Temple of Love, a place we both love and respect. He agrees. We confide in four women especially dear to my heart: of course, Rev. Grace Bradley; Rev. Rose Pellegrini of St. Petersburg (her mother Mary Rossi makes my wedding dress); Thelma Carlysle and Fran Ward of Gainesville. Everyone is sworn to secrecy.

I am giddy, happy, and scared to death. Who knows what Charles, the carefree bachelor, is feeling? We write a small, personal service, with only those present who can support us in this effort. Believing no one will understand, we do not tell our families. We are from very different worlds—his so formal, mine so suspect. It is 1975, and new thought is truly "fringe."

I manage to scoop up three of my children. They drive up with Grace. They all know

Carol Parrish and Charles Harra on their wedding day.

Charles, but they know little about the day until I tuck their new clothes into suitcases that morning. "We are marrying Charles today, and you get out of school." My hands shake as Grace loads them in her car.

Two wondrous phone calls come that morning before Charles arrives to pick me up. The first, Dr. Iswar Sharma, a frequent speaker for Association for Research and Enlightenment (ARE), SFF, and Florida Humanistic Institute, says, "Blessings, Carol, for you and that wonderful man from Sarasota. Today is your wedding day, yes?" I sputter. He has met Charles perhaps twice at programs. "How did you know?" I ask. "Oh," he says, "I got it in meditation this morning." I thank him and feel heaven confirms our event.

Within minutes, the phone rings again. This time it is Dr. Ramamurti S. Mishra, a dear friend I have known for years, as have so many in St. Pete. I see his little brown face, his orange cap, and his loving smile as I write. A frequent visitor, he has laughed and played with my children as we devour ice cream and I tell him how my heart aches to go to India. I know I have left something there. Now he acknowledges he knows today is the wedding. He assures me, "It is ordained to the two of you, a blessing you have earned. You are to serve God and grow together." In a few months, he comes to Florida to bless us in person.

What comfort these calls are for this young woman in love, scared, and battered by her own past. Now she must go forward courageously. These calls of reassurance carry the spiritual endorsement so helpful to proceed happily, embracing the changes of the unfolding plan. Now I see Charles fulfilling the promise, "A man will come into your life and help you." Indeed. Here he is, and indeed he has worked so tirelessly and unceasingly to support the Work!

The Adventure Expands

Charles has been on his spiritual quest for years—reading, meditating, quietly investigating. Our lives entwine wonderfully, and we see the benefits of coworking daily. In 1976 we establish Villa Serena, a small spiritual center in Sarasota where we rejoice in truly and wonderfully living one day at a time.

My correspondence training with Vera continues. Because Charles loves England, having been stationed there, we find ourselves traveling to and fro and building close ties to Vera and her husband, Aage Larsen.

Vera is a successful portrait painter in Europe, as well as an author.

Interesting, both she and Ann are artists and writers. I too painted briefly. Some of my first experiences of lost time were when I planned to paint for an hour or so, and soon dawn was breaking. Concentration and focus open the serene place for many it seems; time stands still when so engrossed.

Aage Larsen and
Vera Stanley Alder.

The Way We Were

After a visit with Vera in Bournemouth, England, in 1980, I go to India for the first time. I have been studying with Vera for some time now. Special love is felt for a mentor, and I am grateful to acknowledge the treasures passed from this soul to me. Ours is truly a love story.

Born October 29, 1898, in the late 1970s, Vera Stanley Alder is ageless. Young beyond her years, lovely beyond her physical attributes, proud to be a Scorpio (Leo rising, moon in Taurus), her visionary ability charms her friends. As her student, you know you are privileged. Her home is mysteriously charged with the atmosphere of a world server. The corner serving as her office holds an imposing world map of her contacts; every correspondent has a pin, and she knows who is in most every country.

She takes me to the map and tells me stories of how she longs to help each take part of the Plan to weave humanity into the future of the great possibilities she discloses. Vera puts into words a picture of the evolved humanity she envisions through the mists of time. Her students are to see that it happens. She is an agent, and angel, of transformation. Whether writing you a directive or looking into your face with full earnestness, she lovingly charges you to go forward into planetary service.

Since reading *Finding of the Third Eye*[1] in 1972, I have been under Vera's influence. Her materials are clearly in harmony with my message; those who are ready for a bigger world picture need a clear, concise introduction to the teachings. Her work fills me with such joy. She graciously picks up the threads of spiritual development begun by Ann Manser, still living but not well. Ann had taken a baby student and given her concepts, words, and direction. Vera builds upon what Ann set into motion and brings sophistication with both her English charm and boldness.

She sees herself as preparing me as an international worker for the Hierarchy. She is looking for the next generation of those touched by the Hierarchy. We spend hours probing the relationship with Masters and teachers who prompt our actions. Both of us have experienced intervention from the Unseen, so we have a tie only that can bring. Raphael has given Vera a mission and continues to guide her thoughts, and Master Morya has left an indelible mark upon me.

Our passion is dedicated to laying the foundation of a world yet to be, our hearts bonded in the immediate task. Vera seeks those she feels are dedicated to the Great Work, so she blesses me with her fervent awareness and her prize of knowledge.

A modern woman long before it is fashionable, Vera is, in her words, Bohemian, and proud of it. On one visit when Charles and I are staying in a charming English bed-and-breakfast around the corner, we are invited to dinner with Vera and Aage. When we arrive at Vera's flat, she is already in the drawing room, looking lovely. She asks us to be seated, saying Aage will be along shortly. Indeed. Down the sidewalk he comes with a dinner cart! A white tablecloth covers our meal, Aage pushing as fast as he can so the food will not get cold. The table is set at Vera's, but Aage has prepared the meal at his flat several houses away because Vera does not like the smell of food to linger in the air at her place.

Vera Stanley Alder

At the time of her marriage, Vera was living with her dear friend and long-time secretary, Norah. Having worked together for years, she will not allow their world service to be disrupted; yet Vera fully accepts that Aage is her soul companion. She had seen his face in meditation years before. When he appears at her flat in London to inquire about wisdom teachings, she knows him to be the helper she needs for the rest of her life. She recognizes (and loves) his Danish blue eyes immediately, yet her sense of loyalty to Norah is immense. How to resolve. On February 16, 1963, Vera and Aage marry in Copenhagen, where Aage stayed a few more years to complete his employment. Coming to England as a pensioner to be with Vera, he moves Vera and Norah to Bournemouth where it is warmer, fulfilling Vera's desire for sunshine every day and a garden of her own.

I know Norah—a bulwark of strength to Vera—only slightly. The two have the dedication required to conduct the worldwide letter-writing campaign called "The Order of World Guardians." They answer letters daily or work on a manuscript. Aage is the spark of laughter, fun, and charm needed to lure the women away from work, to eat, take a walk, or enjoy the garden.

When Vera writes the foreword to my first book, *A New Age Handbook on Death and Dying,*[2] her support means so much. We discuss Alice Bailey having written the foreword to Vera's *Finding of the Third Eye*[3] and that by Vera writing for my first book, I carry the lineage of regal women. Vera often refers to me as her spiritual daughter. My spirit rejoices each time I consider how the grace of earlier work has flowed to me, through me, and to new generations of their world servers.

If you take a piece of sculpture and give it form, others seeing it will say, "She made it." Some will say, "Does it not remind you of her?" Perception reveals the link to our creations, just as we are linked to God consciousness through the stream from which we have come.

Message Carol received July 10, 1980

During these years, I become increasingly aware of a nagging ache to go to India. I cannot get over my love of India. I have made peace time and again with my Western self, yet my heart aches to go to India. I have an inner contact and an outer teacher who meet my needs—what do I want from India? I do not know, but I am certain India is pulling me to her. On my way, I decide to introduce students to Vera.

At her home Vera charms visitors with futuristic ideas that engage imagination, then demands to cross examine how and why these may come about. This exercise transpires when I take a group of students from the U.S. to meet Vera in 1980. They should know this genteel English woman who works diligently for World Guardianship. A trip to England's sacred sites and a brief visit to Bournemouth, then off to India we will go!

In 1984, after years of loving friendship, sharing, training— sifting through concepts, books, and manuscripts half completed, ideas scribbled on pieces of paper—I am on my way to be with

Vera again when she does indeed slip away in her sleep, May 26. Upon checking in at the hotel in Bournemouth, the clerk says, "There is a message for you," and I know, "Vera is gone." The note is from Aage, who is awaiting my arrival. It is Sunday afternoon, and Vera had not awakened Saturday morning.

Aage is numb, and grateful I am here. I am stunned. Though not ill, Vera had become increasingly fragile, simply disappearing before our eyes. Each visit she was more easily fatigued and more intense about the Work. Now we are all sad. I go immediately by cab to Aage. Our tears mingle as he tells me how much she was anticipating my visit and meeting this new group of friends. He has not begun to arrange anything but has waited until I arrive.

Ten students are with me to pay this tribute to my dear teacher who has blessed all of us. The funeral service is attended by only six or eight English people, her beloved Aage, myself, and the ten Americans who had come to say hello, but instead are privileged to represent all world servers who love and appreciate the service of this soul. Vera will be honored later in a memorial service in London by many who love her and the inspired work to which she dedicated her life. Back home we had already planned this day to be a special Sunday for Vera: *Celebrating the Life of a Living Legend*.

Agni Yoga, a Contemporary Path of Ethical Living

After the visit of Master Morya, guidance intensifies. I follow it as clearly as possible, carefully evaluating its effects on my life and often sharing it with wise ones who provide additional insights. One such piece gives me the words, *Agni Yoga is your way*. As the words enter my head, I ask, "Is this a telepathic thought from another mind or an insight from my own High Self?" I do not know. Later, the words appear again in a writing, *Agni Yoga is your way*. I keep searching. I thought I had ended the pursuit of the Eastern way. Having chosen and been ordained in the Christian tradition, I felt I had made peace with my personal struggle with the Church and believe this is the right path for me to follow.

But my search for Agni is launched, as repeatedly I ask, "What is Agni Yoga?" The response is, "Agni means fire. It is not a way but a word." I visit *ashrams and teachers throughout the U.S. I open the subject with each yoga teacher I discover. They all know the word but not a path by that name, I am told again and again.

Then one day in 1977, a small booklet, *The Hierarchy and the Plan*,[4] mysteriously appears on a table in my library at Villa Serena. In it, I find:

> In conclusion I will remind you that the yoga of the *New Age will be the Yoga of Fire, Agni Yoga, which will deal with the secrets of the Spiritual Triad and the technique of making the personality a pure channel for the expression of the divine fire within, the Spiritual Triad. The next step then will be to reach the essence of the human being, the inner fire which is the True Self.

Hooray, I am at countdown. I have found Agni Yoga. The booklet is by Torkom Saraydarian, an Armenian born in Turkey, a profound thinker who will stir the boiling pot of my life for some years. When I write to Aquarian Educational Group in Agoura, California, for information about Agni, asking the wrong questions, they refer me to the Agni Yoga Society, New York City. Writing there and asking how to reach Mr. Saraydarian, they direct me back to Agoura. Then I write to him. A letter quickly arrives in Torkom's free-flowing, open handwriting, "It is so beautiful to know that people are working in the Light of the Lord. You want to tell me how you met M.M. and to be informed about Agni Yoga. I will be very glad to hear about it."

Agni Themes
Striving
Humanity
Self-sacrifice
Future
Freedom
Harmony
Community
Responsibility
Service

I jump for joy. I have connected with Agni and "what to think about M.M." as well. I rush to place the call that will take me to California to meet Torkom. I devour all I can find on Agni, which is not a lot.

I read my first chapter on Agni in Torkom's *Science of Meditation*.[5] As I search, I find the names of other teachers, and discover that Agni is a contemporary, still-emerging teaching, rarely identified as a yoga. Alice Bailey materials make a few references to Agni Yoga, but so hidden it is hardly recognized even by

Agni Virtues		
Enthusiasm	Love	Harmlessness
Beauty	Purity	Fearlessness
Universality	Reverence	Humiltiy
Leadership	Transformation	Joy

Bailey readers, to whom I had inquired. One can only conclude, the time was not right.

Agni Yoga challenges me in many ways. I continue this study, love my discoveries, and totally accept it as the way of the future. It may not be offered the way people expect, but I see it blessing the lives of awakened ones it touches. Through fervor and vitality, many beautiful beings are fulfilled (they do not really need a name for what they are doing); Agni is subtle. Since the word *yoga* is often perceived uncomfortably, only as a physical practice, Agni is often entitled the "science of ethical living." It is ever clearer to me, Agni is my way.

As Agni themes and virtues are integrated, it is easy to see similarities to Buddha's Eight-Fold Path. They provide guidelines to those on or not on a path of religion. Each focus amplifies an ethical standard within the devotee. These modern tools enhance lives, especially combined as it is with much meditation for clearing away barriers to greater light.[6]

I rejoice in an active role in the Esoteric Christian tradition, out on the fringe originally but watching as others are ever moving into a position of ecumenical, interfaith appreciation. A wonderful time nears for revitalizing Christianity through the integration of a deeper awareness of the profound message of the Christ. Through inner processes, awakening ones will more clearly attain the spiritual life they prize Through rediscovery of the vitality and truth of the early church, powerful changes are occuring.

When students started asking for correspondence courses, the idea of personal development courses blended with esoteric Christianity, Kabalah, and Agni Yoga (Ethical Living) seemed the answer. The course is now published in three volumes: *Adventure in Meditation—Spirituality for the 21st Century.*[7]

As life unfolds, I believe Ann's, Vera's, and Torkom's influences cause me to relate to the entire world, not to believe one part is more important than another. When I received my first passport, I felt I had broken through a *ring-pass-not; since then, I have traveled to many places and found sincere seekers of high consciousness in each. We once spoke of how some were holding the light behind the iron curtain; now we visit Siberia, Russia, Turkey, even Mongolia, and know it was so.

The vision of the future etched in my memory long ago in the presence of the light blends with Ann's, Vera's, and Torkom's and is reinforced each time I say the Great Invocation from Lucis Trust. As of January 2000, this beautiful, universal prayer is available with gender-friendly wording.

The Great Invocation

From the point of Light within the Mind of God
Let light stream forth into human minds.
Let Light descend on Earth.

From the point of Love within the Heart of God
Let love stream forth into human hearts.
May the Coming One return to Earth.

From the center where the Will of God is known
Let purpose guide all little human wills—
The purpose which the Masters know and serve.

From the center which we call the human race
Let the Plan of Love and Light work out
And may it seal the door where evil dwells.

Let Light and Love and Power restore the Plan on Earth.

Mystique of India and the Ganges

I sit back in my seat and close my eyes as the plane takes off from Delhi, wondering if I will look different to people upon my return. I try to recall how I felt as I eagerly left for India. Has it been only three months since I set out to fulfill my dream? It seems so long ago.

What have I gained? Adventure, for sure. So much new awareness. How can I put into words the encounters with the paradox of India: shock, anguish, and then, stunning beauty.

Only once do I really come apart. The hour for prayers arrives as we are visiting a mosque in late afternoon. When the men in the mosque start yelling at us, I become frightened. Having heard of the beating of two Western women in blue jeans in the Moslem section a few days earlier, I urge the women traveling with me to hurry back to the bus. This is our third day in Delhi, and the pitiful sight of the beggars affects me acutely. All those black-haired, black-eyed children remind me of my two-year-old granddaughter who had died only a month ago. I repeatedly fight back tears as I see the forlorn little ones and deal with the grief of losing my daughter, only twenty-two, and her darling little girl, Alexis. Perhaps India can ease my grief and calm the painful emotional ups and downs.

Sharp tapping on the half-open window beside me causes me to whirl around startled. A frail girl, perhaps ten years old, grins at me and thrusts mutilated hands into my face. Her fingers had been cut off at various joints. As her hands push through the window at me, I scream and burst into sobs. Tears consume me. I bury my face in my lap and cry it out. Then, leaning back in the seat, eyes closed, I listen to the background of strange sounds, allowing the chatter of our group to soothe me. Breathing deeply, I calm myself.

What a place of contrasts! Every aspect of human life is in India, and blatantly. The most profound moments of quiet versus the constant turmoil of human life. Great beauty, art, and architecture form a backdrop for grisly human squalor, misery, and disease. India teaches because she is like us: filled with every trait, traits we push away so that we do not see. We carefully learn to ignore the unattractive us and in our culture. With everything so new to us, so carried to the extreme—seemingly squared, then squared again—we cannot push away the bombardment of our senses in this profound place. Intensity jabs us from every side. Sensory overload kicks in, but on its heels comes a higher level of awareness and new objectivity.

Is this not unlike what happens when someone dissociates during pain? When we can stand no more, we shift to another stage of awareness. When people jog and feel the body cannot take it, if they push on, a breakthrough occurs; suddenly, no longer pressing against the body, one suddenly breaks free.

Coming to India has been like this for me—breaking free to find a new place in myself. I am another me now. I have gone beyond my capability and found a new place, new energy, new knowingness. I have found two pieces of the puzzle. First, my parameters have expanded: I am stronger, more able to endure, less needy, more secure. Second, *Babaji affirmed this newness in me. He gave me the touch needed to anchor my new consciousness.

When he touched me, I realized the truth about what Ben Osborne had told me years ago about not yet having put my foot on my work-path. (Ben, a dear friend now deceased, helped plan a list of the most important places to visit on this lifetime dream of mine.) In that frozen-in-eternity moment, as I stood in front of Babaji and he placed his lei of flowers around my neck, I realized with awe that when I moved my feet and took the next step, I would begin anew. Another time capsule ignited my life, and the whole process of adjusting to a new stage began. Do I have to think about this now? I am excited to be returning to my husband, family, and friends. I am going home, eager to share what has happened in these wondrous months.

My trip to India began in my mind about 1970 when a home movie about *Sai Baba shown by Roy Eugene Davis[1] touches me so. I had studied *Vedanta, the *Upanishads, and the *Vedas and enjoy the beauty of Eastern philosophy. I feel such a pull, the movie makes me "homesick." That night I know I will go "home to India" someday. It has taken nearly ten years for the right time to come. Our trip is planned for September.

The preceding May, my friend Grace brought me a magazine article. The question, "Have you ever heard of this guru?" leaps to my attention. My eyes scan the page. "*Babaji* is in body again. Babaji can be seen in India. Babaji has a body and is seeing people." My mind reels, "This is why I am going to India." I sit down and read the lengthy magazine article. I quickly write a note to the author, but my whole being is still. I know this is where I am going. I whisper the name "Babaji" and feel great peace. Yes, Babaji knows I am coming to India. I sense it deep inside me. Perhaps I have been called, I do not know. All that matters is that I will get to see him.

Just in the way it should, the response arrives. The ashram grants us permission to come. In September we are on our way. Our large group travels together for most of the trip, but for a brief week, four others from the Sarasota community and I slip away and go to Babaji. What will he be like?

Only half way to India we get our first shock when suddenly two MIGs pull alongside our Air India jet. A lengthy message over the public address system in Hindi is followed by a brief explanation in English. War has broken out between Iran and Iraq and the air corridors over those countries have been closed. We are being escorted to Kuwait while a new flight plan can be negotiated. In strained silence, we look at one another. An hour later, our plane lands, taxies to the far end of the runway, and we are surrounded by armed Arab soldiers.

In the hot afternoon desert sun, the plane becomes increasingly uncomfortable. Babies cry. Tension is revealed in tones of voice. Three and a half hours later, comes, "The plane will be serviced, refueled, and we will be on our way to Delhi." The service crew carries off our litter and refills water tanks. The lovely Indian flight attendant coming through the aisle says, "Do not drink the water." Soon we are on our way. Looking back, I see the symbology: confrontation, change of plans, refuel, keep the faith!

I am unprepared for the airport. The sea of brown faces, the babel of so many tongues, eyes peering at us from the glass-enclosed balcony. Now six hours late, exhaustion has long since numbed us. A tour guide locates us and takes us through customs and the crowd to a waiting bus. Our typically Indian bus, ancient, seems held together by hopes and ropes. The friendly hired host gives us his tourist-guide speech as he drives to the hotel. We look at the countryside, stunned. As dawn breaks, it seems a nightmare. People sleep in the street, beds by the roadside. People squat to toilet. People eat by tiny fires. Bicycles, cattle, and water buffalo vie with us for the road. Bird calls are so loud, smells so strong. The ride becomes a blur of agony. Do I look? How can I not?

With our hotel check-in, we experience how tedious paperwork is in India. At last the fourteen of us are registered. Upon settling in our room, we shower and are ready to eat, after being up all night. Breakfast is served in a huge, antique, slightly musty dining room. The table is set, and fried eggs languish on our plates, long since prepared.

Our first outing will be the Mahatma Gandhi Memorial Gardens. Ben engages

Mahatma Gandhi Memorial Gardens.

the guide for our 9 A.M. trip to the gardens and the eternal flame. We gladly finish our meal and push on to the spot where Gandhi's ashes are preserved. Placing flowers on the memorial, I am overcome with awe for such a person. How can such a great soul as this be truly appreciated? Dear God, bless this one so wise, so gentle, and so strong.

Years later, when the epic movie *Gandhi* is released, the public finally has an opportunity to comprehend the work of this mystic. His powerful vision led a country to freedom without a shot fired. Can the world realize his great spiritual influence, to have accomplished so much? What kind of change might we create if *large* numbers would live in such a way? Grand possibilities could be realized if we but held his example in mind.

From here, we visit temples. Everything seems so vivid: the colors so bright, the sounds so loud, primitive, shocking. Buildings badly crumbling. Hot. Dear heavens, is it hot! The guides say approximately one hundred and five degrees. Monsoons just over, the humidity makes it seem hotter. The hair of the children is often bleached red on top by the sun. Wild pigs root through the streets and along the roads devouring the waste.

Myriads of bikers clog the streets in such traffic as I have never seen. A disorderly conglomeration—trucks, cars, buses, bicycles, as well as a wagon here and there—clamors for right-of-way. Whoever makes the most noise seems to win. As our bus rushes full speed ahead, horn blaring, I often close my eyes, convinced we are about to mangle anyone in our path.

Shrines are beautiful from afar but lose much of their charm up close. We visit Embassy Row, and I am thankful the U.S. embassy is subdued. The country of Kuwait has a fine building, and I gratefully remember our fleeting visit there. Thank goodness these two governments get along. Most hotels and public buildings look tattered from the outside, like old elementary schools. Banks remind us of stale notary offices. One bank guard seems like a toy soldier as he stands proudly with a stopper-like object on the end of his gun.

A few days later, the confusion of Delhi left behind, we visit Agra and the Taj Mahal. As I step through the door of the protecting wall for my first glimpse, I have a familiar feeling, wanting to genuflect. The beauty impels me; like a fish being reeled in, I feel immersed in complete and holy silence and move effortlessly toward the magnificent building rising before me.

Taj Mahal

I recall young Carol as a child cutting a picture of the Taj from my grandmother's Bible-school magazine and pasting it on my wall. I told her it was the most beautiful cathedral in the world. She patiently explained it was not a church at all but a tomb. Encountering such beauty, it still seems like a cathedral to me. I move quietly down the long walk, climb the steps, and enter. As the local guide explains the building and its history, I fight emotions stirred by such beauty. That night we return to have the Libra full moon meditation on the grounds. Afterward, watching the mist rise from the river behind, I realize, yes, I have come home. For what, I do not yet know.

The next day, we push on to Varnasi, another place of wonder. Even midst the pain from the deaths of my daughter and granddaughter a month before, I *knew* I was still to go to India. Now I somehow know I am here to advance my healing and hope. It is hard to feel sorry for oneself in this place.

Varnasi, holy city of the Hindus, is often called the city of death. For so long, I have wanted to be in this reverent spot at sunrise! Each Hindu prays to come here at least once in a lifetime. The fervent desire to bathe in the River Ganges pulls pilgrims from all over India to its banks. So, too, it has pulled me.

We start the trip to the river before daybreak. The dim ride in a bicycle rickshaw jostles me. The small, muscled body in front of me pumps the pedals, breathing hard, pulling me forward. Noisy birds and other strange sounds float in the air. It is so exotic, I thrill with anticipation.

As we wind through the darkness, I distinguish the sounds of distant temple bells and ancient chants offered to strange gods with strange names. The shrill language seems scary. Shadows shift, come close, then pass, filling the air with labored breathing. In the pre-dawn light

I notice the shirt of the small dark man in front of me becoming speckled with sweat. *By the sweat of his brow* forces its way into my mind as I ride behind this human engine.

We pass still, shadowy forms. I glance at the bodies lying along the road side. The smoke of morning fires fills the nostrils. Men squat on either side of the roadway as the rickshaw crawls on. We must reach the Ganges before the sun rises.

After five miles or more, barely escaping collisions with cows and trucks, we turn into a narrow path, then a narrower path, and finally we stop. Now I must leave the rickshaw and walk. The street is so narrow I could stretch my arms and nearly touch both sides. Tiny old people patiently squat. Now, close to our destination, more noise reaches my ears. A child cries. Flower vendors

The burning ghats on the banks of the Ganges —a most sacred place—present foreigners with a different perspective of death.

are already in place. The river waits. My special interest in the field of *death-and-dying assists me now as I observe the elderly in their preparations for death.

People emerge from every doorway as life descends to the Ganges. We go to the river steps, quiet now, silent as the unborn. Deep in our own worlds, with closed eyelids, weeping, remembering, breathing, we sit and wait. The guide calls softly, "The sun, she comes." Opening my eyes to see dawn's first signal, the warmth strokes my heart.

Turning my eyes to the river—silver on silver, cool, passive, slow and silent—it looks like shiny, thick mud, darker silver silhouetting the lighter. All life seems to be suspended. The sun's warm pink glow slowly ascends to kiss shimmering buildings. This fresh stream of light climbs into the heavens, holding a straight line now in full view. Its glorious gold color expands earthward. The silver ribbon of river turns golden. The stream of gold in the sky touches the stream of gold across the water. We wait, frozen in place.

Travelers pause to refresh in the shade after washing in a stream beside the roadway.

For a time, only the birds dare disturb this peace. Then, movement; a limping widow arrives to pay her call. Her flowers fall into the water as she sets aside her cane. Slowly, gently, she enters the golden muddy water for her morning bath. She chants her plea, "Mother River, Mother River, release me. I am ready. Release me. I am ready."

Her wet garment hangs on bone and little else. Gnarled hands roll and unroll the wet cloth; the ritual takes care of itself as she smiles at the sun. Finishing, she crawls to the edge and stands. Wrapping in her other rag, she deftly slides the dry over the wet, swift of hand. She is done. Gathering her incense urn, her bag, her rag, her lot, she climbs the stairs. I watch. The press of the crowd affects me. The beauty, the strangeness, chanting voices calling to God seem unreal, a remote dream.

High drama—life and death collide every minute. An old man breathes a deep sigh; the next moment, he is done. A beggar moans, a donkey brays, a child cries. I weep from the crush of such stark exposure to reality. Watching boats glide effortlessly over the water, I become detached as my heart drifts with them. The pain passes, the fervor in my chest subsides. In this ritual of life coming to the sunrise, my heart opens and swells in its quest for understanding.

Dipping my cup into the river, I pour the water over my head. My need to come to the River of Things Ancient has been met. Now I am ready to move into the present. I feel the deep bond of humanness, rejoicing in a sense of oneness with all life. "Dear God, let the light shine more radiantly within me," I send my prayer heavenward.

In the next weeks we visit Bodh Gaya, Gaya, and Sarnath. As we enter the temple at the Park of Buddha at Bodh Gaya, we are greeted by a monk and a huge golden *Buddha clad in orange cloth, flowers strewn everywhere. Barefoot, we step on coins left by others. We sit silently awhile, then climb to a second floor to walk about the roof on the high, narrow temple porch. Our heads are in the leaves of the Bo tree. Coming down the steps, I stand on the slab where Gautama Buddha sat. Walking the grounds of the temple that King Asoka had erected, admiring the railings—a wall carved with characters and symbols preserved the teachings of Buddha—I realize I am standing on the soil upon which Buddha himself walked. I feel every bit the pilgrim I know myself to be.

We walk to the lotus pond where, centuries before, Buddha washed. We descend the steps and silently, reverently wash our dusty bare feet. The pond is enclosed by a grassy slope where teachers sit and talk. Special devotions are being offered for departed parents today; many others wander about thoughtfully. *Mantras are chanted—the people responding to the priest. As I listen, I recall the Christian Mass for the Dead.

For days, we chant, look, pray, contemplate. Staying at the government rest house, we awaken many times each night to the call of holy ones as they chant. The *Om* floats across the dark valley.

We survive energy shortages. Temperatures are well over one hundred degrees, and electricity is in short supply. While the fan hangs silently from the ceiling, we "feel" the meaning of "no energy, no electricity." At night we use candlelight for dinner. We dress

At Swami Dwarko Sundrani's girls' school at Gaya, from left, *Swami Dwarko, a worker, Elizabeth Cherbonneaux, Joyce La Luzerne, Carol Parrish, Lois Sadler.*

and swelter in this land where electric fans are luxury. We are learning.

A kindly Buddhist monk told us one day, "Buddha gave a great commission, as Jesus did. He told his devotees to 'go now and preach the doctrine to the masses.' Two great Masters ruled with compassion, Buddha and Jesus." Everywhere in this setting we are reminded of Buddha's message to humanity, *If thou would worship in the noblest way, bring flowers in thy hand. Their names, the flowers, are these: Contentment, Peace, and Justice.*

Next we visit the school of Swami Dwarko Sundrani at Gaya, which we have financially supported for some years. The good swami, in memory of his wife who died giving birth to their first child, a girl, began a school for poor girl babies cast out to die or raised to beg and suffer all their lives. Swami collects these waifs, educates them, paying a monthly stipend to their families in return for the girls so they need not help support their families. After the girls are raised, Swami Sundrani must find husbands and dowries for each.

Today he gathers twenty to twenty-five girls, six to twelve years old, to sing Hindi songs for us. After a few songs, he tells us the girls have prepared a special song in English to thank us for our assistance. As they sing "We Shall Overcome" in English with their clear, young voices, tears run down my cheeks. The memory of my beautiful blond daughter and her brown-eyed toddler returns. The pain of death seems so close, yet here we see what life is all about. One step at a time, one human at a time doing what s/he can. As their little voices sing of hope, peace comes.

From Gaya we fly to Katmandu, Nepal, to enjoy its temples, its art and mystique. A cool land, comfortable and clean—the population is smaller and the food is better. A week to rest, browse in shops, and tour the countryside fortifies us for another month in India. Our thoughts turn excitedly to Babaji and our next adventure. As we fly back to Delhi. Five of us will leave the others and trek to the hinterlands to meet Babaji. We are frightened to go so far off the beaten track, yet this is the big moment for which we have come.

To unaccustomed eyes, India looks like a gracefully shaped silver dish with most of the silver worn thin. The patina of the carved patterns has dulled with so much time and service. This beautiful antique country has had hard daily use, with little repair, painting, or maintenance of buildings, no major replacements, no inventiveness since the British departed. The fervor of new independence shows, right next to the barrenness of harsh human living. The few new buildings of brick and plaster are often left unpainted. The glamour of a rich past is unmistakable in its once-upon-a-time state, but with an absence of vitality. With so many needs, no one can determine what to do next. Honored old philosophies prevent India from confronting the tough business of progress or initiative. Yes, I do think like a Westerner!

I had been drawn to Roy Eugene Davis after I learned he had studied with Yogananda. Once during my meditation I had an image of a holy Being in front of me. When I glimpsed him in my inner eye, I had been filled with peace. This great peace seemed like recognition and wholeness. It drew me into close communion and led me to study more about the Eastern way. I later found a copy of *Autobiography of a Yogi*.[1] In it I found the picture of the being who had appeared to me. The book called him Babaji and introduced him to the Western world. I determined that if Roy was of that lineage, it would be to him I would go. I was initiated into *Kriya and settled into my practice. The breathing exercises caused me trouble. I found myself returning from unconsciousness time and time again. I finally gave up the technique, but not the relationship to the tradition.

Blessing from Babaji

n Delhi I am to lecture for the Indian Federation of the United Nations. A special
friend and former member of parliament, the
late Madame Savtri Nigram, then-president of the
national Indian Housewives Federation, has arranged a gala evening.
I am honored to be invited to the palace to meet Premier Indira Gandhi
the following day.

Arriving there, we wait a short while in a sitting room with half a
dozen gentlemen in traditional turbans and clehortis, a man's skirt
pulled up between the legs and tied. Straight chairs line the walls of
the simple room. In time, my name is called, and a secretary escorts
me into the office of Madame Gandhi.

She is smaller than I expect, so lovely. In a flowery pink and white
sari, she looks soft, quite unlike the often grim-faced woman of news-
paper photos. She is interested in spiritual teachers, she says, and has
visited several since her first son died in 1980. In fact, she lost her son
about the time I lost my daughter, so we share our love of our children
and our pain.

With the official photo taken, the historic occasion passes. As we
leave, Madame Gandhi wipes her eyes and hurries across the grounds
to a pavilion to address an ever-waiting crowd. Soon we hear her voice
over the outdoor P.A. system. I feel I have glimpsed behind her public

demeanor and seen the real person, one who few see. How beautiful and delicate she seems.

After my public lecture, a friendly gentleman introduces himself. He is manager of the Imperial Hotel where we are staying and offers his assistance. The next day, I share with him my anxiety about five ladies traveling alone. We will leave the more populated part of India to seek Babaji (Herakhan Baba) in remote Himalayan country.

Asking how long we will need a driver and car, he says he can guarantee our safety. His

Carol and Madame Ghandi exchange personal stories.

genuine kindness calms my concerns. As he arranges details, we rest in his assurance. We study the map, find Haldwani in the foothills, and soon depart. We will be gone for over a week.

His Holiness Shri Babaji has received your letter and he sends his blessings to you. You are welcome to come to Herakhan to worship at his Divine feet.

To reach Herakhan you should take bus from New Delhi to Haldwani—in Haldwani you should go to the Kailash View Hotel where the manager will assist you to reach Herakhan.

It is necessary to bring a sleeping bag, a wok and your own plate and glass. . . . Women should equip themselves with a sari and a bathing suit (not bikini). It is necessary to change money in New Delhi as it is not possible to change foreign currency here.

We recommend the repetition of the holy mantra of Shri Babaji: Om Namah Shivaya (I take refuge in Lord Shiva) which will help you as a preparation for meeting the Great Master.

With best wishes.[1]

Before leaving the States, I had received permission from Babaji to come to Herakhan (the ashram) and complex directions to find a certain guide in Haldwani. Upon arrival in India and learning where Haldwani is, our adventure becomes uniquely Indian. Recalling our six-hour train ride from Varnasi to Bodh Gaya and realizing we cannot handle a bus, we hire a car—more comfortable and less expensive than we imagined. We leave the city behind.

Our driver speaks little English, and we struggle to communicate. Behind the solemnity of this handsome, stately *Sikh we wonder if he is laughing at these strange American women who stop to take pictures of huge vultures, water buffalo, and naked children. Sikh guides are prized, for when they accept a charge, they swear to give their lives before letting harm come to the person in their care. (Since two trusted Sikh bodyguards of Madame Gandhi have since assassinated her, one wonders what has become of this time-honored custom.)

Lack of bathroom facilities makes travel in India difficult for women. Men relieve themselves anyplace; it would seem women have no such needs. A subtle, cultural means to keep women at home is to not build public restrooms, then forbid women to toilet in public. Restrooms exist in Western hotels sparsely sprinkled in larger cities. In the country some cafes and public buildings (airports, train depots) provide this luxury, often with deplorable conditions. Travel for women is uncharitable at best.

At one place our driver locates a cafe with garden for us to have *limca,* a popular lime drink. A clean restroom is of major importance; alas, we are favored with a small room with a faucet and a hole in the floor. We wait in line to enter one at a time. Far from an area frequented by travelers, we are an attraction. A crowd soon converges to watch us stand outside the bathroom.

Leaving the enclosed garden, we discover over two hundred people assembled to stare. They point at my blue eyes and grin—friendly, openly curious, eager to make friends. While beggars and poverty are shocking, instant acceptance and open affection encourage us. Everywhere we go, they and we try to bridge the communication and culture gap.

As a lengthy train blocks the highway in Haldwani, an excited schoolboy bikes over to our car window. He stares right into my face. Having traveled six hot, dry hours, we are slightly giddy and thrilled to be nearing our destination. As I speak, "Hello. How are you?" he lets out a squeal and replies, "Hello. My name is . . . ." Adding more barely comprehensible English, he whips out his school composition book to display his writing. As I read his pages aloud, he grins from ear to ear. He says he has never spoken with "an English," and I reply, "We are Americans." The train pulls away. Brimming with joy, the boy excitedly discusses our interaction with his peers.

We soon find our way to the Kailash View Hotel. The sign is in Hindi, and having communicated so poorly with our driver, we wonder if this dilapidated building is our true destination. No one is in sight as we drive through the gate to a walled enclosure. The driver stops, and everyone just sits. I feel I earn a medal for bravery when I get out and call for someone. No response. It is dusk, and we are increasingly ill at ease. In a back courtyard, an old man is stirring a pot of food over an open fire with a stick. As I speak, he carefully turns with a flow of Hindi words. I shake my head and say, "Manager, please." He shakes his head. My heart sinks. "The manager is expecting us. I wrote from New Delhi. Manager, please." He returns to his pot.

Then from behind me a commanding voice speaks the King's English, "What can I do for you? What do you want?" I whirl around with delight and relief, but his manner is distant and cool. "The manager, please, is expecting us. My name is Carol Parrish. Are you the manager?" He responds, "What is your business here?" At the end of my rope, I ask, "Is this the Kailash View Hotel? I have a letter directing me to the hotel." "What is your business?" he asks again. Now I respond, "I am to see Babaji. The directions are from him."

Instant success! The gentleman in a Western, grey-striped seersucker suit breaks into smiles and bows from the waist. He has heard the magic word. Now he shakes my hand, apologizes, and yells at the old man in Hindi, who hops to his feet at full attention!

Back at the car, the others wait for me to reappear. Our driver has never moved; he has delivered us to the destination. The blessing in disguise is that Mr. Shrivastava (the suit-clad gentleman) arrived earlier in the afternoon with the news Babaji is coming here in two days. Mr. Shrivastava becomes our instant friend and confidant, taking our care upon himself.

After seeing the dinner stirred with a stick, I decline for all of us when asked if we want to eat. We ask for hot *chai* (tea). We have bananas and apples—scrubbing them with Basic H®, the traveler's essential—and wheat bread from Delhi. Peanut butter, wisely brought from home, becomes our staple. We settle in and eat in our room. Advised we are being put in the room Babaji uses when traveling here, we are honored. The quarters are rough, but we rejoice in a bathroom—small, faucet just off the floor, and the usual hole. Here we bathe, do our laundry, and use our own private luxury toilet, Indian style. Later, two of us notice a large furry creature sharing our quarters, a jumbo-size rat, but we do not tell the others. Things are hard enough.

From my diary. "I observe my inner feelings and ask why the Master or Masters are hidden here. Does India realize what is concealed in these mountains among the people? I ask Mr. Shrivastava 'No. Not .001 percent of the people know anything. They think this is a fakir's game.' He talks of the *Om*, its sacred meaning. He tells stories of God setting all into motion and his firm belief that Babaji himself is God. Here we are in the Himalayas in a glorified hut—excited, a little scared, out of touch with our world and our realities—hearing exciting, miraculous tales of God. We prepare for a night's sleep. A fan hums softly overhead, as we place a sheet over a bed made of strips of board with a thin cotton coverlet for a mattress. We use cotton sheets from our pack and save sleeping bags for when the night becomes cold. We are international searchers—blessed, frightened, growing, one step at a time.

"Lying on our uncomfortable beds, we speculate what Babaji will be like. I wonder if I can see through the surface of this culture and find the holiness of anyone here. Can I see the light of God in these circumstances? Humanity's eternal struggle is to see the light wherever it flows. These people so easily worship Babaji as a living incarnation of God. They need no theological explanation, only incredible stories. Perhaps everything is believable to them. I do not want to resist in such a way that I fail to be receptive to the joy, love, and divine power which are also present.

"After fretting, I finally realize I do not need to say anything, particularly to Babaji. If he can see my love and my pain, he will respond. If he is divine, he will know. If he is not, he doesn't need to know. If he knows at a deep level, I think I will see it in his eyes or hear it in his voice or words. If he knows it at another level, and I believe this is so, he will let me know if I need to know. So much wondering about to what others grasp. Why do I have to strive for acceptance even here? Why am I asking myself this? I have already had so many powerful insights, do I require still another?"

How does one go to meet a guru? *Free yourself from expectations*, come the words from inside. *Expectations block the flow of grace. Be receptive to what happens. Do not anticipate. Just be here now. Feel. Learn the cultural patterns, and try to accommodate them. Allow as little resistance as possible. Remember, rules are structures to let us know what to do, so try to be comfortable. If we recognize this, we can "resist not" the guidelines.*

Why such esteem for the guru? The Christ-Within should respect every living thing. We amplify that respect, often through status games. True deference to saints comes from realizing how hard life is; we honor the effort holy ones have made in their own patterns. Pay homage, for the one we watch draws others to the God force. The spiritual teacher tries to grow and guide at the same time. Each is on an individual path—no two alike. A teacher may shed light upon our path, and then we give thanks. A big question for now: Can we receive the grace of a great being in a setting so strange, even uncomfortable? We will soon find out.

There is a tradition of Babaji that goes back thousands of years. Twice in the past hundred years Babaji has appeared, lived and taught in the tiny village of Haidakhan in the Kumaon foothills of the Himalayas. In the 1980's, He built the temple on the top of the hill where the Ashram is located. During His ministry from 1970 to 1984, nine small temples and several more ashram buildings were built. His association with the village and ashram has given Him the name of Haidakhan Baba, among many other names.

Babaji comes to teach humanity a way of life which He summed up in the words "Live in Truth, Simplicity and Love and practice Karma Yoga." He taught that the whole of Creation is the manifestation of the Divine Energy and that humankind must learn to live in harmony and unity with all of the created universe. The Energy of The Divine is in every created element and all things must be treated with love and respect.

Babaji said of Haidakhan: "Here in Haidakhan the old world has been destroyed. I am teaching you this: THE NEW WORLD BEGINS FROM HERE! I want you to be happy and in peace."[2]

Several times we have opportunities to observe new beings, new ways. We pray and cry, attempting to grasp it all, and both fear and joy visit us. We seem to know this special one will ignite our quest even more. I recall C. W. Leadbeater teaching in *The Masters and the Path*[3] that placing ourselves in the presence of a great one increases our ability to see our own imperfections more clearly; the great light or aura focused directly at us illumines weak areas in our nature. Unfinished efforts will be ignited and unpolished parts activated, enlarging so we can see them better. Yes, this is why we have come here and why we are so uncomfortable at times.

Three a.m. sounds awaken and mobilize us. Cold baths from a faucet eighteen inches off the floor take time. The mountain air is frigid. We must bathe, wash our hair, and be ready for meditation by 4. We understand little of what is told us except, "Today you will meet Babaji. You are so blessed he comes to you." This we know. We have waited for this day!

Our moment of meeting happens on the mountain. The jeep races along, climbing ever-steeper, narrower trails. Our small, hired tourist car tries to keep up. Our driver is good, or we would not be here to tell the story. *Why are we the only ones following the jeep with Sri Ramesh and his driver?* We have the only vehicle, but the jeep only has two people in it, and it could hold two more. Everyone at the hotel seems to have much to do. The Haldwani ashram is a block away, and a festive air is everywhere. Lost in our thoughts, we wonder, *Is the jeep really going to meet him or going somewhere else?*

These strange days challenge each of us. One woman, picture pretty, attempts to keep her hair nice. Another, her depression long past now, is cautious, participating more and more, finding her inner strength, and trying to reserve judgment. She catches herself checking, judging, erasing, grappling. A third woman, newest to the group, is far more egotistical. She tries not to be offensive, handling well Mr. Shrivastava's remarks regarding her ego. Though misunderstood, he reprimanded her when we first met, hoping to spare her public humiliation later.

None of us enjoys the dirt, the discomfort, or the confusion. We dress carefully, preparing inside and out for the day. Wrapped in white muslin saris, one step removed from bedsheets, none of us feels like a beauty queen. However, we truly believe we have paid our dues for this occasion. Sleeping on board beds and living in strange quarters, no mirrors, peculiar food—the starch is out of our sails. We are told, the custom for the first time you meet a guru is to present yourself in white. Not knowing this until Delhi, we outfit ourselves there with simple white muslin saris.

Mr. Shrivastava has spent two days "getting us ready," filling us with wonder, steeping us in Indian mysticism. Our heads are swimming with tales of *Shiva, *Brahma, and *Vishnu. He attempts to teach us etiquette as well: how to enter the room, to bow, to present gifts, to eat, and so on. He takes pride in preparing us, and his love for Babaji expresses in many ways. He speaks of his family's relationship to Babaji and how his sons feel. He dreams of serving him for years into the future.

The trek up the mountainside becomes even scarier as we look off the edge of the trail to the treetops, seemingly thousands of feet below. The small deserted trail commands our attention. With the driver in the front right seat, me beside him, and the other four women in rear seat, the small car is very full.

Suddenly the jeep, with our car close behind, rounds a curve, and we meet a truck adorned Indian-style with trinkets, pictures, statues, and leis. People sit four abreast in the front seat, and a half dozen or more stand up in the back, looking over the cab. Just as instantly, the jeep is thrown into reverse and backs down the hill and around the mountain, as does our driver. I close my eyes. Finally the trail widens enough for our driver to back off the road safely. The jeep backs by, and the truck passes us to come to a stop. Leaping out of the jeep, Sri Ramesh and companion run to the truck, their arms full of flowers. Now we realize Babaji is in that vehicle! Our driver does not move. Sri Ramesh gives no sign as the truck roars off down the mountain; the jeep races to keep up with it, and we swing into the line.

Where have all these people come from? Now they line the trail, shouting, waving palm fronds, throwing flowers before the truck. Out of the jungles, the mountain people have gathered. How did they know Babaji was coming this way? Minutes before, not a person was visible. People spread their robes on the road for Babaji to drive over; others hold babies high to see him. As branches are waved and flowers are tossed to him, I think of the triumphant entry of Master Jesus into Jerusalem.

The trail widens a paved mountain road. As the truck stops, so does the caravan. A figure clad in green silk disembarks from the truck. Another runs to the stream and returns with water to pour over the tall person's hands. From the distance we see someone hand him a towel. He turns. As he moves gracefully toward us, I think, *Is this a man or a woman?* Our driver opens the door and falls at his feet as Babaji comes to our car window. He stops and looks directly at us—into us.

All the preparation and good manners taught by Mr. Shrivastava disappear when we look into this face. Even as I write this today, my heart responds to the memory of such love. To describe the face, the expression, is beyond words. His eyes examine me. Hot tears pour down my face as his eyes explore the inner, as well as the outer. He does not mind staring, with the piercing scrutiny of the Indian people. His clear, brown eyes are steeped with love. I think, *I bet Jesus' eyes were like this, such compassion and complete acceptance.* As he continues to look deep into me, I remember my manners; placing my hands together in prayer posture, I attempt to bow from the waist as deeply as I can from the confines of the tiny front seat.

His eyes leave me and travel to examine each person in the back seat with the same lengthy review. Finished, he smiles warmly and converses in Hindi to two companions standing close behind. He speaks to our driver, waves, and returns to the truck. Someone in the back seat asks, "Why did we cry?" and I realize tears are flowing down every cheek. Each of us has experienced a powerful rush of emotion.

Our driver is ecstatic. His English, so limited we can hardly communicate even with patient effort, now is useless. He babbles with joy. He has seen Babaji before. He loves him. Baba touched him. He will serve us forever. Babaji accepts us, he says. The driver promises he will take care of us, protect us—not to worry—beaming a lavish display of teeth, respect, and love.

We follow the truck, captivated by the drama. Flowers are everywhere. Babies are blessed. Men and boys shout, bow, and wave.

Drivers wind slowly down the mountain. Triumphantly we return to Haldwani with Babaji, to the ashram prepared for his coming.

Staying in ashrams—U.S. or Indian—is a remedy for many *glamours and *illusions. Experiences of joy and love are real, and when abroad, cultural aspects add charm. After the new wears off, required hours of sitting on the floor challenge us; my active nature grows restless. Having experienced American ashrams,

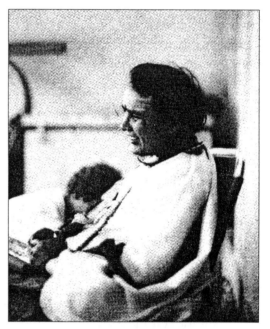

Carol performs her assigned service at the ashram as Babaji addresses devotees.

I find this atmosphere little different, though Babaji keeps me enthralled.

Babaji's face defies description. He presents different aspects daily. I often look at him and realize how visibly he has changed from an hour before. First he is young, then he looks old. Yet, no gray is in his hair, no lines on his face. His face reflects the room, the people, the feelings about him. Always aware of his audience, he watches their behavior, their moods. He amuses them, plays with them, accepts their love in unique and peculiar ways. One morning, he holds an elderly woman so tenderly; he kids her until she hides her face, then he sings to her. Sometimes sadness seems to inundate him.

The day's business goes on in front of everyone. After the appropriate bow, people ask questions, receive blessings, present babies, and converse. They come to him to settle quarrels or solve family problems. They bring letters for him to read and discuss business matters. Like a day in the life of a king and his court, village life turns on his word.

He calms people, and he reprimands them. He takes time to teach a bit; he calls people from the audience to give *shakiputi.[4] We watch, amazed and bewildered. I realize I would not want to stay here long. A wonderful place to visit, but I would not relish this environment all the time. Babaji knows we struggle, and he lets us, enjoying the watching. He sends us goodies to eat and tosses smiles and love across the room. Now and then he calls someone forward playfully, talks to them, smiles, and jokes.

The Blessing

Upon entering the room, when Babaji sits—usually on a kind of backless couch—custom is for one to go before him and bow, touching one's head to the couch or to the floor. One day, upon respectfully bowing, Babaji takes my hand and says, "You know where you live is not safe." I hear myself calmly respond, "Yes, I know." The truth is, I do not consciously know it, or perhaps do not want to. Our life in Sarasota is great!

For sixteen years, since 1964, Charles has handled the financial affairs for New College: budgets, personnel, purchasing, computers, buildings, and grounds-experience—which proves essential, you will read later. Together we renovated a beautiful old Mediterranean apartment building to create a home for spiritual students. Villa Serena (page 116) is as the name implies, an atmosphere of peace and healing. Beautiful gardens and a banyan tree *par excellence* grace the grounds. A second building serves as offices, chapel, and classroom. Our needs are well met, and I do not want to think of change.

Everyone in spiritual studies has heard of challenges predicted for the turn of the century. According to Edgar Cayce, earthquakes and weather extremes are expected, perhaps even a pole shift. I had avoided such negative subjects, not wanting to face them. Now, I hear myself respond, "Yes, I know."

Aware of my height among small Indian ladies, I sit at the rear of the room. As chants are being sung one morning, a devotee with shaved head and orange sari approaches me, "Babaji wants Swami to talk to you." "Am I to bring my friends?" She replies, "If you wish."

In an adjoining room a white-haired gentleman in the orange robe of a swami is seated. Babaji has asked him to tell us many things,

Babaji

so Swami Shastriji teaches us several hours daily: of God incarnating as man repeatedly, always in the Herakhan area; of Babaji creating a body, yes, manifesting a body vehicle in 1970 to teach again and to be with his people during the end of the *Kali-Yuga, which we are in now.

We are told of the mountain people seeing a light on the mountain side and searching through the jungle to find in a clearing a young man sitting yoga-fashion with a radiant light about him. For forty-five days, it is said, they watched; he did not eat, drink, or toilet. More people gathered. One day, he stood, looked at the people, pointed to a disheveled hut nearby, and spoke, "Clean the hut." He had established his place, and his people had found a teacher.

Stories become more and more miraculous. Swami says, "Do you know Jesus the Christ came to the Himalayas two thousand years ago before he began his public ministry?" Yes, we know, so we proceed.

Babaji reveals many things to his devotees about the challenges ahead, preparing those who come to see him to live simply, to love clearly, and to maintain a state of goodness and grace through trying times. Part of me thinks, *I already know this.* Another part does not feel in touch with it. I recall thinking, *Here, nothing seems real or unreal because everything is so different. I cannot trust my judgment because of the culture shock. I will think about this again after I go home. This is not the time. Just listen now.*

Babaji Sends a Gift to Oklahoma

Carol Parrish-Harra, an American mystic teacher, lecturer, and the founder of the spiritual community of Sparrowhawk, near Tahlequah, Oklahoma, tells this story of a connection with Babaji, whom she met briefly in 1980 during a trip to India.

Carol says the peacock has been a strong symbol for her for many years. As long as thirty years ago, the symbol of a peacock would come to her in her meditations. She has a collection of peacock artifacts of various materials from all over the world.

In 1981, after the 382-acre Sparrowhawk community was formed, a peacock appeared in the back yard of a family that lived just off the community land. People tried in vain to find the owner. Finally, they built an aviary on top of the Sparrowhawk 'mountain' for the peacock.

During this time, a friend of Carol's from Cincinnati, Ohio, had gone to Haidakhan to visit Babaji for a month. On his return from India, the friend called Carol from New York to tell her about his trip. At the end of the conversation, he added, "By the way, Babaji told me to ask you if you received the peacock He sent you."[5]

Swami tells us Hindu parables. Presented in broken English, we often do not know when the story is about Babaji or another great saint. For hours we listen to talks of future happenings, devastated humanity, and the coming conflict between darkness and light. I realize how similar *good and evil, light and dark, *salvation and *sin are in every culture and religion. I am relieved when Swami sends us back into the sanctuary with Babaji.

I sit on my zen bench daily with my eyes closed, centering, re-establishing a place of peace within myself, emotions so mixed. Babaji has invited me to travel with him for a period of time. I have declined. Part of me so wants to; the other part remembers those waiting for me in Delhi.

I think, *Do not try to understand, just be,* when unexpectedly a voice speaks to me inside my head. "Look at me," it says. My eyes fly open—not in obedience but in surprise. He is smiling at me. I look away, closing my eyes in total confusion. Again the voice, "Look at me." I open my eyes. He winks at me and smiles. Later he speaks again, and when I open my eyes, he playfully tosses me an apple. Then, "Look at the door. A woman with a child is going to come through the door." The windowless courtyard has no outside view. A mother

Carol at Babaji's ashram
—a life-changing experience.

carrying an infant soon enters. For the next two days, he demonstrates this telepathic ability to me from time to time.

Babaji's teachings are simple and clear. He says time and again, with the aid of interpreters and the swami he assigned to teach us, to realize four things one must do to live a spiritual life. He implores all to:

1. Treat all others as God.
2. Feel empathy for others.
3. Know all have God in them.
4. Serve those about you as you would serve God.

"Do these things daily. Let work be your meditation. Do not be lazy; do not shirk duty. Meditate briefly; work hard. Love all others as God." When I ask, "Does one have to do *kriya?" he replies, "No, any way you love God and keep the name of God on your lips is fine. My way is a universal way. Love God your own way."

On our last morning with Babaji, we are told to be at meditation by 4 A.M. We arrive early, but everything seems to be in full swing. Lit torches are mounted on the walls. The courtyard is only partially roofed where the women are seated. Pulling our shawls and saris close, we chant in the cool night air. The purification ceremony is performed, each person smudging with incense. Trays of paschad (blessed bite-size treats) are distributed. A festive air is created as drums beat and the peculiar music of India sweeps us along.

Now all becomes quiet—the only sound, gentle breathing. We are so close, so many, in such a small place. The American women, as we are known, are in the very back of the room. Less comfortable with long periods of sitting, we wiggle more than others but try not to distract the small, silent, patient Indian ladies about us. We are unsure just how to get up and down in our saris, always feeling just one wrong pull and all will be revealed. We settle in the deep quiet. Time passes slowly.

The breathing seems to be in rhythm when a voice speaks in my head, "Come up here." My eyes pop open in shock. There he sits, eyes shut and quiet. I close my eyes. Again, the voice says, "Come up here." I keep my eyes really shut now. I wait. I do not hear a sound. A third time his voice speaks, "Come up here." I think I am going to cry. I cannot move without disturbing others. There is no aisle. We are sitting across the room among a solid mass. I take a deep breath and open my eyes. Babaji looks at me and smiles. I struggle to stand, trying to be careful of those about me.

As I get to my feet, the ladies part to create a path to Baba. When I look at him, he stands, and I move slowly to him and go down Hindu fashion and touch my forehead to his feet. He reaches down and draws me to my feet. Tears are in my eyes. The room is breathlessly quiet. He speaks in Hindi. He takes the garlands of flowers off himself and puts them around my neck. He blesses me, speaking gently, "I bless you, and I bless those you bless." He says more in Hindi to the people. The conch shell is blown, and the room explodes in praise, "Bhole Baba Ki Jai! Ki Jai!"

In the midst of people yelling, chanting, and jumping up and down, my years of astrology study prompt me to look at my watch to see what time it is.[6] My mind seems detached, yet fully alert. He touches me again, smiles warmly, turns, and is followed closely by many male devotees as he files out and climbs into the decorated truck.

Exultant Indians jump up and down, yelling and touching me. My head says, *It is all going to be new now. This is a new beginning, a next stage.* As my feet take a step, I know I will establish my work path now, as Ben has predicted. Consciously exploring these thoughts, I move back to my friends. In the medley of sound and excitement, Babaji leaves to travel. Our driver, now indeed respectful, sees to our every need with fresh enthusiasm.

When you come into the presence of a great being of love, it clarifies your own ability to love. As you experience the ability to see more clearly, accept that God energy and do not judge it. This energy of God is stepped down to you. The major question is, what new awareness, clarity, or purification happened within you as a result of the outpouring you received? You are offered an opportunity through this blessing. What will you do with it?

Message Carol received January 15, 1981

With the concepts of the East and of Shiva (the destroyer) clarified, we realize more explicitly the approach of the end of an age or era. Babaji dwells passionately on duty, love, clarity, and ethical living, pushing us to heal our lives, settle debts, do service, love others. Be ready, he says.

All of these ideas are present in Christianity and in the ancient wisdom teachings. Channeled materials, as well as our own Native American traditions, warn of a closure period. The more fundamental approach to Christianity speaks of a great *tribulation approaching. Messages of endings and challenges for a new dawn abound if one is courageous enough to look.

Shiva,
the destroyer.

For me, being blessed by Babaji is an ending. I feel the connection clearly. His love surrounds and strengthens me, creating a cusp between what has been and what is to be. I become aware of a new concept of *grace*, an apt word for Babaji. It streams from him to others, affecting each differently. All of us are deeply touched. As we review our experiences, we realize how diversely we were moved. I observe levels of myself responding in distinct ways. When I comprehend how deeply we received, it seemed each grew according to her capacity; he revealed what we could perceive.

Returning to the city, my heart sings. The heavy sense of loss I had carried is gone. I feel buoyant. I do not know where or how I will proceed, but I am grateful a new cycle has begun.

Babaji's blessing brings to a loving conclusion my captivation with the East. I believe I am to travel my path of blending and bridging, not to look back to what was. The energy flowing from him is compassionate. He challenges: Build no illusions of the future, simply do what needs to be done, now.

Babaji left his body February 14, 1984. His work continues in both India and the U.S. Many said he would return after 1995, so devotees watch eagerly for his reappearance. Stories of Herakhan Baba are many. *Autobiography of a Yogi* has introduced many Americans to this remarkable saint.

atha Sai Baba awakened me to India, so no trip would be complete without a visit to him. We are told he is traveling back and forth between Puttaparti and Whitefield. Engaged in talks with government officials, private appointments will not be possible. Ben and I immediately send Baba thoughts, "We are coming." As the time nears, we send our mental message, "Come to Whitefield." Joyfully, we pray, and hope, and work telepathically.

We arrive at Bangalore at seven in the morning from Bombay. As soon as we sit down for breakfast at our West End Hotel, the manager brings a message: Sai Baba arrived last night at Whitefield. He will have darshan (a devotion at which the guru gives blessings) in half an hour. We leave our meal and rush for cabs, our hearts singing. We were heard!

Today, "Indian time"—a fact of life to all who have been there—saves us. We arrive, find our places among the many, kneel, and try to calm our excitement before the palace gates open and a cluster of people walks toward the small pavilion, protection from the hot sun. A delicate, saffron-clad figure approaches amid a half dozen men clothed in white. Familiar with his picture, I know this is Satha

Sai Baba

taking prayer requests, blessing, touching, our eyes meet and hold. His face shows strength and assertiveness. The atmosphere about Sai Baba crackles with energy, an intensity any sensitive would detect. We sense the passion here. Sai Baba strives to move people ahead, to awaken them to make progress, NOW. The energy is a surprise. This is not peace, love, and softness, but *power* of a new sort. The aura about him is charged with excitement. The strength of his soul makes itself felt, like mighty, humming generators. I smile inwardly as I think, no wonder he can manifest objects. As our eyes touch, I discover humor behind his serious demeanor, and I think, *How great he is*. He knows all of this is God's great game. Though he goes through a lot of "hullabaloo," he is not trapped in ego.

Our days in Bangalore fly. We go to the ashram morning and evening for darshan. Each session, almost an hour, consists of the same procedure: visit bookstore, copy thought for the day, converse with others, compare notes. Rumors abound throughout India. Technology is antiquated, but whether in a city, sitting under a tree, or on ashram grounds, news drifts like a breeze. Sharing hopes, crowds quickly add more glamour to each statement. No one knows how long Baba is to be here, so rumors spawn, elevating the anxiety of those wanting to see him or to be touched, for no one wants him to leave.

A common story about Sai Baba is that often travelers return to America to tell of going unnoticed or not seeing him until their last day there; then Baba acknowledges them and notes their departure. The old story hardly needs retelling, but now we will experience it. Each day, as we join the devotions, he greets none of the ten of us.

Picking his way among the men and women, he blesses, touches, talks—but not with any of us.

On our last morning in Bangalore, we go to the ashram. Rumors are, he leaves today. Many stay, hoping for another glimpse as he drives off the grounds. We purchase books and admire the spectacular Indian architecture. Satha Sai Baba is recognized for the way he pushes his people. He approaches his role with a more Western, intellectual, achieving attitude than is usual for an Eastern guru. He demands quiet and respect, tones down the adulation most gurus cultivate, and has standards less devotional, more oriented to activity. He campaigns for education, speaks out for equality of the sexes, and works with the government for contemporary social action. His innovations bring much criticism from more traditional Indians. I see in him an activist, a change agent not content with just spiritual mysticism but wanting to thrust his country and his people forward. The power of his personality is noted by both those who love him and those disconcerted by him.

The morning disappears, and we return to our luxury hotel. After a swim in the pool, we pack, and talk about going home. Our plane departs at 6:45 P.M. At 2 P.M., we discuss evening darshan but find no way to visit the ashram and make our plane. At 4 P.M., I decide I must try one more time. When I mention it to the others, three decide they too want to try it. Leaving our luggage secure with the group, we eagerly depart in a cab. Is Baba still there? Upon arriving, we find the front row kneeling positions are taken, so we, three women and one man, separate to find places in the crowd to kneel. No two of us are together. An Indian lady on the front row beckons to me and gives me her place. Thanking her, I settle down.

Beads in hand, I quietly say my goodbye to Sai Baba and to India. I thank God for a wondrous trip, such a shocking exposure to life, and for the privilege to be in the presence of holy ones, recognized or not. My heart is full, happy, settled. I say thank you to Babaji high in the mountains and to Sai Baba for this extraordinary place of learning. I feel we have been seen because of the recognition I saw in his eyes the first day and because he came to Whitefield after our prayerful telepathic messages.

Suddenly, excitement stirs in the people and Baba walks across a clearing surrounded by swamis, going straight to a woman in our group. He speaks to her in English, blesses her, and moves through the crowd. In a minute, he places his hand over the second of our women. Again he has acknowledged guests on their last day. I smile and think *thank you.*

He crosses to visit men on the other side of the pavilion. Then he turns and comes directly to me. He blesses me, touches my head, the beads. As I bow, he reaches down and, smiling, pulls aside his skirt to place his foot directly out to me. Overwhelmed, I bow my head to his foot. He speaks to me softly; I feel his friendship, his well wishes, the power of his being. His pleasant eyes smile, and I am charged with energy. He moves to others.

Darshan is soon over. We gather, overwhelmed by wonders yet unfolding. Turning our eyes to the palace to say goodbye, we run for the gate, then collapse with emotion inside our cab. We connected with Baba! Wait until we tell the others! Baba has done it again. The airport ride is a happy blur. We are going home! We are going home!

What Have I Gained from My Trip?

Serious awakenings. I realize how Western I am. I love and have learned from the East; now I truly know I am a Westerner. Motivated from the subconscious in their daily lives, spiritual teachings run so deep in Indians, it shows in all they do. I would like to see spirituality so interwoven into Western life. I so appreciate the remnants of India's rich culture and am overwhelmed at how fast cultural growth and achievement fade when a society declines. Recalling India's splendor of six hundred years ago, it is hard to reconcile it with today's problems.

The idealized Eastern spiritual life is rarely found; ashram life is not as blissful as expected. I know I will work even harder now to facilitate the Western tradition of enlightenment for which the West is primed. The light of wisdom that rose in the East now hangs high in the Western heavens. Richly blessed, we must use our opportunity well. Our time is nigh.

What happens to a soul born to the opportunities most Americans enjoy? If there truly is a law of cause and effect, what happens to people who have so much and appreciate so little? When most of the world labors to just eat, what happens when one wastes so much? What about souls who have time to learn, express, and serve, yet they choose to desecrate good fortune almost daily? I ponder the reasons I came into body: to teach and to be here now.

As the plane rushes through the night to take me home, love floods me. Feeling expanded insights pulsate through me, I take out my pen and write. Comprehending the meaning of the Christ more fully than ever before, I work with the idea of the Christ in the kabalistic manner of breaking a word down and meditating on each letter. The body and fullness of the meaning of the word Christ reveals itself anew. This is the *Christ* I see in many beings and the Christ I have found.

C The moving *charisma* of the dancing holy spirit, the fire that makes itself felt.

H *Hope* and the presence of God are easily felt as they spring into the heart, abounding full and rich, the hope of being One with the great hope of the world.

R *Reassurance.* Realizing the struggle to be in the presence of the light carrier is worth the pain it takes. Required effort realized brings assurance at another level, and peace flows to our lower nature.

I *"I am that I am."* These words are felt, known, and comprehended in a new way inside my being.

S The *stream* or current stirring the living *spirit* merges into one happening: fully human–fully divine. Spirit arcs within my personality. The steady, sustaining stimulation of cleansing moves through me.

T Now is the *time* for fullness of Self. Tenderly, gently, I allow the outer world to be. I think of nothing; I am completely here, aware of the presence of saintly being. I drink from a cup of clarity and holiness in a way that is timeless.

Words and symbols preserve the importance of fervor in the spiritual quest. Words such as *passion* for God—or the Holy Spirit, the spark of God, or Divine Fire—express fiery feelings. It has long been recognized, fervor is necessary on any holy path in order for one to pursue, persist, and endure. Among the Hindus the word is *Agni*, meaning "fire," "the flame." My journey on the Agni path is strengthened by participating in devotion with others—others so different from myself, yet so similar. This flame of love, devotion, and intensity purifies and guides to an ever new awareness of the Inner Presence. For me, it is the *Christ*. Called by whatever name, it encourages those who strive to demonstrate high principles, love, compassion, and spiritual power.

For centuries, those longing for closeness to God have prayed, lit candles, fasted, and chanted to stimulate the flow of adoration. Many people today find it strange and awkward when the fervor of the soul breaks forth and challenges materialistic values.[1] Yet, in the last half century, an especially large number have felt a stirring to search for *something more*. Some Westerners, while leery of Hindu mantras, finger rosary beads and chant the prayers of the West.

Diverse paths become one at the point of God Realization, when we comprehend we are one in God. In the Hindu tradition, Shiva is the God of Fire, the destroyer of all that is unclean so the pure and real may be revealed. We fan the divine fire within that we might be *born again* to a higher level of spirituality, to stand anew, strengthened, and ready to go forward with that which is ours to do. We are fortified with spiritual insight for the challenges of our time, both individually and as part of the collective human family.

Love of Self

Loving self is understood most correctly if we realize that which we love regarding self excites us when found in others. The mirror that shines the light to us cannot do so unless there is light to illumine the mirror.

Resentment grows toward traditions that reflect our pains and discontents. When we are ready to look for help but are given the vinegar of life, we are disappointed. We want a tenderness that allows us to find the gentle spot within ourselves. If we can find the calm inner place, we deal more encouragingly with self while we grow. If we find no grace, mercy, or love within, we brace even harder toward our ills. We cannot get well if we remain full of hatred and anger. In softening

*and forgiving self in the light of tenderness, healing may find a place to
begin.* Message Carol received July 10, 1980

We must be ready on a daily basis to relinquish our glamours and
illusions, our games and manipulations to become a clear mirror,
tried and tested, which reflects the multiple qualities of God. The
fervent one vows to watch for clouds of distortion, seeking to view
life with more clarity.

Just as the storm refreshes the environment, today's chaos prepares us.

The path exists, often believed beyond human reach, a goal
unreal. Hidden in the crevices of life, the door is found when the
heart can bleed no more and the mind ceases to judge. A new birth
occurs, out of sight, often unrealized for a time, sought through the
fervor of inner resources. The clarity of inner peace steadies the
aspirant who has contacted the goal, whether or not it can be
defined. New energy currently hitting Earth intensifies everything,
both to awaken and prepare humanity for coming challenges. This
holy bombardment stimulates, even when we do not know for
what we hunger.

Struggling to find new and different values, we long to heal
what has disillusioned us. Many examine religious rites of other
faiths. An insatiable desire for *meaning* expresses itself—in mundane, everyday goals, then in pursuit of enduring relationships.
Painful setbacks confront us until we realize we are to look *within*
for the holy of holies. In one, then another, the light of personal
guidance kindles a vision of the possible human.

Call it superior intelligence, group consciousness, or the Plan
of God, today's challenges require participation from each of us.
Dynamic changes lie ahead: good, necessary, valuable, and little
understood. Just as the storm refreshes the environment, today's
chaos prepares us.

Walk-ins are messengers trying to deliver hope and help, to
stimulate potential, and to accelerate human evolution. Jesus re-

peats in John 10.34 what is found in Psalm 86.6, "Ye are Gods."
In John 14.12, he says, "Even greater things than these shall you
do." Awakened in past human lives to an awareness needed now,
walk-ins come to arouse other players because the need is great.
They are messengers ready to suggest creative solutions to the
critical situations humanity faces.

A combination of false beliefs, untruths, greed, inertia, and
apathy has constructed a group consciousness so mesmerized by
materiality that humanity has inadequate desire or stimulation
to "get on with it." Spiritually stirred walk-ins and those awakened by other means struggle to take action. Whether or not logical reasons exist upon which to base their feelings, they detect
time running out. A critical sense of timing and need impels awakened ones to search and experiment. The restlessness astir in humanity resembles the animal kingdom as winter approaches.
Whether or not we comprehend all that is happening, we sense
something momentous in the atmosphere.

From the plane, June 12, 1978—

The mountains are handwriting in the sand,
character lines in God's face.
Tears stream down my cheeks.
Does my God cry tears? We call them rivers,
rivers we drink to live.
Perhaps I cry my tears to live better.
Does the God I adore shed tears to give us rain and water
because that Love must flow for us to survive?
O God, I care.
I see the mountains, the wrinkles in your brow.
The smooth plains roll gently with your laughter.
Thank you for my life.

10

The Lord Said, 'GO'

And the Lord said, "Go."
And I said, "Who me?"
And he said, "Yes, you."
And I said,
   "But I'm not ready yet and there is company coming and I can't
   leave the kids and you know there's no one to take my place."
And he said, "You're stalling."

Again the Lord said, "Go."
And I said, "But I don't want to."
And he said, "I didn't ask if you wanted to."
And I said,
   "Listen, I'm not the kind of person to get involved in controversy.
   Besides, my family won't like it, and what will my neighbors think?"
And he said, "Baloney."

Yet a third time the Lord said, "Go."
And I said, "Do I have to?"
And he said, "Do you love me?"
And I said,
   "Look, I'm scared. People are going to hate me and cut me up in
   little pieces. I can't take it all by myself."
And he said, "Where do you think I'll be?"

And the Lord said, "Go."
And I sighed.
   "Here I am, send me."

—Author Unknown

Home from India. What will I do? I recall more and more of what was said and shown when the Light Being was making itself felt from deep within. My personal life, happy and good, seems to hang on a thread. I fear Charles will not want to give up all we have for a new mission. He will never understand why I feel I have to start over. Perhaps India has gotten to me. A knowingness that began as Babaji touched me continues. New insights surface every few days.

Mother Earth is in danger! Humanity is to be tested. I am to speak out! I am to create a place of greater safety and encourage others to do so. I fight the disquiet that threatens. I cannot imagine beginning again; life is hard enough. I am serving. I work hard, I teach, I share. Struggling to live one day at a time, I do not want to think about the future. I find comfort in waiting for Torkom Saraydarian to visit. When he arrives in February, we will talk about it, and he will tell me what to do. He knows how the Villa is growing, how well things are doing, what is being accomplished.

Charles and I have already created a spiritual community where we practice ethical living, sincerely work on ourselves, and try to impact the outer world. The residents of Villa Serena, a ten-apartment complex, are in the studies and gather each morning for meditation and most evenings for study. We each volunteer in the greater community, seeking to serve with an attitude of love and joy.

The teaching program has grown to over one hundred local students; many others travel long distances to be with us. Study groups are developing in other cities. Our seminary for ministers and teachers is gaining recognition. Why must all of this change? My logical mind argues, fights, and torments me. Deep within, I already know I am to

Villa Serena in Sarasota, Florida.

move. I have to take a next step, but I am not ready to face these thoughts.

I remember the warning I carry within a secret part of myself. Standing in the Presence, waves of information that permeated my being so long ago are surfacing. I feel the urgency to speak of danger, yet I prefer to be silent.

I recall Master Morya's words that I would carry a grim message. I am already considered strict, even harsh by some. I have reached a stability I have sought all these years. My home life is gloriously happy and secure. I love my husband, Charles, so much. Why must I confront more controversial issues? Representing the studies is hard enough. I see myself as a mediator to bridge that painful place between emerging spiritual concepts (esoteric) and the more mainstream Christian approach (exoteric).

By 1981 the Cuban crisis has complicated matters. Racial tensions mount, crime soars. Miami has its first race riots in May 1979, and unpleasant incidents are on the rise all over the state. This is not the Florida of the past—easy going, safe, relaxed. With rapid population shifts, our state is one of the fastest growing in the nation. City services can barely keep up with demands. Florida is changing.

One morning in meditation (my notes read September 1979), I am told, "In five years you will not want to be in Florida." I cannot believe this. I love Florida; there is nowhere else for me. I was a child here. Florida is my home. Why would I want to leave? Something is wrong here.

In February 1981, Torkom arrives at the airport with a warm greeting. He is scheduled to lecture within an hour, so I decide to hold any questions or comments until later in the evening. Within minutes of getting into the car, Torkom says, "You know you have to move out of Florida, Carol." I hear myself saying again, "Yes, I know." I look imploringly at him. "Please talk to me about this while you are here. I do not want to move. What do you think is going to happen?" We become silent, closing the conversation for now.

Later, we speculate well into the night. Such talk continues all week. Predicted times of challenge are nearing. Spiritual teachers must be the first to demonstrate principles of flexibility, ecological concerns, simplicity, and community. Torkom stands firm in his idea that leaving Florida is correct. He is in the same predicament. He will leave Agoura, California (north of Los Angeles), as soon as possible, at least by the end of 1982, he says. He has chosen Sedona, Arizona. Perhaps we would like to join him, he suggests.

The weeks after Torkom's visit are painful and confusing. I pray for guidance. Charles and I talk and struggle. He is at the height of his career. Renovation of Villa Serena has just been completed. Financially, we are secure. Why not wait a few years until his retirement? Calm down, Carol. Why such a sense of urgency?

At a retreat (April 1981), I share my guidance. Everyone wants to know why I am leaving Florida, but I have no ready answer. My guidance is to *go*. It is not about anything wrong with Florida but about what I am to do next. I cannot tell others to "follow your inner guidance," then not listen when mine is unpleasant. I must follow the inner voice to maintain my own integrity. If I stay in Sarasota under these circumstances, I could not continue to teach. A loving group in South Dakota wants me to consider their state. The Florida community encounters many emotions.

A week later, I have a clear guidance dream: Going through security check in an airport, I must choose one of three gates. The first to the left, wide and attractive, is labeled "Sedona." The far right, again wide and attractive, is "Rapid City." The sign over the middle, small and plain, reads, "Other." With a feeling of resolve, I lower my head and go through the middle gate. I awaken knowing it will be neither place I have been considering.

Soon after, the answer comes. In my meditation I am in a large room with maps on all four sides. In front of me a U.S. map fills the entire wall. My inner teacher, standing behind me, reaches over my right shoulder and places his forefinger directly on a spot on the map. To see clearly where he points, I step closer. I am stunned to see the shape of Oklahoma, the name clearly printed across it. His finger directs my attention to the northeast corner of the state and a strange name I have never seen before. My heart seems to stop. I cry out, "Oh no, not Oklahoma— not *Oklahoma!*" I snap out of the vision. My heart aches. I cannot believe it. I have never been in Oklahoma. I do not know a single person there.

My mind races, *Oklahoma—flat, dry, brown*. I love water and greenery. How can I manage? Why Oklahoma? With a heavy heart,

I hesitate to tell Charles, keeping my guidance to myself for several days. After talking and tears, we decide to fly to Sedona to confer with Torkom. Charles, as stunned as I am, shares his most bizarre experience with me:

As a young Air Force pilot, about age twenty-four, Charles's commanding officer is retiring to Colorado. Suddenly Charles has a premonition and says to those present, "When I retire, I will retire to live on a mountaintop out West," an unusual remark from a young man who grew up in Florida.

Nothing has ever tempted Charles to leave Florida. His family lives in the Tampa Bay area. His career has advanced; he loves the water, sailing, flying, soaring. Neither of us has experienced much cold weather, and we were raised to enjoy "southern hospitality." What would we do in another part of the country? The inner voice says, "Learn."

Charles and I are on edge as we fly to Sedona. Our moods are not eased as we hear talk of the danger of nuclear war and other painful predictions. We have read Bruce Clayton's *Life After Doomsday*[1] totally supporting the idea of people surviving such an attack, pointing out that, whatever happens, it is better to be knowledgeable than ignorant. Clayton emphasizes preparedness for any emergency and provides material on tornadoes and earthquakes. Other advice includes what to do in case of riots, how to prepare in case of food or energy shortages.

Arriving in Phoenix, we look forward to talking to Torkom. Will he still think my message is valid? Torkom listens patiently as I share every detail of my guidance. He smiles kindly and says, "Well, Carol, it seems you have your guidance. I think you should move to Oklahoma." I know it is so. My last escape route has closed. I have known all along. We try to enjoy a happy time with friends in Arizona, but our hearts are heavy. Flying home, we agree to go and see.

I recall enjoying living in St. Petersburg until I was shown a building in meditation. I discussed this several times with Charles. One night, having dinner in Sarasota, the subject came up, and he commented, "I bet I know this building." We rush to the location, and there is the building, needing repair, but with beautiful Mediterranean lines! Alas, the building is not for sale, but we make an offer anyway. Several out-of-state owners come to an agreement, and soon we are proud owners of Villa Serena. I happily remember friends helping us create this place of healing, joy, and love.

We love Villa Serena, every inch of the buildings and grounds. The seminary program begun in 1978 is developing nicely; classes are well attended. Our dream has come true, and we are happy. We suffer to think we are to leave it behind. I recall the grief when I left St. Petersburg and how, when I came to Sarasota, I had remarked, "I am here until I am told to go elsewhere." That time has come.

Remembering, I know what must be done. The call is for spiritually awakened ones to speak up and change the consciousness of society. It is no single person's task. It is our task. The "Aquarian conspiracy," not just a book[2] but the master Plan, is at work everywhere. One book after another—health, business, child-rearing, as well as spiritual upgrading—calls us to holistic living and notes the changes as they happen. It is not yet as it will be, but it has started. Intentional communities are social experiments of cooperation developing here and there, a test to see if we can practice what we preach. We who say to God with passionate eagerness, "Give me a great mission, I am ready," will get our chance. We feel so sure we are prepared, we even ask for a test. Now the cosmic clock calls us to action. We shift into preparation, for the time of change nears.

Until recently, Oklahoma seemed an outpost of civilization in most minds. When I was impressed to come to Oklahoma, it held no attraction, but I knew it was mine to do. I would go, from a sense of obedience. I said, "Okay, since this is what was shown to me, I will go and do my best." Some of us make peace with fate easier than others. I know I have had excellent guidance. Time and again it has proven itself. I have seen it.

Today (2001 update), I see numerous reasons why Oklahoma is the place for me, for Sancta Sophia Seminary, and for the community. I can expound at length upon the beauty and wholesomeness of this astrally clear area. But my guidance set it all into motion. This seems to occur when I get to a certain point of agony or intensity. All of a sudden, a plan or a knowing comes—a lot like labor pains!

Pull the cloak of Christianity close around you for ten years. After that time, greater acceptance will manifest among God's children. Challenges that come now will be met with the protection of your heritage. In the future, each one shall say "yea" to others, and no one will think he rules the Earth. Allow yourself to be guided to the summit of experience, and fear no evil, for my rod and my staff will comfort you. Shanti.

Message Carol received February 1981

My whole spiritual life has been impressed with a desire to do my part. When I experience an inner drama—seemingly power-filled—the next step becomes apparent. I wish for an easier way, but I have not found it. After knowingness comes, or once I discern what is mine to do, I can allow my mind to work on it. Usually I find the intuitive answer is better than anything my rational mind might create.

My answers do not always come in the same way. I may hear an inner voice or see a picture. Sometimes I gather data from the dream state. Most often, I just know. This is increasingly clear; a feeling of inspiration or guidance permeates the answer. Though it seemed absurd then, in time we find much about Oklahoma that makes sense.

Hidden, subtle signs prod us. But, it is not just this experience; I base these remarks on guidance of more than thirty years. As a plan forms, I try to be flexible enough to allow it to adjust and come alive, to unfold and grow. Many pieces add to the merit of the plan if we can avoid locking them out by too much logic or rigidity.

To the Sooner State

The weekend comes when Charles and I fly to Oklahoma City, rent a car, and drive to Tulsa. Having examined our map, we head toward the "directed point." As we leave Oklahoma City, we both feign cheerfulness. We are dedicated to the test at hand and prepared to "keep a stiff upper lip." As we near Tulsa,  rolling hills turn green and lush. It is May and very pleasant. With map in hand proclaiming "Green Country," we concede, "Yes, the land is different in this area." We like Tulsa. We take the interstate to Muskogee. All interstates seem the same, but this gently rolling, green land is picturesque. I recall thinking, with a few white rail fences this could be Virginia.

In my guidance the unrecognizable name I had seen I now believe was Tahlequah. Calling home to check with my office, Susan Hyder has phoned from Atlanta the night before, and Stan and Helen Ainsworth, Clearwater, have left a message. Both had received guidance to indicate Tahlequah was the place for us, and the office was to let me know. All systems look go, so it is on to Tahlequah.

As we come into town, Tahlequah feels right. A friendly Chamber of Commerce gives us brochures and information, and we locate Northeastern State University. I have never lived in such a small town, population ten thousand. The countryside is fabulous. We drive through town, turn around, and take another route, checking outlying areas. We discover we are in Oklahoma's recreational area— lovely rivers, creeks, mountains, and woods.

Nestled in the foothills of the Ozark Mountains, Tahlequah enjoys a rich Indian heritage as the capital of the Cherokee Indian Nation. In North Carolina we had heard of the Trail of Tears and the displacement of the Cherokee Indians. Guess what? This is where they came. I feel great empathy, for I, too, have my trail of tears.

I am amazed to learn this is Cherokee country; my father, whom I hardly knew, was part Cherokee. My parents divorced before I was two, so my father had never been part of my early years. At thirteen, I met him. When I asked about the "Indian side of my family," his bitter retort was "Forget it. No one need ever know; I have suffered enough for all of us."

From Pinnacle Peak, a favorite hiking destination, we capture a lovely view of the river and valley.

Born in 1912 at the height of prejudice toward native people, his father walked away when Dad was five. He never saw him again and felt the discrimination focused on his half-Cherokee father was now directed at him. Seeking to escape painful years in Arkansas, Kansas, and Kentucky, Dad went to California where his dark skin went unnoticed. His friendly, eager manner allowed him a fresh start. Now I find myself in Tahlequah, capital of the Cherokee Nation, and hoping to learn about the lost side of my family. Again I see the wonder of guidance. It is no accident I am directed here.

Tahlequah, the first incorporated township in Oklahoma Territory, was home to the second female seminary in the nation. Known as the "Athens of the West" in the mid-1800s, now it is a pleasant small city where the South and West touch. I am intimidated by the harshness of the West and find Tahlequah much gentler than Arizona. The relaxing bit of southern influence reminds me just how southern I am.

Charles and I think in terms of a large piece of land. One hundred acres is large to two Floridians. Later, Charles will be the one who finds the exact piece of land. Although we go home knowing Tahlequah is the area, we do not find an exact site. When a realtor has properties to show, Charles returns to Tahlequah, but when he sees what he has, "No, that's not it." Charles shows on a map the area he wants to explore. His own in-tuitive guidance—hunch, if you pre-fer—leads him to a piece of unlisted property. They go in, and the rancher shows the two of them around.

As they view the property, Charles *knows* this is it and calls me to fly out the next day. When he meets me at the airport, his face is shining, his aura dancing. The next morning, we rent a small plane to survey the adjoining country-side. I, too, know it is right. It is not logical, but it attunes to the plan for us. Being led by spirit can be exciting and wonderful, or it can be painful when you try to resist!

Villagers enjoy a mile of river-front property.

As we attempt to negotiate for one hundred acres, the owners say it is "all or none." We swallow. We

Wild turkeys and deer abound at Sparrow Hawk. These young does pose for the photographer.

know we want more space than we had in Sarasota, enough land to build a community geared to new ideas, as well as a campus for the school. We know this is it, so we accept the challenge and adjust our idea of what is a lot of land. Before the day is over, we have a contract for 330 acres on Sparrow Hawk Mountain. (Since 1981, we have acquired adjoining small pieces until we are now at 442 acres.)

We want to consider self-sufficiency. When it comes to land use, most of us are not very good stewards and waste a great deal of space. We think the cluster concept may be the way of the future. It is a wise way to conserve land, instead of dividing pieces of land into squares and building one house in the middle. Then we can allow more natural areas for wildlife, the first occupants. New land-planning concepts are not easy to introduce. The American penchant for status often propels us to want more than our share. It is an emotional issue even when we try to be logical.

We hope for a community willing to bridge concepts of enjoying individual homes and sharing property. Each family might own its own homesite, choosing a cluster home with less outside footage and a common courtyard or a three-quarter-acre piece of land. Families with children or other space needs might select the larger pieces.

With the aid of Ohio land-use planners, we create plans for approximately one-third of the land reserved for farming, one-third for homes, one-third to remain in its natural state, including the riverfront property. We hope this means all villagers will take an interest in protecting the entire grounds. Ideally, through honorable stewardship, we will all care what happens to wildlife, the woods, meditation cave, and our river-front campground.

11

Creating Sparrow Hawk Village

etrospectively, Charles, Grace, and I seem to have been "prepared" to dare to develop Sparrow Hawk Village by diverse experiences but particularly by our communities of St. Pete and Sarasota. Investing all we had in each of these—physically, monetarily, emotionally, mentally, and spiritually—they provided rich experiences of learning, encouragement, and building confidence. I feel blessed to share meditations, classes, and life with sensitive, caring people, finding increased inner connection in each special environment. I glimpse more and more potential and hope for humanity.

If fear had been in the earlier nature of Carol, now it ebbs. Friends important to me in St. Pete support and encourage us: Rose Marie Pelligrini, Bill Anderson (deceased), Bethany Link (deceased), Joan Pinkston, Grace, Thomas (deceased) and Marie Gilchrist, Jeannie Thayer, and Frances Farrelly (deceased). Others who participated in classes and grow as I do are a part of happy memories. Two dear friends, Rusty and Jim Petters—the first individuals to ever invite me to do an out-of-town lecture—add advice and friendship.

We learn an important lesson from the first community: too much togetherness causes children to resent no private time. Community members eat one meal a day together, usually at my house. Friends, especially Grace, help with my children and share my life.

For the first year of our marriage, I live in St. Pete and Charles in Sarasota—with much kidding from friends who remind us that others live together without benefit of clergy, and here we are married and living apart. We indeed have a unique arrangement until 1976 when Charles led me to a lovely old building I had "seen" in meditation a number of times. He had recognized my description of it, and soon we began a gracious, comfortable, rewarding life at Villa Serena in Sarasota. The embodiment of all I wanted, this "Camelot" served many well. A slightly different style of living—meditating, teaching, sharing obligatory community service—wove all of us into a serious commitment.

At Sparrow Hawk Village we find ourselves creating once again. I thank God for Charles, his love, and his talents. Guidance comes as we explore the new property: *Pay attention to the *leys[1] and to energy patterns of the Earth.* Having no experience with energy leys, I am intrigued.

I send maps of the property to two special friends, Terry Ross (deceased) and Sig Lonegren, internationally known experts in the field of dowsing. They understand techniques for harmonious application of Earth energies. Divine proportions, the golden triangle, and other mathematical keys enhance beauty and proper ratios for the well-being of humanity. Hopeful the community will come to live in harmony and beauty, we rejoice in their assistance.

Our graphic symbol of the sparrow hawk, shown here, is taken from a wooden label three thousand years old, found at Abydos, Egypt.

From the maps, both believe the property contains a potent energy center (where a number of leys converge at one point). But I am getting ahead of my story. In naming our land development, we react most positively to Sparrow Hawk, the name given long ago to the mountain, once home to a sizable rookery of the small, plentiful local falcon. The sparrow hawk, or kestrel, a sacred symbol of ancient Egypt, represents Horus because it can hover and fly straight up. Thus it became symbolic of levitation and *ascension.

One weekend the first winter I am here, I go to the mountain with a small set of dowsing rods. I play with them but am not adept. My hands are sensitive from healing work, so I am more comfortable holding my hands extended and walking the direction of the energy, feeling it with my palms. At last, energy begins to lead me. I feel as if I am standing in a fountain of water, like energy is bubbling up and spraying in all directions. Excitedly, I pile a mound of stones upon the site.

A few days later, I get a real test. In the forty heavily timbered, flat acres atop the mountain, I cannot see through the woods to locate the pile of rocks. I have to start over and locate the highly charged area a second time. This time I borrow a red bandanna from one of the young people walking with me and tie it to a stick for an easily seen marker.

You have been guided to the energy center for it is to serve a holy purpose. The very energy of the Earth given here will aid in sustaining physical life, food for the spirit, and energy contact with the one of light who protects and guides you. For centuries, ones have been made ✳ *aware of holy ground under their feet. While charged in such a way, many are cleansed and awakened to higher awareness. It will be especially beneficial in the years fast upon us.*

Know yourselves as children of spirit nourished by Earth. Matter must be blessed and dedicated to spirit; spirit must freely communicate with matter. Thus, mother and father are one, and the new can be born. This period is the travail of childbirth—a feared time, yet anxiously awaited, a time when new life on Earth can begin. Those who guide you, not fearfully but tenderly hold such a vision. We would comfort you and help you through the experience of the agony.

Message Carol received February 11, 1982

Timing and further guidance lead us to invite Sig Lonegren from Greensboro, Vermont, to come out to designate lines and details of the center, wanting to make the most of the spiritual energies to bless those who will come. From ancient times, history reveals humanity has established places of worship on leys to enhance its relationship with both God and nature.

When Sig arrives, he locates the area in a much more sophisticated manner. It is impressive to watch him work. He looks like a young Santa with a pack on his back. He got my attention when I saw the surveyor's tools, compasses, and a variety of dowsing gear. He checks, measures, and maps as he goes. The net result is that his mark is about one foot from my stones; we both express respect for each other's "tools."

Sig Lonegren

Sometime later, Mic McKay, church architect and dowser from Rapid City, South Dakota, comes down to study the church site, again dowsing the spot; it had shifted again, back one foot toward the point previously located by hand.

In a quick telephone call, Sig explains what is happening. Energy leys are living streams of energy that undulate slightly. A strong ley may be several feet across, running like an invisible river and with a similar rise-and-fall pattern. Thus its center may move a bit one way or the other from day to day; the larger the stream, the more likely its fluctuations.

Understanding the ley as a natural resource of our property, we review the exacting details of Sig's work in his comments below. For centuries, spiritual centers have been constructed by precise formulas and dimensions to enhance sacred sites, assisting humanity in ways little understood. With this in mind, Sig helped us design the sanctuary.

The dome of energy, where five leys intersect and from which veins of water flow, is under the center of the altar. The pattern of the leys, or veins, flowing around the dome is similar to the pattern of the Native American medicine wheel, which seems appropriate for a sacred space where people might heal and harmonize lives. We so appreciate Sig's vast store of knowledge as we strive to use the holy ground upon which we so appropriately build.

The color of the energy center, purple, will enhance the power of our spiritual action. Energy centers are said to heighten sensitivity, enhance meditation, assist in healing, stimulate dreaming, and help balance energy centers, or chakras. Aware of the concentrated energy and other natural gifts of the area, villagers seek to work in harmony with the natural order and to honor the beauty and integrity of the Earth Mother.

The Sanctuary of Light of Christ Community Church
by Sig Lonegren, 29 October 1982
Astronomy • Sacred Geometry • Earth Energies

This sanctuary has been designed, as were so many pre-Protestant–Reformation sacred enclosures, to enhance the possibility of heightened spiritual awareness. Three factors seem to be found at sacred spaces such as Stonehenge, Solomon's Temple, the Great Pyramid, Chartres Cathedral, Aztec and *Mayan temples of Mexico, and many other places where men and women go to draw closer to their Maker:

1. These temples are *oriented toward significant horizontal astronomical events.* Think of the Summer Solstice sun rising over the Heel Stone at Stonehenge or Solomon's Temple being oriented to the East so that when the East Gate was opened (only the Lord could enter through the East Gate), the rising equinox sun illuminated the Holy of Holies at the back of the temple.

2. These temples were built with certain repeating ratios, referred to as *sacred geometry,* e.g., the Parthenon, using a ratio called *phi,* or 1:1.618. The Greeks

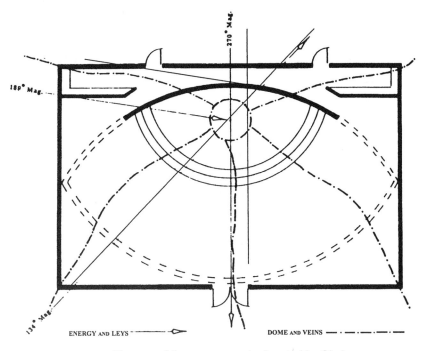

ENERGY and LEYS ⸺⸺▷   DOME and VEINS ⸺ · ⸺ · ⸺ · ⸺

Diagram of the energy center located by Sig Lonegren
and how the geometry in the sanctuary is used.

called this the Golden Section, and it was the fundamental ratio that led to the perfection of their statues, vases, and buildings. The ratio of the Parthenon's height to its width is exactly 1:1.618. For the Greeks, *phi* was synonymous with beauty.

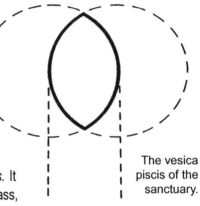

The vesica piscis of the sanctuary.

Gothic cathedrals employed another sacred geometry form considered to be particularly Christian—the *vesica piscis*. It is created by making a circle with a compass, then, using the same radius, put the point of the compass at any point on the circumference of the first circle, and create a second one whose circumference goes through the center of the first. The vesica is the saucer-shaped figure formed by the intertwining circles, the top half of which creates what is called the Gothic arch.

3. The third common theme found at sacred places is the notion that the ground itself is holy. We hear this alluded to in the Old Testament when Moses encounters the burning bush. The Lord tells him to take off his shoes because he is on holy ground. Native Americans of the Southwest have the same notion in sacred enclosures they called kivas, circular temples constructed on holy ground, or power centers.

Different cultures use different techniques to determine where this holy ground is, where on Earth's surface to place their sacred enclosures. The tool of most modern investigators is dowsing, using implements like the forked stick or a pendulum to determine things that would not ordinarily yield empirical answers through the five senses. Most people have heard of dowsing in terms of looking for water. Indeed, underground water is one of the manifestations of the Earth Mother found at every power center (holy ground). Ezekiel talks about this phenomenon in Ezekiel 47.1 when he tells us that a river of water "was issuing from below the threshold of the temple toward the east (for the temple faced east); and the water was [also] flowing down from below the south end of the threshold of the temple, south of the altar."

Along with finding water at power centers, dowsers also detect straight lines of male, or yang, energy they call leys, closely related to phenomena noted in Great Britain, South America, and other places where ancient civilizations built holy sites in straight lines. These lines come together like spokes on a wheel at especially sacred sites like Stonehenge and in Peru at the Coricancha, the major temple of the Inca capital of Cuzco. These alignments of sites are called leys.

Astronomy, sacred geometry, and Earth energy centers—the LCCC sanctuary was designed with these three components in mind. The front door of the sanctuary is oriented toward the setting sun on the equinox (spring and fall). This means that when the front door of the sanctuary is open, the rays of the sun as it touches the western horizon on those two days illuminate the altar and the cyclorama behind it.

The geometry of the sanctuary incorporates two basic sacred geometrical forms. The room itself is a rectangle that yields a ratio of 1:1.618 width to length. This use of phi creates a sense of harmony and beauty in the proportion of the room as a whole. Since the sanctuary serves as a vessel to carry the light of Christ into a new era, the Christian *vesica piscis* is an appropriate symbol to focus attention on the altar and the power center underneath it. The vesica is created by a line on the flooring on one side, and the cyclorama on the other. In a sense, the cyclorama serves as a parabolic dish to focus these energies on the altar and on the congregation.

Earth energies come together at the altar. There are two through energy leys, and a third one ends, or goes to Earth, at the point of the altar. The water underneath manifests in what dowsers call a dome. Unlike surface water derived directly from rain, primary water comes from deep within the Earth itself. Perhaps it seeps there from fissures in the floor of the ocean. In any event, it rises under pressure through cracks in the rock, like the geyser Old Faithful, and ascends toward the surface of the Earth until it hits an impermeable layer, then water. From above, the dowser perceives this dome as roughly circular with the veins exiting, like legs on a spider.

Energy leys intersect over the dome, and five veins of water exit from the dome at the Sparrow Hawk Mountain power center. Four exit the sanctuary at the corners of the phi rectangle, the fifth exits out the front door.

When used in the construction of any sacred space, astronomy, sacred geometry, and Earth energies, among other facets, will make for better meditations, increase the possibility of spiritual healing, and enhance the potential for heightened spiritual awareness. The LCCC sanctuary is a true sacred enclosure.

✳

The church and fellowship hall are situated on the wooded mountaintop. At first, we choose a conventional approach to con-

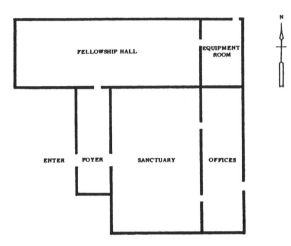

Solarcrete™ Construction Details: Developed by Solarcrete Corp., Erlanger, KY, the concept calls for the walls of a building to be a sandwich of expanded polystyrene (E.P.S.) enclosed between layers of gunned-on concrete. In our case, the styrofoam-like core of E.P.S. is 6" thick and the concrete 2 1/2" thick on each side, reinforced with steel rebars and keydeck mesh. The rebars are tied together through the E.P.S. with special steel clamps to create a truss effect that results in an especially strong wall system. Other benefits are a super-insulated (R-26) wall, a very quiet sound transmission rating of 61, a seismic-3 rating, making the system appropriate for earthquake-prone areas, and a two-hour fire rating.

struction, easily tied to the natural setting, aesthetic, and in keeping with the planned design of cluster homes to go nearby. Our designs for comfort and simplicity simultaneously feature energy conservation.

Charles asks the general contractors bidding on the church to give him an alternative bid using Solarcrete™ for the walls. Charles discovers Solarcrete when Jim Moore, Minneapolis, mentions it in a phone conversation. Checking out the patent, Charles discusses it with a local structural engineer. This innovative approach to wall construction immediately excites him.

When the contractor offers to try the system at no increase in price, he is promptly awarded the contract. Having no experience with this new system, the construction workers are reserved, but they are quickly converted, some even planning to build themselves a home using the concept. Charles introduced several "state of the art" construction techniques that make village buildings more interesting than they might be otherwise. The floor plan of our first Solarcrete building is explained in the diagram above.

The split-level fellowship hall on the north side of the church may be entered through the church foyer. A handicap entrance and a walkway for the future Wellness Center are added in 1992. Fellowship hall is earth-sheltered for energy efficiency with two feet of earth over its concrete roof. In Oklahoma a minimum of two feet of earth maintains sufficient moisture to grow grass; otherwise, the soil would dry and lose its insulation value. The roof slopes to a height of fourteen feet against the north wall of the church, protecting the church from cold north winds in winter. This high wall provides a wonderful openness, as well as a spectacular space for banners and artwork. The space is well graced by our numerous artists.

Villagers at Meditation Cave. The cave shows signs of use, probably by Native Americans.

In August 1984, prep students design a meditation trail and name it the Path of the Initiate. Susan Barrett, who has worked throughout the U.S. and abroad with Earth energies, gemstones, and crystals, supervises the project. She is greatly assisted by Ken Bucholdt, Sue Brown, Melva Mellinger, Jane Traeger, and Randy Doyle.

On April 6, 1985, at 9 A.M., at full moon, a medicine pipe ceremony at Meditation Cave blesses two specific stones that anchor energies between the first and seventh chakras. A rutilated quartz crystal is buried at Meditation Cave, and a quartz crystal cluster is placed in the power center of the sanctuary after the full-moon ceremony. When the connection between these points is made, the task is to sense the natural design running between them.

In following weeks, five remaining points are marked and traced. Stones to anchor the line along the complete path are placed from Meditation Cave to the sanctuary. The cluster used many years under my altars in St. Pete and Sarasota is tenderly placed at the sanctuary's power center.

Later, a dear friend, Thelma Carlysle, will bring a 140-pound amethyst cluster from Brazil as a gift to the church. Residing on its own circular base on a place of honor, it reminds us of our spirit-matter connec-

The church (1983) located on the left and office building (1989) located on the right.

tion. Each power point has a concrete marker with the pertinent word expressing the positive energy for that center. A map of the trail with words, stones, herbs, and chakras is found in the booklet, *How to Use Sacred Space for Problem-Solving and Inner Guidance.*[2]

Artist Cynthia Taylor Lightner has contributed a great deal of beauty to the village. Her inspiring sculpture in the church sanctuary is called "Embracing the Light," and her mural of changing seasons in the Fellowship Hall is subtle and relaxing.

Our love of art and our tenets embracing beauty are expressed in many ways. A highly visible display is a series of banners proclaiming meaningful messages. A long-time resident, now property owner, Rev. Cedar Carrier patiently led students each summer (1984–1994) in the creation of lovely banners. Eight banners grace the sanctuary, three large banners bear the symbols of Easter, Wesak, and the Festival of Humanity. Stitches sewn by hundreds of friends, lovingly placed in these artful pieces, remind us of the love and support that sustain the holy work anchored here.

By 1989, villagers and friends have raised funds to build a library and office building for the seminary and all who are interested in esoteric studies. When a particular amount had been raised, a most generous member donated enough to make an expanded building available. Our library collection, among the most outstanding for its field in this country, continues to increase.

Church offices, originally on the east side of the church building, now are located in this second major building, as well as the gift shop, administrative offices, and Sparrow Hawk Press; on the second floor the large esoteric/metaphysical library doubles as a classroom. Each building must be desperately needed for us to build. Dedicated to good stewardship, we raise funds and plan carefully. When the office/library building was completed, all areas were bursting at the seams. Charles's unique talents as a planner combine admirably with his background in college administration to serve the village, the seminary, and the church.

By 1995, we have built three major buildings, and all are used heavily. Our first, the church, was built with funds from many, including several large donations. The second, the office/library building brought a year of fund-raising, wherein many assisted, then a generous gift put us over the top. The Wellness Center was completed in 1995, and we are particularly indebted to Rev. Ninette Peterson for making this third building possible.

Each temple and church is meant to be a community of like-minded people, and they are to care what happens to each other. Cities are merely many neighborhoods rubbing shoulders. I do be-

The Wellness Center (1995).

lieve this may be the time to rethink "small is beautiful" or at least "we are in this together." Keynotes for the era ahead are cooperation, communion, and community. At one time, when I was considering a major change, I was told in meditation, *When you were weak, you were forced to become strong. Now you are strong, it is time to learn cooperation.* I pray many will respond to the call to community, the hope of our new emerging civilization.

When Sig returns to teach a week-long class on sacred geometry, he guides the building of an outdoor labyrinth, another tool to assist villagers and visitors. It is wonderful to walk the labyrinth after a full-moon service—so powerful and beautiful in the bright moonlight! Now we have a small booklet[3] presenting a simple overview and directions to guide this wonder-working process. Do add it to your list of things-to-do-while-at-the-village.

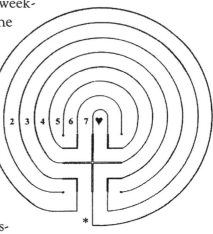

The classic 7-circuit labyrinth.

My sixtieth birthday in January 1995 inspired me to start the planning necessary to perpetuate the work of LCCC and Sancta Sophia Seminary. The village holds its direction and service through the residents; it is truly theirs to create, maintain, and support. My thoughts now, however, lead me to intensify my search for future leaders of the seminary.

Overlighting Angel Shelters, Nurtures, Inspires

The overlighting angel of Sparrow Hawk Village appeared one night after two or three years of consistent group meditation in the chapel. In addition to daily morning meditation and Sunday worship services, we said—and still say—meditation every Monday evening for the planet's well-being, for the community, and to link with the network of world servers around the globe.

This special time begins with about ten minutes of soft chanting, which often includes chants to the Divine Mother—the divine feminine, called by many names—for the village was dedicated to Our Lady on August 15, 1982. We sit quietly for about five minutes, then pronounce a seed thought, bringing the group mind into a singular focus to sensitize ourselves to impressions from spirit.

We close with the World Healing Meditation by John Randolph Price and the Great Invocation. With guided thoughts, we envision our network, linking ourselves to other groups, communities, and

In 1992, Sig returns to the mountaintop to advise us on an outdoor labyrinth, again using the power of Earth leys. The labyrinth invites powerful walking meditation experiences.

world servers across the country and around the world, all of us in harmony with one another as we find find our work and our places.

One special evening, a radiance fills the room with sprinkles of gold, silver, and pink. Three of us clearly see a large angel above us, arms outstretched. A silver mantle cloaks her, and lavender energy streams down, almost like a skirt covering us, taking us under her protection, sheltering us. We all realize at the same time, we have at last attracted to us an overlighting angel.

Sometimes known as the angel of the shrine or angel of protection, the work of this angel is one of security and love. This presence provides a representation of the higher world at all of our functions. The angel watches over us—cleansing and clearing *thoughtforms and vibrations of our chapel and the work, especially the teaching and healing done within its presence. An overlighting angel, or deva, as they are also called, gradually expands its sphere of influence, granting its qualities of harmony and well-being to the surrounding countryside. For this reason, a group welcomes the sign of this heavenly one and rejoices that the devotion of the group has earned its presence.

After that wondrous time, we sketch the angel as best we can. Others select fabrics to represent the effect as nearly as possible and make a beautiful banner to hang in the chapel. Now we can share our first impression of the angel we attracted to this sacred space.

137

Since this day, about 1984, the angel has grown larger. She is often seen by people driving up the road approaching the cluster of buildings, the church, and homes atop the mountain. Some report as they look back to say goodbye, seeing the gentle, loving face of an angel smiling at them. Villagers often feel her vibration miles away as they return home, and some arriving for the first time may comment, "I felt something special a good distance back as I approached Sparrow Hawk Mountain." We smile and think, "Yes, our angel watches over us and all who come here in light and love."

Angel of protection banner.

The 100-foot–high water tank towers over the church. Its 38,000 gallon capacity serves the community of Sparrow Hawk Village from the mountain top. The cross arms, 40 feet from tip to tip, do not contain water.

12
Village Life and Philosophy

I live at Sparrow Hawk Village because I was led to be here, and this is likely true for every villager. We dared follow a trail that brought us here to experience growth, and we make of the event what we can. The energetic light, love, and power stir the best and worst in all of us. Life demands we release that energy—be it sexual or prayer and meditation—into some activity. Energizing one's divine potential is designed to make us miserable until we "turn 'round right," as the song goes.

From its inception, the foremost goal of Sparrow Hawk Village has been to create an environment that fosters personal growth, an atmosphere of mutual sharing and respect so that individually and collectively we mature spiritually. *Sparrow Hawk Village is a spiritual community with an educational focus, providing a supportive environment for the practice of ethical living,* a credo begun when the three founders attempted to define our purpose.

"In the village our determination of status has shifted from that of material possessions to that of personal development and social contributions," Charles says. "We believe we are relatively well prepared to sustain an acceptable quality of life. You can see a clear determination by villagers to succeed at this. Ultimately, we hope to have one hundred and fifty to two hundred families, large enough for a diversity of knowledge, skills, and talents, yet small enough to remain close and to care about each other's well-being."

Today, humanity is experimenting with spiritual lifestyles in a fresh, contemporary fashion. Sparrow Hawk Village attempts to create a middle-road tradition for the Western way, each person striving to grow spiritually, respect the needs of others, and to be about "their Father-Mother's business." While integration of spirituality into daily living forms the basis of this new-millennium community, we believe the spiritual nature is best realized through healthy integration of religion, philosophy, art, and science.

> *You are developing a householder tradition for the Western world that is satisfying to the development of spiritually searching souls. The monastic system is exclusive; the Christian tradition for home-makers has become ineffective. A system of practices, private, yet communal in the sense of "communion of souls," must be built and become sustaining, so those needing guidance in developing their spiritual life are encouraged to feel the Presence.*
>
> *Your expression is of this responsibility. The entire pattern of your personal life is to give you understanding in developing this concept. Use your own life to direct you in setting up guidelines. It takes struggle and inspiration. The seeker brings the pain and struggle. You are to supply the inspiration. Teach devotion as a strengthening force, and orderliness will emerge.*

Message Carol received March 24, 1977

The Importance of Trust

People with a healthy sense of worth can trust themselves and others more readily than those who lack self-esteem. Forceful egos may irritate, but loving hearts survive community friction more easily than those who misinterpret and take offense readily. Communities need leaders and followers, although leadership and duties often change with the events of the moment and talents at hand. We all become team players.

The guidance I receive is always important to me. I especially remember a line, *As we give in to fear, we return to darkness.* Again and again, I have been warned of the danger of fear and about accepting people into the community who come to "escape" what they fear elsewhere. Fear of the world is a poor reason to join a community. We come to community in order to live with like-minded people. Communities seek to create cooperative and supportive settings wherein, I am told, *we live good lives whether in the best or the worst of times.*

At the village we take careful steps by asking, "Is this a good decision if times are good? Is it a good decision if times are hard?" If we can answer "yes" to both, we proceed. Right now, top priorities are self-sufficiency, learning to cowork, being inventive and resourceful, developing natural healing abilities, and meditation work—enriching outer life with a rich inner awareness.

Masters do not choose their helpers because they are perfect, but because they are willing.

Through the years, guidance has suggested we maintain silent prayer and meditation groups for the well-being of the work anchored here. A small group of anonymous villagers meditates together every Saturday—a practice we initiated in the spring of 1982—and though the faces change, the meditation link-up continues. A position of great responsibility with no ego rewards, each serves in a quiet, unassuming way. Dedication maintains the highly charged magnetic oversoul needed to insure longevity and guidance for the part we play in a greater Plan.

Three additional silent meditation groups are vitally important as well. These workers bridge the planes between the intuitive higher reality and the physical. They buoy us upward. We salute our unseen helpers who join from their respective places across the country and beyond with focus groups located here, a work vital to the well-being of any spiritual undertaking. We respect and take seriously these invisible helpers; some do not grasp the etheric work, but we do.

In the first years, construction of roads, houses, wells, and other physical needs occupies most of the time and energy of villagers.

As those materialize, more attention becomes focused on relationships. The high energy at Sparrow Hawk acts as a magnifying lens, enlarging whatever we bring—virtues and "baggage." It seems to accelerate things, making both strengths and weaknesses highly visible. We all learn, there is no place to hide in a community. We seem to live "in the eye of the hurricane." Because of the intensity, every unkindness is greater than life, even the unspoken. We strive to live a balanced life in a highly potent current.

We consciously practice a distinct, extraordinary intimacy—love of extended family—and simultaneously preserve space for privacy. We truly believe humanity is becoming one family. So as we share, we must also balance the personal responsibility with maintaining our own family and lifestyle. We learn what part of information and relationship is communication and networking and what part is gossip to be thwarted.

Our response to people wanting to move to the village is "First, come and see." Aspiring communitarians need to ask why they want to be here. Is it a pull to spiritual community and/or the studies, or are they avoiding the world? What do they *bring* to community? How willing and ready are they to trust, cowork, follow guidance? Can they be stewards of abundance? We believe each of us is charged to use wisely the resources and talents we possess. Can we build the skills needed to communicate, share, and serve a group?

The lives of those most greatly concerned with materialistic endeavors will be the hardest. If you choose to build up your treasures on Earth, prepare to be challenged. You pit your strength against the strength of heaven. Many have tried this, and it cannot be done.

You, Humanity, call yourself "awakened." Can you live in stewardship rather than ownership? You own nothing except your body. It is yours because you created it to experience the physical world and your life here is always dependent upon maintenance of your creation.

Ignorance is thinking without illumination; the light of high consciousness is not turned on. We rejoice in the researching for new insights. God is the source of light drawn into dedicated lives. Stewardship is enlightened participation in the maintenance of that which you perceive as good. When any creation is no longer good to you, no longer give to it. It will die or be picked up by others ready to support it. Move on to your next area of stewardship.

Message Carol received November 1982

In the Beginning

Ask any of the villagers about the early years, and you get a mixture of humorous anecdotes, nostalgia at the intimacy of the community, disbelief that so much has been accomplished in so short a time, and immense relief those years are over. Retelling it cannot totally capture the personal effort, pain, and courage demanded of every member, nor the wonderful growth experienced. In April 1983, with the church only partially built, the basement was used for a c-c-cold Easter service. The only warmth, Susan Hyder noted, was the "warmth of community." Indeed.

"I sort of see my function as that of historian," Grace Bradley remarks. "We come from a history of garage churches. I am sure many remember our chapel on the south side of Tahlequah. Now we have this beautiful building. I hope we don't get so fancy or fine that those in the campground feel uncomfortable with us or that we forget why we are here."

"We can all be proud in our accomplishment. When you mention Oklahoma, some think of oil and refineries. Well this is a refinery too," Charles contends. "We are working not with oil but with spirit. It has been a privilege to see so many refined spiritual approaches at this facility."

My role as founder, spiritual mentor, and "average jill" member of the community challenges me. I feel obligated to be as clear as possible as I respectfully practice tough love and to call the shots as I best see them. A major test for me is determining what is mine to do and what is someone else's. The village is not the right place for everyone, and we continue to face hard decisions as we grow. As workers for the future we envision, we dare not be overly dependent in any area.

The village welcomes opportunities to share its information, research, results, and game plan. Communities fulfill a variety of needs—nice neighbors and an excellent process for personal commitment; but selfishness, competitiveness, ego, love of status, fear, and pride prevent any neighborhood from becoming a caring community. We strive to be group-minded yet independent, responsible, and self-reliant.

I envision coworking as vitally important to one another and to future humanity in this Aquarian era. *We do not have to like each other, but we must love each other.* On a day-to-day basis, everyone will not enjoy the same people or even want to spend time together; some chemistries just do not combine.

Just as our homes form a circle around the natural energy center in the chapel, we seek to use that purifying essence to assist expansion of consciousness. Hopefully, our intent reflects in our daily lives of meditation, work, study, and bonding. We are at once contemporary contemplatives and highly social monastics, our integrated selves soaring as we proceed with the work.

As the middle-road spiritual path stretches before us, the village spreads its wings of insight over vast areas. It contains love enough to do many works, not the least of these in our own backyard. We write so often of glamorous travels or inter-disciplined openness, it is good to share our down-home reality too.

Some years ago, struggling desperately to be perfect in all endeavors, I was told, *Masters do not choose their helpers because they are perfect, but because they are willing.* This has comforted me many times when I struggle to do what is needed, yet often feel limited. Even if it were a goal, I have learned it is not possible to meet people's expectations, which are so varied and conflicted, so I do the best I can one day at a time.

I know we are a part of the emerging new design: an awareness that changes lives and brings renewing vitality as old ways fade. In the early years, a dozen or so of us would sit and share our guidance with one another. We envisioned the community we were birthing in much the way parents dream dreams for the unborn child. We hoped to lay a foundation to honor both genders and to keep rules and regulations to a minimum.

We use the expression, "The church is theocratic, the village is democratic." While not always understood, this is clearly to say the church has policies, plans, and responsibilities in keeping with specific direction received from the higher world, while life in the village is to unfold in an organic day-to-day manner through the consciousness of villagers. Using a one-lot–one-vote system, we elect a property owners Board of Directors which includes two cochairs—one male, one female for equality and balance. At the Monday evening community meditation, villagers attune themselves to one another, to the mandala of action which we have brought together, and to planetary well-being, acknowledging and blessing the network of emerging light workers all over the world.

We strive to hold our vision, stay on track, and remain open to fresh ideas. Probably our best examples come from village service teams: preparedness, agriculture, orientation, and so on, plus state-chartered volunteer fire department and water board. Each creates a game plan, lets its needs be known, and handles funds at its discretion. Teams share their agenda and accomplishments as needed.

Spiritual achievements of such coworking are unending: leadership develops; coworking demands resolving discontent; communication matures; boundaries appear, move, and are reconstructed or torn down. Clarity evolves in each member as the goal is achieved.

I love to recall Babaji's comments on the work of our time: "Learn to talk less and work more. This is the field of spiritual practice. Karma is the highest way of perfection. It is a great thing to take a human body. Whoever comes to the Earth must do work.

"In the *Gita*, work is said to be the highest form of *sadhana. Everybody must work; an idle man, though he is living, is dead. All who have taken birth must work to be successful. One of the things I want to do is remove idleness from the world."

In Agni Yoga it is said, "This flaming measure of labor must be established. The very approach to the Fiery World demands realization of earthly labor as the most proximate step."

Let us remember Master Jesus' remark in Matthew 25.40, "Inasmuch as you have done it to one of the least of these my brethren, you did it to me." As villagers, we strive to summon these words on days of struggle.

Sowing Good Seeds

In the early days, I was totally unprepared for the grief I would feel when people who had lived here left. I had taken each into my life so deeply, it was an overwhelming loss. When villagers elected to leave, I would waver between grief and gratitude, lamenting my personal loss and the community's, yet grateful they were prepared and eager to serve the larger world. As I mature in my philosophy, I realize how restrictive that thinking is, that indeed the whole world is our home, that people can be anywhere and still be within our hearts.

Gradually I learned to rejoice in the circumstances that bring people to be with us and later celebrate their readiness to go out to share. Creating the future is humanity's current work.

As spiritual students, we realize that challenge and blessing usually are two sides of the same coin. This is easier to recall in times of challenge, harder when we are being blessed. So as we invoke favor, saying, "This is what I want," we admit, the challenge will not be far behind.

In the teachings we learn that those with abundance are challenged to use it wisely, that more is expected of wise ones, and that as karma presents opportunities, we are held accountable. Hence, our challenges and our blessings try our mettle to see if indeed we can be what we know ourselves to be.

Just as powerful energies bombarding the Earth accentuate the good in us, they activate the not-so-good; betrayal, desertion, and crime proliferate around the planet. We must not forget basic laws of integrity, love, and vision and to respond wisely. We learn to face gossip, fears, and insecurities constructively. As we become wiser, our soul searching empowers us to be clearer and more accountable; each experience can become a springboard to new strength. Darkness will beget light only if we find the creative impulse needed.

> ### Enjoy Our Village Lifestyle
> Our intentional community welcomes newcomers. Eclec-
> tic and interfaith in our approach, we respect all practices lead-
> ing to higher consciousness. We each strive toward self-mas-
> tery and the transformation of ourselves and humanity, to make
> our world a better place for all.
>
> Villagers are from all walks of life. We elect the guiding
> themes for our lives and are self-supporting and responsible.
> We strive to live in right relationship with one another and
> the world of nature. Most of us admit we do this better some
> days than others. We discourage actions that tend to lead to
> abuse: drugs, excessive alcohol, offensive sexual behavior, disre-
> spect for others or the environment.
>
> We believe community is the way of the future; thus, we
> have begun. We invite you to come and be with us in voluntary
> cooperation.

Charles, Grace, and I have always realized the importance of
establishing rapport with the greater community of Tahlequah, resolving to link to both city and county. How can we be world servers
if we cannot bridge to the local area? When we find how mistaken
some are about our philosophy, how confused about esoteric Christianity or spiritual development, we work harder to communicate
and live the teachings, an important part of the Plan.

The village is known for larger-than-life ideas, and for service,
kindness, bright minds, and high creativity. We support many activities in Tahlequah: the Chamber of Commerce, Help in Crisis,
Hospice, Habitat for Humanity, Hope House (for the homeless),
volunteering at the hospital, recycling and other environmental
groups and projects, several firefighting organizations, Election Board,
and Community Action Council. Villagers hobnob at the university, participate in art and music events, and find fun, laughter, and
play with our neighbors. We build friendships at the farmer's market
and are known by local merchants as nice folks. For two years, I have
had a Sunday morning radio show, "Building the Inner Life."

While we truly want the people of Tahlequah to better understand what we are about, we realize some do not approve our liberal, ecumenical views; some prefer more explicit guidelines. A clearly defined religious approach is perfect for some, rather than a path as broad as ours. As our local re-lationship deepens each year, we rejoice in acceptance by most.

We know we dare not be so holy we are no earthly good or so grounded the Holy Spirit cannot use us. We strive to be channels of creativity through which grace flows to forge a community that withstands all

Bird's-eye view of part of the village.

kinds of changes. People living in the light of challenges seldom find their lives dull. In a village filled with all the drama of daily life, conflicts, unfinished business, and karmic lessons quickly come to the light of day.

Glancing at a recent issue of the *Community Directory* publica-tion, I think, *There are no communities like us.* I wonder what people picture when they think of us. Aware that every community is differ-ent, I ponder, *How can we most realistically represent ourselves?*

Let Me Paint You a Picture

Imagine a secluded setting on a lush, green mountaintop, where a small campus rests lazily at peace some weeks and hums with activ-ity others. A horseshoe-shaped street travels between the church and seminary buildings among about thirty homes placed carefully for economy of space, good views, and access to the woods. Each house is fairly new—for just a few years ago, only trees and wildlife

The beautiful Illinois River, enjoyed by tourists from all over, winds through village property.

were here. Most have extra bedrooms for guests and students. Villagers welcome opportunities to introduce others to community consciousness.

In the valley, gentle lanes fan out from one country road off the nearest blacktop. Homes of all sizes and values are spaciously situated, with clusters near the river. These homes also welcome visitors. A campground with hookups and cabanas awaits guests. Children play. Here and there individual and community gardens produce. The river winds about the base of the mountain, past the village, and on through the hills of Green Country, a region encompassing several large recreational lakes.

How do villagers look? That depends upon which day. On Sundays we dress up a bit as most attend church services. Light of Christ Community Church (LCCC) becomes the focus of activity with Communion at 10 A.M. and worship at 11. Potluck follows the service, then time to visit, nap, enjoy each other, or participate in whatever lectures, workshops, meetings, or social events may be happening. Most weekdays, our dress is quite casual, like our lifestyle.

But who are we? Middle-of-the-road, we commit to one another, but we are not communal. We share our good times, our troubles, and our support. In fact, we shine in our response to another's need.

One of our most admired policies is to make as few rules as necessary. Honoring the Agni Yoga principle of ethical living, we prefer to use general themes, rather than rules, granting the freedom and responsibility of self-mastery to each. Being free-thinkers, we learn more and more how to work together without working on each other. We may sometimes be too idealistic, but we have many practical people who keep their feet on the ground, even as we lift our minds to a vision of what might be.

The majority of villagers are well educated, well traveled, well read, and well balanced. The school has a *Ray 2 personality of love-wisdom, and its work centers around learning, transformation, and conscious living. The village is more Ray 4 with lots of drama and a wide diversity of personalities.

Sancta Sophia Seminary is the primary cottage industry. The church certifies a network of workers from coast to coast: churches and study centers, teachers and ministers. We are contemporary interfaith esoteric Christians, emphasizing service and inner work. Believing humanity is preparing to take a leap forward in consciousness, our work is to open minds, share teachings, and offer tools and techniques for those who see or would like to see themselves as world servers. We seek to attract people who share our vision of the Possible: hope, love, universality, cooperation, and dedication.

Modern Community Life

Not only is no community perfect, it does not work at all for some. Community falters without effort or when we place too many expectations or restrictions upon coworkers. Raising consciousness is what spirituality is about. For those who have never worked on themselves, choosing to cling to past pain, anger, guilt, and other negative aspects, community presents even more challenge. Said another way: An aspiration to grow and change is needed, *to be the future self now,* for an exciting frontier lies within. We learn not to exact due service. With love and allowing, we grow together. Intimate friendship is not obligatory; we strive to respond with acceptance, to reason with higher perception.

The power of a shared vision is profound. We remember, *when two or three are gathered in his name,* spirituality magnifies. In doing the work, women and men become united and woven into the plan or service that calls them. Only then can the love that binds nourish all. What do we do when we find ourselves in the wrong place? *Is there a wrong place?* Perhaps not, theoretically. We might think we are in the wrong spot when a specific location offers what we do not want; maybe it is time for us to claim our power and move. Many times we stay in a job, a marriage, or a situation long after it is time to make a change. Perhaps the lessons we are to learn from that experience either have not been satisfied or it is time to go to the next adventure.

One of many rewards of living in the village is to see individuals change. I am often asked, "What do you think the village's greater role is?" Perhaps it is an incubator designed to move aspirants more rapidly toward higher consciousness. Should we believe we are in a time of great testing (*initiation) for humanity and our planet, we can see that responding constructively to events and providing spiritual leadership are unequaled opportunities. We witness rewarding events regularly and recognize the impact the village makes nationally and internationally. We are privileged to participate in the externalization of holy thought.

Part of our village's purpose, not always apparent to the outer world, may not be appreciated by passers-through or -by. The light which emanates from here is eclectic, ecumenical, esoteric, disciplined, yet chosen by each, as are all heart-centered paths. We rejoice to be part of the great work that is in progress, the return of mystery school training for disciples. Honoring the wisdom of Kabalah, esoteric Christianity, and Agni Yoga, we integrate step by step. In fact, we create daily a foundation for the now-veiled future. Challenging one another as we challenge ourselves, we will either learn or fail. We prepare to meet the demands and tests of today's world, or we will fall by the wayside—disillusioned and spent.

13

Light for the New Millennium

Living in Sarasota in the spring of 1981, I receive a name for the new center in meditation: *Light of Christ Community Church.* The name surprises me. Previously I had chosen Aquarian Age Forum and Villa Serena for centers, names which seemed more contemporary.

As I meditate on the proposed name, I realize that Pentecost— the flame, or light, of the Christ—anchors inspiration. So with that and a planned astrology chart, we incorporate in Florida on June 2, 1981. Both sun and moon signs of the church's natal chart are in Gemini in the ninth house, making the ascendant Libra. My sun, Aquarius, falls in the fourth house of home—important as we construct an Aquarian home with lots of freedom to choose, think, and serve. Two years after incorporation, I realize Charles and Grace, the two who joined me as original trustees, are Gemini and Libra, respectively.

When we looked at charts and chose a date, we wanted the influence of universality, where people of all backgrounds would be welcome. On each church birthday we recall the love that nurtures this project. We remind ourselves, *church* means "meaningful assembly." Since the formal incorporation of LCCC was on June 2, we observe our birthday each Pentecost Sunday. We pause that day to

In 1991, ten years old, strong, solvent, and deeply anchored in our work, we celebrated the burning of the mortgage on the original land LCCC, Inc., purchased to establish the development that would be the village, home for our collective purposes.
From left, the three founders, Carol, Grace, and Charles.

contemplate our past, acknowledge our strengths and weaknesses, and celebrate our future. We have achieved a great deal, and it shows in those who participate in our maturation.

In the beginning, I had to invoke will in order to survive in this strange, new land. Now I love the mountain and celebrate the love which has nurtured all of us in this glorious place.

We see ourselves as part of a network of inspired temples, churches, and study centers anchoring the vision for the new millennium. We moved into position in 1981, preparing our contribution as a religious society structured to empower its teachers and ministers with immediate access to advantages provided by the religious freedom of our country. With its nonprofit, tax-exempt structure, its privileges allow it to charter churches and study groups so that prepared workers may specialize in ministry and service. We think of our mother church as a tree. Some rest and heal near her trunk, others form new branches. As the legal entity, the church grounds the teaching effort into the physical setting.

154

By 2000, our branches include thirty small churches and study groups. The work grows in response to the call heard and the protective affiliation with the International Council of Community Churches (ICCC). I love this group and appreciate the encouragement of its courageous board who invited me to join the council in 1975. I have been graciously encouraged time and again by the now-retired Reverend Ralph Shotwell and his lovely wife, Virginia. Such leadership serves well both the council and emerging new-thought organizations. Many of our people and loving friends use ICCC as a bridge from which to do their ecumenical Christian work. It is a valued resource that changes lives.

LCCC embraces Christianity as a process of transformation and enlightenment. We believe in an oral as well as written tradition, an inner spiritual heritage as well as an outer form. We recognize in all prophets a harmony, in all scriptures a unity, through all dispensations a continuity. We seek to awaken the Presence-Within and transform our human nature to live in accord with spiritual law. We believe that the divine consciousness makes all sects, classes, nations, and races one beloved planetary community.

> **The future of humanity and the planet depends upon humanity's ability to bring into balance our masculine and feminine natures—individually and collectively.**

The teachings of LCCC encourage and advance spiritual healing. By definition, *wellness* is the optimum condition or point of well-being one can realize at any given time through an integration of physical, emotional, mental, and spiritual awareness, harmony, and balance—of which the Wellness Center reminds us daily.

A post-denominational, interfaith Christian church, LCCC encompasses the teachings of Master Jesus as the Christed One who offers the way to humanity through a contempory Christian faith. As expressed by ICCC, *post-denominational* indicates a time to cease dividing, a time to heal the Christian faith. This is our belief.

Interfaith is a group of Western and Eastern clergy dedicated to bringing people of different faiths together so that we might recognize our common spiritual origin, all people of one God. Each member of the clergy speaks from his or her particular background, while fully recognizing the validity of other religions and supporting them actively, not simply tolerating but accepting them in truth and love.

Under these principles we are dedicated to the encouragement of individual spiritual growth. We salute the Christ-Within and seek to unfold that consciousness in all its beauty. Our annual fall conference for LCCC is always a time to reconnect our lives and inspire each other.

Light of Christ Community Church

TENETS

We believe in One Almighty Power in the Universe, the Cause of all creation.

We believe that in the heart of every living form is found a spark of that Almighty Power.

We believe that each human being can bloom and unfold spiritual potentials and radiate Beauty, Goodness, and Truth.

We believe that humanity is guided by Great Ones, who are the Saviors of the world.

We believe that Christ is the vision of perfection. The teachings are the path leading to perfection.

We believe the spirit of each human being is Immortal.

We believe that all humanity is becoming One Family. We love all religions, traditions, nations, and races, without discrimination of color, creed, gender, or sexual orientation.

We believe that each individual must shine personal light and live a life of honesty, nobility, simplicity, and justice.

We believe in generosity, in sharing, in giving and receiving in accord with the Laws of Abundance.

We believe that culture and beauty will unite humanity, that a life of sacrificial service reveals and manifests inner divinity. It is only in giving of your life (making sacred) that one truly Becomes.

We believe that culture and beauty will unite humanity, that a life of sacrificial service reveals and manifests inner divinity. It is only in giving of your life (making sacred) that one truly Becomes.

Two important works are happening under the auspices of LCCC. The first is the development of the seminary as a present-day mystery school; second, the building of community itself is a human experiment. Can humanity return to bonded interdependent living yet? Have we evolved far enough? Can we value each one enough to trust and grow together?

I believe Charles, Grace, and I were to anchor this work in this unique place. I do not feel this means, even if calamity struck, that we must necessarily be in the village. I might be in New York, New Delhi, or Newcastle. My guidance is to go and do, and I have never had a guarantee of personal safety.

As the village began, LCCC served as an essential parent—an entity empowered to buy property, funded to set things into motion, and with a board that could make decisions as necessary. Committees were introduced and responsibilities distributed to residents.

Dancers greatly add to services at LCCC.

The roles of the village, church, and seminary are rather defined, for the three which make up the one share a variety of talents and expertise. With Aquarius in the fourth house, the village is Uranus-ruled in nature, with an emphasis on Aquarian humanitarianism, love-wisdom, and equality. Coworking is both the challenge and the reward. As we were told in our village guidance, *we are a miniature world and will face the same lessons as the larger world.* Our opportunity is that our lessons are close up, and we can respond consciously to each situation.

Each year, more certified workers, teachers, and ordained ministers, as well as churches and study centers, reap the benefits of LCCC's structure. Our successes are the result of the love and efforts of supporters here and afar. When the message came to create the village, I turned to friends nationwide, and fortunately they responded with vital, indispensable encouragement, dedication, love, and financial support.

Almost everyone is comfortable with our inclusive tenets. We respect all paths; however, so far, most of our residents have been Christian. We welcome all faiths and races; our friends are from many backgrounds. At LCCC, women are in the pulpit more often than men—not by intent but because they are here, well prepared, and eager. We would love to have more men in residence, and we delight as they join us more frequently.

Not feminists *per se*, we do believe the future of humanity and the planet depends upon humanity's ability to bring into balance our masculine and feminine natures—individually and collectively— an aptitude for nurturing each other and creating solutions that lovingly serve planetary life.

People of the esoteric tradition strongly believe, *We have to "do it" for ourselves; no one can do it for us.* The tradition encourages conveying what is acquired through rich lineages—mystics, teachers, and saints who shared with disciples. This tradition still lingers: Helena and Nicholas Roerich, Alice Bailey, Vera Stanley Alder. Ancient wisdom teaches that each of us must birth the Christ-Within and walk our own path of challenges and growth. Spiritual teachings caution that *disciples must not hinder the work of one another.*

The Christian way has always taught that the kingdom is within, yet few truly search there for their divine connection. Speaking mere words does not make a practice. We seek to provide a supportive environment to those for whom spiritual progress is a major life-goal. Values are reshaped here. We deepen our appreciation of all that comes from an inner life; without that, we are bankrupt. Under the canopy of the great world religions, spirituality is gradually emerging; as it does, past prejudices and divisiveness will vanish. Religions once defined dogma and doctrine so we could easily identify differences; today, spirituality seeks to heal separation by encouraging us to see similarities *and* our oneness. Religions offer specific pathways to travel until the spirit matures. Believing the soul creates higher perspectives which will align us to the purpose of our incarnation, at some point we realize spirituality is the right path for us.

Spirituality, an evolutionary impulse, occurs when one's focus moves from personality issues to an awareness of oneself as a spiritual being. Religion and spirituality are often confused, but the purpose of religion is to develop will and social controls until the inner nature awakens to itself. Now spirituality can begin its influence; religious traditions often lead devotees to spirituality.

In *Signs of Christ*[1] Harold Balyoz says that as education, churches, and the Masonic Lodge reawaken to higher realities, each will become a major pathway for building the new civilization. Currently we are witnessing both schools and churches strain to transform. Spirituality flourishes more readily outside than within traditional institutions. Rarely do we see a priest, minister, or rabbi ready to welcome the new (actually ancient) wisdom even when their people clamor for it. Aware ones must search it out, absorb, and return, prepared to share.

In past centuries, structures "parented" members because individual consciousness was so limited. Schools, religions, and societies designed guidelines—from the womb to the grave. Now, from every arena come self-disciplined, sensitive, and wise beings capable of creating a new world view. Others are in personal rebellion against life, an equally valid stage of growth. However, our efforts are to become points of consciousness attuned to the higher Plan and to help bring it into outer reality.

No longer do we dip pen in ink and scribe letters. We enter information via computer programs, search the Internet, and stretch to catch new ideas. The meditations of our group embrace with broad appreciation the wisdom of those who seek and find the Christ, the Light, the One free from the constriction witnessed throughout history.

While the church provides the legal structure for certifying workers, ordaining, and networking, Sancta Sophia is the stimulating educational structure. The village serves both entities, many friends, our nation, and our planet as a retreat, a laboratory in which humanity matures through its experiments with the principles, ethics, and truths which we affirm. Think of this enterprise as a three-legged stool, each leg dependent upon and supporting the other two. Better yet, envision it as a triad of blessed energies. As we place the Christ within each at the core, the Master blesses the whole.

As we try to comprehend spirit interfacing matter, we know reason and appetite are to be reconciled into orderly behaviors that can satisfy both needs and intellect. Humans, it has been proven, can curb sexual drive and convert that energy for healing and creating, rather than hurting.

We are to be people of the equal-armed cross, comprehending Hierarchy as the direction to vertical attunement. As sincere, well-intentioned people of high consciousness, we recognize that personalities are not equal in health, talent, good fortune, or karma. When we can perceive others as souls and address them with noble regard, we create the horizontal arm of equality on the physical plane. The ancients used the symbol $\oplus$ as a balance of masculine ($+$) and feminine (O). The vertical line acknowledges spirit and matter must come together to work together. The horizontal bar is the mental and emotional Earth plane suspended between spirit and matter. At the intersection of the cross, we stand at a point of choice, empowered to lift or lower our nature in search of experience.

We recognize in all prophets a harmony, in all scriptures a unity, through all dispensations a continuity.

Spiritual life creates its environment, honors Hierarchy, and grants equality. Rank, status, prestige, and ego peel away. Conscious sharing intensifies the atmosphere, amplifying the contents of each soul, providing love, movement, challenge, and growth. Participants create a "magical circle" in an agreed-upon designated space. The agreement defines acceptable behavior and style—"how we do it here." Boundaries support those within as they grow in right-relationship, companionship, and service to one another. Congregations become an environment of transformation in this mystical place of spiritual influence. By placing ourselves at the intersection, we activate our karmic pattern and hasten new realizations. True equality occurs as each experiences being at the center. We await our fate, bowing to the Higher and what it will bring.

The Ray 7 influence now coming into power calls us together to re-form and re-order churches, communities, centers of commerce, and so on. From these, new life force will emerge to nourish the kingdoms, to embrace rituals of transforming power, and to place tools (money, energy) into the hands of world servers.

A Time to Fill the Lamps of Enlightenment

The frightened, the fear-mongers, the malicious and judgmental work under old banners. It is not enough to simply applaud courageous light workers. We must fill their lamps with oil to brighten the twenty-first century. Sancta Sophia, LCCC, walk-ins, new-thought teaching centers, light workers, and all awakened ones need support: supplies, helpers, currency, and encouragement. Many have heard the benefits of the wisdom way in the last twenty years but are not yet committed to supporting the new. The projects of many messengers suffer for lack of a firm foundation upon which to build. By supporting whatever works we choose, each messenger can serve the future more dynamically.

Spiritual ones create thoughtforms of possibilities and embody techniques of transformation. In the midst of family, society, and business, disciples strive to exemplify a life of nobility and integrity. Wherever we are, we are charged: *Weave your path, and make it sacred.*

The temple of instruction truly abides within; the outer merely bears witness to the halls of learning we discover. The community is a haven in which to share our truths, our knowledge, and our healing power—not just for the physical body, though we all aspire to that end, but for the consciousness which needs balance, peace, and positive purpose. Disciples go within to realign with the Divine.

The ashram or sacred place is coincidentally of benefit to its surrounding area as well. For centuries, areas have been considered fortunate when a spiritual center is situated in the countryside near them. Such a place holds the energy needed to bridge the inner and outer, a spiritual lighthouse. Energized for growth, the site clears astral negativity, brings good weather, a positive atmosphere, and good fortune to its people. It is taught in the Orient that the ashram invokes prosperity. We think of this as abundant life—not just material resources but a wealth of what the soul needs in order to learn that for which it has incarnated, and thereby mature.

Wherever there is an ashram, a guru, or a temple with a holy one, Eastern teachings consider that area blessed. The opening between the planes allows a bit of heaven on Earth, and the consciousness and lives in the area are uplifted. We might say, this creates good vibrations and brings good karma. When we attempt to express this, it seems vain, but it is imprudent to deny the higher nature. We become the good karma of our home, our families, our employees and employers in our various areas of influence.

The Ashram
The ashram is a gift of the Siddhas.
It is an outer expression of the Guru's inner state,
a place of immense power and beauty.
Where a Master of meditation dwells,
a vast reserve of energy accumulates.
This subtle energy pervades the trees, vines, fruit,
flowers and leaves, the soil and lakes,
springs and streams.
Partaking of the water, food and fruits
of such a sacred place,
even smelling its flowers,
awakens the spiritual energy in a human being.
—Eastern writing, source unknown

The spiritual *focus* blesses, and without a spiritual foundation, there could be no society. Even a whispered prayer sends vibrations to grace and heal, bring joy and harmony, add protection, and neutralize hostilities.

Transcendental Meditation™ made a great effort to prove statistically that one percent of the population meditating made a measurable difference in crime rates of U.S. cities. Thus, a group working together regularly invokes a creative response from the world of higher reality.

Our Western world is charged to create a middle-road path in the midst of extreme materiality. *Materialism is a belief system that nothing exists beyond that which can be explored by the physical senses. Science, limiting at times, has persuaded us to deny the nonphysical; spiritual teachings acknowledge the values of the soul. A middle-road path includes both material and spiritual realities without extremes. Today's emerging middle-road path differs from those of the past in that we do not turn our back on the world and withdraw. Releasing money, power, and status as goals unto themselves, we choose to use those energies to create a life of right-relationship with the world.

We learn to use energy in the form of

PHYSICAL	both labor and sexuality, as well as currency;
EMOTIONAL	drama and sensitivity;
MENTAL	creative consciousness taking responsibility to express positively; and
SPIRITUAL	the Self-Within reveals its love-wisdom.

Love unveiled through family life, honorable vocations, and voluntary simplicity transforms both our lives and the world around us. We recall the great good is to be fully human and fully divine. Spirit emphasizes the importance of placing oneself in the loving embrace of group prayer and meditation. In the village we see the lives of those who participate in morning meditation and community prayer-work consistently reflect expansion of consciousness. Changes occur more rapidly in those dedicated to their inner work. Remember, lip service is much easier than knee service.

Once upon a time, I was shown a view of this country dotted with little temples all across the land, each representing a small, dedicated group. I was impressed with: *it is not size but intensity that is needed right now.* We must commit to making a difference. Too often we lose the impetus, the inspiration, the moment of opportunity. Spiritual living allows for little hesitancy; it is so tenuous, we lose our vision if we become too rational, too materialistic, too consumed by the *maya of the world. Spiritual questing is like love—it is not rational and never will be!

14

The Power of Incarnation

Myriad souls clamor to incarnate in order to participate in this momentous period in time. Most souls in spirit wanting human life now are not novices but experienced, highly evolved souls who want to grow through the opportunities of the next fifty to one hundred years. Ready for testing, they have knowledge to contribute, along with a mature capacity to receive guidance. They can rapidly recapitulate accumulated wisdom; most are not immersed in materialism. Many are scientific with highly developed minds; others are quite sensitive to nature. The bright-eyed babies we see today can lead humanity toward peace and security, to a new collective awareness.

The 1960s and '70s frightened scores of people as they watched many rebel, stretch, break through. New boundaries were established, not because authority or perimeters were bad but because rigidity demanded resistance. Since then, we have been rethinking and redefining all human values. The slightly awakened may return to sleep and let it all pass, but a sufficient number have been jarred to keep asking questions. Many would like to go back to sleep, but change commands their attention. A beseeching humanity is being answered. Invited guests—walk-ins, messengers, angels, terrestrials, the Hierarchy—are here to assist the planet and the collective.

In the 1980s and '90s, humanity takes important steps toward manifesting new spiritual concepts. Bookstores stock shelves with esoteric, metaphysical, and mystical writings. Conferences and conversations buzz with talk of UFOs, extra-terrestrials, and in some circles we even hear discussion, empathy, and acceptance of walk-ins. Angels are "bursting out all over"—in debates, art, stories, and TV shows of miraculous happenings. We are finally asking about other life-forms. "Do you believe in angels?" is more easily answered than "Do you believe in UFOs?" We are witnessing a collective expansion of consciousness at a relatively easy level.

Expansion of consciousness means we stretch to see more of life and how it functions; we would perceive, intuit, and know the universe in a new way. Each soul incarnates for this.

Are We Devic, Terrestrial, or Human?

Why is it so difficult to be a human? Not only does this Earth dimension, thus humanity, vibrate at a slower frequency than some places and planes, this is intentional. Earth is designed to be a place of lessons! Shustah teachings refer to this as a "dark planet," a seeding place—not dark like "bad," but dark like a womb, where embryo souls get a start, like seedlings in a greenhouse.

Wisdom teachings present ideas about souls from families other than humanity learning lessons here and experiencing energies and bodies that do not exist where they originate. The teachings acknowledge that few of these "greenhouses" are in our system, so Earth's role is vital. We hear references to Sirius, Pleiades, or Arcturus, and we wonder what Earth has that is nowhere else in our solar system or so important.

Let me suggest that a variety of beings (evolutions) incarnate upon this planet—some because it is their home, others come to learn. Going away to school means different things to different folks. We are told three parallel families inhabit Mother Earth: humanoids, angels (i.e., devic kingdom), and meta-terrestrials (spacials native to this planet).

Humans vibrate to the densest bodies, angels to the astral, and terrestrials to an even subtler dimension. While terrestrials, sometimes called meta-terrestrials, are Earth's own version of "space beings," they are native to the Earth's mental plane, not travelers from another place and not extra-terrestrials. Think of them as nonphysical residents of Earth's higher vibrating frequencies.

At this eminent time of measuring planetary progress, all three families are important. These three evolutions, *all natives* who love their Earth home, are involved in the approaching planetary initiation, so the total planetary vibration includes them. Each of these shares responsibility for the condition of Mother Earth. Others are guests here (extra-terrestrials, for example); but, while they enjoy time here, this is not their home.

The diversity of Earth provides many opportunities for expansion of consciousness.

What makes it so difficult to be a human? First, we must learn to care for our body, a denser form than consciousness. Called a school, here we discover in slowed motion the power we possess. Many of the physically, emotionally, or mentally impaired are souls new to this body, gaining experience at creating a new type of vehicle of expression. When walk-ins enter, they must heal and coordinate with the inherited body; lessons come to teach us how.

The astral essence for *angelic* ones is light, easily reenergized by light, color, and sound, and with an emotional focus. Being in a dense body is burdensome, but imagine adding strong emotion too. Not to say that our devic friends do not enjoy emotion; indeed they do. If things get too calm, they will stir things just because they love passion and drama. Earthlings plod, which holds little charm for angelic ones; they would rather dance in and out of fun events but depart when the going gets tough. Being tender-hearted, they love to rush in to help; afterwards they are shocked to discover they have become stuck.

Terrestrials have extra-sensitive mental capability and relish using it. These friends love chemistry and complicated math, so they become our physicists and computer programmers. In fact, computers duplicate *their* fabulous minds. These academics resist feeling, so Earth provides opportunities for the heart. Relationships being so scary, they fight this little-explored, little-understood territory; after all, they are to learn to love with heart instead of mind. Impersonal and unconditional love is their goal. Their detachment encourages humans to let go and augments their inventive capabilities. In scientific and scholarly fields, terrestrials will lead us to discoveries now waiting "at the edge of mind."

When they access other realities, these two evolutions may feel homesick, stuck, or lost. At times, they resist human participation and may want to escape, but the axiom to recall is: *what we desperately love OR hate traps us*. Until unconditional love prevails, we are linked karmically. Until these souls surrender to meeting their challenges wisely, they must stay. So far, it is not easy to "phone home."

And how do *humans* relate to all of this? Slowly! Earth beings evolve slowly, upward and onward, often getting stuck. Earth Mother appreciates mud, clay, stones, gems, sculpture, working in gardens, loving children, and just living life in a practical, "down to Earth" manner, with an appreciation of slow, regular steps, little things like flowers in bloom, and the feeling of energy moving through the body. Often stuck in slow-moving lives, they mature through experiences others might find boring or dull. But here rests the stability of the planet.

From time to time guests come to see what is happening in this garden—extra-terrestrial visitors who are not natural inhabitants of the planet. Some have good intentions and some do not, it is said. Some are evolved and compassionate, while others, still attached to lower awareness, are very mental, no more spiritually aware than unawakened humans. Fear elicits concern in them, as it does in humans unconscious of the spiritual self. Such visitors who reach this planet carry an inventive mental mechanism and often are quite intense. They seem to think little of examining specimens they find and may not believe humans to be "as conscious" as they are.

Some walk-in messengers are revealing themselves as travelers from elsewhere, while others are more experienced human souls. This is not to say "perfect" or "perfected," for ALL who choose to incarnate do so to learn, grow, and serve.

As the walk-in from other dimensions slips through the doorway into human form, additional adjustments are to be made, similar to seeing through the eyes of a newborn. Time and again, we hear people say about infants, "If s/he could only talk." The child gradually learns motor control, language, communication skills, and acceptable social patterns. In contrast, the walk-in opens the door and finds her- or himself in the driver's seat of a new vehicle—wiring intact, gas in the tank. How does s/he learn how to operate this vehicle? Can s/he remember her purpose? where to start?

The diversity of Earth provides many opportunities for expansion of consciousness. We need to remember: 1) we have a Hierarchy of wise, perfected ones who have passed through the human family, 2) humans are now passing tests of initiation, so 3) more and more are assuming leadership. Earlier helpers are advancing into new roles, and as Earth gains new status (after the leap forward we anticipate), the planet itself will vibrate less densely and will be less difficult for everyone.

Walk-ins must consider two major points. First, they may or may not be of human origin but have entered a body to facilitate higher consciousness here, beginning with refinement of the lower sheaths of the inherited form. Each cell is in training to align to higher purpose. The soul is a great general; body organs and systems are the troops under the high command. It is not easy to create harmony within one's nature, but for health, energy systems, and high forces to move easily through a vehicle, it is necessary. Second, should one be a transferee from the devic or terrestrial evolution, s/he will probably have more struggle and differences in energy patterns; if s/he is of human evolution or has had previous human incarnations, it will be easier.

Lastly, we may ask how many devas are in human form, how many terrestrials. No one can say truly, but the general idea is that about fifteen percent of all humans are from the angelic kingdom. They migrate toward theater and the arts, and sexuality is a powerful attracting force. About ten percent are terrestrials or space beings who enter to learn about heart, to slow down, and to live on several levels, not just in the mind. Less than five percent of these incarnate from outer space. Most travelers do not choose to live in this slowed-down reality but are involved with experimentation, visitation, and inspiration. Basically, nearly seventy-five percent of the folks we see walking around are of the human family. The others join them in learning the lessons available: how to handle body, sexuality, materialism, time, money, relationships.

Becoming dependable, developing respond-ability, retaining the ability to love and care while being mindful in our actions are our work orders—not easy when we are all learning. We recall Lord Buddha's words, "It is not enough to cease to do evil; it is time to do good." If we believe we are a messenger, we should measure it against this adage which has stood the test of time. Then we will strive to live the Lord Christ's primary message: "Love one another."

In these trying times, disciples/world servers must remain strong. Our inner nature longs to be made whole. Of course, personality often suffers hurt. When congealed balls of "stuff" cause divine discontent, we attract incidents which cause us to review, study, and heal our blocks. Then the restricted energy is freed for more positive use and new endeavors.

As we live through our tribulations one by one, we encourage humanity's rehearsal for the coming of new Light. We dare not waver in our commitment to the service of that Light and to the network of world servers wherein we are all one. We know we are fortunate to participate in a work that is greater than ourselves.

Today's challenges focus more on the psychological level than the physical. Tests persist to see if, indeed, we can walk the way of love-wisdom. Clearing ourselves of the glamours of emotionalism and sensationalism, we strive to erase distortions of illusion and separatism. We are tested to love impersonally and to stand for principles that demand allegiance, even when painful, rather than making decisions purely from personality. All of this forces us to grow.

As we strive to embrace group work, we observe the stages disciples must achieve to prepare for service. What more can be said? This universal message is open to all who choose to "take the higher by storm." The challenge: do we have *ears with which to hear?* At a time when groups often are classified as cults and spiritual life and study are suspect, each of us becomes a role model. Our behavior is scrutinized regularly. How sad to realize how easy it is to harm one another and spiritual group goals.

A major technique for using creative power is envisioning, a tool to bring into focus the part of the Plan we can perceive. As more of humanity advances in chakra development, these senses become increasingly powerful. Different from visualizations but, of course, similar, envisioning begins with a picture—let us say, like a forest. The vision appears brimming with wholeness. But just as each tree has its unique aspects, so do we; thus we are little understood by others. Like the trees of the forest, we contribute to the whole, even with our personal conflicts. As we appreciate the whole, we focus on our own segment. To bring both into form, we envision the whole, then shift to our personal part. Envisioning is a process of sustaining the whole while energizing our little piece, yet grasping the importance of both.

Each inspired activity contributes to the creation of the new civilization. As old world views collapse around us, many incarnated today, particularly messengers, are like little shoots of new growth; valor sprouts even through the clutter. World servers construct new forms and invite others to nurture their potential.

The first step for any creation is to have a holy idea, a vision, a fervent desire. A swelling of great love and enthusiasm translates into energy we use to enhance the blueprints for our Plan. Image that a drafting department "in your mind" is creating blueprints; each day the planners are busy drawing designs for your hopes and dreams. The most knowledgeable, expert parts of you try to charge those blueprints before your attention shifts. Allowing the intensity of the emotional nature and highly focused mind to work together, what a team we forge. We can do anything. All things are possible!

Without a vision, the people perish. What blueprint are your inner specialists working on? Visions are fundamental to our creative abilities. They keep us excited about life, opportunity, love, and the use of potentials. If I had to state what makes Sparrow Hawk Village most wonderful, I would have to say, together we envision a place of sharing great love, healing, and hope. We have chosen to be a point of light within a greater Light and a channel for God's grace to touch others. As we hold such a vision, we each help others carry it. When one fails, is too tired, has a bad day, another reaches out, takes the load, and keeps the Light shining. This is the vision that gives us meaning and purpose. The village stands for group discipleship.

And to the Source We Return

Esoteric Christianity teaches, our evolutionary ascent back to the Source has begun. From the time of Jesus, the *historical Christ, a higher way has been proclaimed. Few have *the eyes with which to see and the ears with which to hear*. Yet, through the darkness of the past two thousand years, the message survives and continues to inspire, planting precious seeds of love and acceptance. Wondrous words clearly remind us, "You are the Light of the world." Too few understand, yet the message persists, threatened in a thousand ways. But as the golden age now dawns across the heavens and within our hearts, we grasp those words with new depth.

Messengers who proclaim the way are granted a brief time in which to be heard; then the spotlight moves. This unrelenting light illuminates inconsistencies, errors, and the foolishness of any prized ideology, simultaneously reflecting the lustrous gold of each design. We see great truth expressed. Life's lessons teach what can be understood, then spiral back to rest again. Each embodied soul works to reestablish a hold on body, emotions, and mind. It takes years to construct and reenergize usable vehicles, as well as to build the base of operations for this life's work. As soon as integration is validated at personality level, the soul makes its impact—the moment awaited, for the highly aware. The soul pours itself into its task.

For a walk-in, the message is the gift. In an exchange the two lives merge, as remnants of the original builder mingle with the messenger's fresh energies. The second soul directs the life, maximizing opportunities through the design of its inherited personality. Relationships are modified. Relatives, intertwined after a cycle of seven to nine years, may become family; they have the opportunity to become true family, as closely woven as adopted children, parents, or friends we lovingly embrace. If the incoming soul cannot elevate relationships to the new frequency, relatives assume the role of mere acquaintances with no special rapport. In this interim, the incoming one either has been able to personalize ties or not. Intimate ties must be adjusted to the new soul frequency to continue; otherwise, they tend to dissolve.

"The work" becomes the very reason for being. For the awakened, it colors all relationships and occupations. As one becomes aware of the inner presence, life and lifestyle change, old values and current means of expressing are revamped. Each area of life is upgraded. This age-old pattern repeats, hastening our enlightenment and the collective's as well.

Today the trauma of this revitalization reflects in the spiritual pain of thousands. Combined with the restlessness of an impending sense of participating in a special event, we grasp the opportunity that calls many souls to enter (walk into) adult bodies (by-passing the time and energy demanded to grow through two or three decades) to serve as focal points of inspiration and to bring their stimulating energy to assist humankind.

Most of those arriving can be called "bridge people." Experienced in human life, they are to master the lower nature—physical, emotional, and mental—as quickly as possible. They know that, while the past equips us for the future, it must not dominate it. Many carry a vision to guide them and work closely with the higher worlds. Whether embodied or standing in the wings, holy ones guide thousands who attune to their directions. As teacher of angels and humanity, Lord Maitreya, or the *planetary Christ, directs all beings; thus the message delivered two thousand years ago still reverberates.

We recall Lord Buddha's words, "It is not enough to cease to do evil; it is time to do good."

Humanity *can* choose change; we can be saved from darkness, ignorance, and materialism. The absence of light—understanding, perception, spiritual insight—is darkness (called "sin" by some, unaware of the Christ-Within, the divine Self). Absence of light begets ignorance. Many are misled by identifying solely with material/physical life. They delude themselves, believing the Game of Life is limited to mastering the physical plane. A truer definition of *sin* is "missing the mark." If we forget we have come here to attain our divine potential and only participate as a physical being, we have, in fact, missed the purpose of having a learning experience in a human body.

Mature ones long to see the meaning behind each truth, teaching, or spiritual law and begin to comprehend the wisdom bestowed by those who have guided humanity. Again, this is only possible for those who have *the eyes with which to see*.

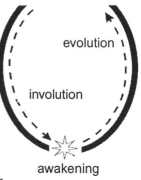

evolution

involution

awakening

The descent into matter requires far less effort than the path of return demands. Symbolically speaking, the pull of gravity assists the descent; being spun into orbit, we respond to the thrust whirling us toward density. Awakened, we seek to reverse that direction, even as personality tends to restrict. It always takes more effort to change direction than to go with the flow. Since the human current moves slowly, it is easier to become engrossed in materialism than to trust our other levels of being. Just as self-doubt curtails hopes and dreams, logic negates our intuitive promptings. While it challenges some to believe we are a body with a spirit, enlightened ones know we are a spirit with a body!

Enclosed in egoism, we may feel separate or superior. We learn through daily world news, we either become better stewards of Mother Earth or she sinks. Terra Firma, or Sophia (often called the world soul), is awakening her children one by one. This awakening is happening in every field of human endeavor—education, philosophy, art, religion, science. Restlessness prevails, a call to the perimeter of understanding, stretching us to a painful breakthrough in every facet of societal life. The divine feminine quickens.

15

Awaken to the Plea

The decision to share such personal information as is in this book created a formidable challenge. Who would dare or care to reveal that you listen to an "inner voice"? This seems incredibly precious and private. Does it serve a purpose? Biblical words ring in my ears: "Do not cast your pearls . . . ." Yet my *promise* to the Light Being was to do just this in response to the emergencies of our time.

As a walk-in, my mission is guided by periodic "time capsules." A segment of information is revealed, then more details emerge, resulting in a leap of understanding. As my outer life view adjusts to include the new data, another puzzle piece falls into place.

Realizing how consequential the story can be for two audiences, I agree to share much of my inner life. The first audience is messengers (walk-ins) trying to comprehend their own experience and mission. Mostly intense personalities, these souls feel an ever-increased pressure to discover their purpose for incarnation and how to make it happen. Some may not consciously realize their mission. Identifying with my story, perhaps some messengers will hasten to acquire new knowledge and proceed with intent. As each shares, others may find support.

When the incoming one surmounts being dazed and disoriented, the work commences. Each struggles to summon remembrances. A major problem for the walk-in is not having confirmation of these rememberings. When those around the walk-in deny the possibility of different realities, consciously or unconsciously, the walk-in may feel rejection or even more "peculiar." As experiences continue, the newly arrived one has to be strong enough to accept her/his personal reality or surrender to depression, confusion, and doubt.

The second audience I hope to reach is spiritually stirred people from all walks of life around the world who sense a crisis in the making. In the U.S. and elsewhere numerous respected human-potential educators and spiritual teachers acknowledge concern about disastrous possibilities: nuclear war, economic collapse, civil unrest, Earth changes, or other events of nature leading to painful human experiences. Both the spiritually stirred *and* everyday people—politicians, diplomats, artists, educators, journalists, visionaries, mystics, spiritual teachers, and some scientists—feel compelled to stress our ability to determine the path of the human future. If we have an option, as I believe we do in many areas, should we not be heard? Certainly we want dangers defined and suggested solutions aired.

Humanity is in a process of choosing light over darkness, peace over war. Can governments work toward coexistence, cooperation, common concerns, health and well-being as peace-keeping policies? Or will countries stockpile weapons and produce terrorists for fear of vulnerability? Spiritual attitudes are as confusing today as were worldwide issues in the past, from slavery to voluntary water rationing. Suspicion, distrust, and thoughts of superiority and competition dominate contemporary life as we approach the awakening of whole societies to new levels of awareness and power.

Future Communities

In 1980, I was shown a map of the United States divided into seven bioregions, each small and with independent laws. Then I saw countries around the world divided similarly. I was told, Small is beautiful; peace will come as the culture of each region is recognized. A bit later, I was given information about seven prototypes of communities emerging for the coming period. I believe Sparrow Hawk

Village is one of several paradigms being developed by Hierarchy for the advancement of both humanity and the planet. People who feel guided to communities might do well to determine which prototype best serves them and in which kind they can best serve.

We live in a deciding time. In the next few years humanity must rise to new consciousness or many will recede into *pralaya. Change is everywhere. The Masters' emerging influence is impacting the lives of humanity. We must all be ready to face the great questions.

Discipleship at the Group Level

If we think of ourselves as disciples working to prepare for a heavenly consciousness on Earth, we evoke the finest within ourselves, and in the process we unveil the talents and capabilities needed. As we each find our place in the great whole, we attract others to the part of the Plan that has been perceived.

From the inception of the village, we have always needed more hands, hearts, and minds than we have drawn. Emerging communities seem to attract more independent, creative types than cooperative team players; then everyone grapples with this imbalance.

We send out the call for dearly needed practical helpers: those who would like to start a restaurant, housecleaners, jills and jacks of all trades, transportation providers, and other practical assistants. Many love to do readings, or massages, or officiate at church, give sermons and workshops—a wonderful group, but we also need diligent, capable people who wish to serve, grow, and happily do part of the behind-the-scenes work.

Sometimes someone will say, "I have no talent and I really want to work for the Plan, but I can't do anything special!" "Hold it," I say, "I know just the place." *Is that discipleship too?* Yes. To do gladly whatever wherever whenever is a major virtue. I got to Oklahoma by just doing what I thought I was to do, one step at a time. Ego pay runs out, but work does not. Those who desire to advance on the spiritual path must recognize this. It matters not which rung of the ladder one's feet are upon; each brings challenges and rewards. This is the need—not escape from the planet, but to love it to excellence.

My work is to assist in the emergence of spiritual education within the framework of the Lord Christ, on the second ray. Christianity

Seven Rays, Seven Prototypes

The seven types of communities are best delineated according to the *rays and their purposes.

Ray 1 centers are disciplined places for strengthening will and invoking change. Many activities emerge along the lines of recovery programs—twelve-step–types such as AA, ACOA—straight rules to enable the development of will, proper boundaries, the ability to close tightly the door to destruction. The use of personal will later becomes *will-to-good.

Ray 2 highlights education. Communities constructed around the teachings and preparation of teachers train others for initiation. Esoteric schools are led by Master Morya, so the Masters and their goals can emerge. Disciples prepare for sharing through healing and teaching. Esoteric churches are Ray 2; institutions such as LCCC and Sancta Sophia vibrate to this area.

Ray 3 communities emphasize specific philosophies; a host of ideas will produce assorted experimental lifestyles. These people and centers will attract the intellectually curious. Talk on every subject will abound, with less stress on self-discipline, a good place for conversation and those drawn to interactive learning. The nature of Ray 3 indicates less structure and more movement toward experiential concepts. A variety of ideologies becomes important here.

Ray 4 ashrams appeared some time back as places of high creativity for artists, writers, musicians. Talented ones congregate to share art forms. Currently these exist helter-skelter, mostly around large cities where emerging talent can more easily break social tradition and display unique flares. We watch movies of ET or read science fiction. Remember the troubadours, Bohemian in nature. Ray 4 colonies prompt us to soar, to break free, to create thoughtforms useful in the process of change—sometimes good, sometimes destructive, but all urging humanity forward as they stir emotions in radical ways. The village has a surprising amount of Ray 4 in its heart.

The *Ray 5* frequency gathers scientists, engineers, an array of technicians. Learned ones in specialized fields prove their hypotheses or denote specific dangers and methods of correction in their labs. Their new ideas (solar homes, greenhouses, computers, Earth- and energy-sustaining methods) are appreciated in such environments. Good examples are Robert Monroe's laboratory in Virginia where he taught *OOB experiences, the biosphere in Phoenix, and a community gathered by such as Buckminster Fuller, the inventive genius who created the geodesic dome.

Those who serve here require an imaginative, intuitive nature, combined with well-developed mental skills. Currently, this aspect of planetary life is guided largely by incarnated space beings. In the third millennium, these will provide solutions merely dreamed of today, solutions which will assist all as collective problems are recognized. Technologies for survival will be created, proven, and shared. These will also be responsible for accessing unknown dimensions and traveling through time portals to explore the nonphysical world.

We may best understand *Ray 6* ashrams, the passionate path, for humanity is replete with fourth and sixth ray natures. Here the devotee continues in the faith of choice, often devoted to a particular aspect. Monasteries and ash-rams sustain the more traditional adherents, while others stir the unorthodox. Here the past is often honored as protectors of culture, world religions, and ideologies form kibbutzim and conclaves for time-honored practices. Loyalty reigns in these collectives, yet a new passion to serve and benefit all creation begins even as humanity constructs a world view devoted to eclectic interfaith communities.

Reflecting the ancient allegiance to duty of the Elder Brothers, Ray 6 initiates hold the heart light as humanity matures. Here, a new kind of work with animals begins—to allay their fear of the abusive human, preparing another swarm ready to evolve into the human kingdom. The power of dedication keeps producing. Also, much interaction with discarnates will come to pass as *there is no death* is proven.

Because of humanity's misguided concepts, perhaps the work of *Ray 7* is hardest to comprehend. Long absent from Earth, this ray is little understood consciously, though powerful on a subconscious level. Here are found many beneficial measurements: economics, recipes, formulas. Ray 7 introduces probationary practices, simplifying the point of focus. Floating in a sea of ancient, timeless wisdom—vague but powerful archetypes, mandalas, and symbols—it simultaneously builds in the here and now. This ashram manifests through each of the other communities, proficiently weaving past and future, male and female, spirit and matter, right use of ritual, meaning and value.

With its respect for efficiency and order, alchemists, shamans, and priests will receive training here, as will a growing group of ones emphasizing voluntary simplicity and order. Angelic forces interact with the human family for mutual lessons, sharing wisdom and power. Feminine energy encourages the planet's inhabitants through Sophia, our intuitive guide, to be orderly, practical, and effective. Without such temples of ascending comprehension, humanity would go in circles; history would repeat itself without learning; there would be no quest for a higher way.

Also under this influence a collective will emerge that understands the use of currency as a tool for the well-being of all world economies. These powerful ones will create new systems of distribution to meet human needs. Count St. Germaine is connected to Ray 7 spiritual groups to inspire through his legendary powers of manifesting. The new civilization will be built under this leadership.

for the third millennium is being formulated today. We are now in the midst of a Second Reformation of the Christian tradition.

With women rapidly moving into places of leadership, Christianity will change. We have moved into the era of the divine feminine, and she is everywhere. At the edge of our minds she whispers how it is meant to be. Call her Mary, the personification of Sophia, the Bodhisattva of Compassion, or divine mother—she loves all humanity. To be the mother of all, she loves all her children, those judged to be good *and* the not-so-good. The reality is, we are ready to know a more perfect relationship to our Father-Mother God.

We often forget we are part of an ever-transforming, alive-and-well school of thought. It may not seem so when we see Christianity freeze-dried until all the spirit dissipates or over-cooked till not a living enzyme remains. Real loss occurs when we forget the splendor of transcendental experiences held in the privacy of holy moments.

True spirituality is about celebration of *contact*.

We are foolhardy to expect others to grasp our mystical experiences; they cannot. We hardly can ourselves. But we can respect everyone's inner exploration and encourage each other to keep questing. Expanded awareness allows freedom from time restrictions and includes past lives and future events. As we accept that the power is in the "knowing," we surge ahead in our quest. If our heart is all-embracing while the world goes crazy with its ethnic cleansings, its hatreds, and its power struggles, we are blessed. We are to hack our way through sky-high congestion of restrictive thoughtforms to broaden the path of light that assists the survival of all planetary life.

Bodhisattva of Compassion, outside my studio window.

Esoteric materials suggest that for approximately the next two thousand five hundred years (an age), only through groups will anyone receive initiation. That means we need to find and contribute to the group of our choice. Learning to consider the well-being of the whole leads to a deeper meaning of community and coworking. None of us wants to be a monkey wrench to the group plan.

A period of human development designated for the good of all will tame extreme individualism. We will buff the sharp edges we developed as hermits and ascetics. In the past, spiritual seekers needed hidden paths to survive; we were loners, leaving the collective to itself. Now with courage developed, a sense of will, and a higher consciousness, we must find a way to co-exist for the good of the whole. Better still, our light will awaken more light.

True spirituality is about celebration of contact.

If we think of the Christ as a point of light, a holy principle, a focus for all, we will find the path to unity and peace. We do not have to work for peace; as we work for right-relationship, peace will take care of itself. If *peace* is too abstract a concept to visualize, focus on right-relationship among people or with the soil, plants, and animals. We do this privately until we find our group; then we grow, learn, and create together a work greater than can be done alone. Prayer, meditation, acts of service, ethics—all are vital.

Jesus specifically said, "Love one another," an ideal with the power to heal injustices. Contemporary teaching suggests we will learn to live in peace and cooperation in the era ahead or, should we not, destruction will occur. With a few left, humanity will be forced to cowork just to survive.

As I update this book (2001), television often shows cities digging out of blizzards, tornados, and volcanic eruptions; earthquakes are so common, they receive little news time or space; life is slowed to a crawl by severe, more frequent blizzards; areas ravished more frequently by hurricanes and floods; violent weather patterns and global warming. We watch concerned citizens working to save lives and property, for the threat of nature unifies; disaster stirs us to oneness.

When we have no specific insight about what is ours to do, we await the moment of hearing the inner voice. Until then, we serve the highest calling we perceive. Time is allotted to awaken, cleanse, and change harmful patterns. Still we question: Are enough thinkers wakening from the lethargy of materialism to realize where our acts and attitudes are taking us?

Should enlightened ones not achieve an impact on the masses, we must assume a second responsibility. As pockets of people committed to high principles create special opportunities, as they preserve wisdom teachings, applying spiritual beliefs to daily life, they become role models of right-relationship. Just as monasteries preserved education and culture during the Middle Ages, spiritual centers and communities may be the ones to anchor holy wisdom in a modern chaotic period.

Predictions of natural disaster provide enough cause for alarm even without fear of wars and nuclear danger—and now germ warfare carried in an aspirin bottle. If humanity continues to develop cooperative groups and to reject violence, working through inherent arguments by the power of mind, we will decrease numerous predicted Earth traumas. Adjustments on the mental and emotional levels lessen the degree of physical cleansing the Earth must face.

Today, some call themselves "God's people" yet judge and condemn each other, shatter respect for new ideas, hate other races and religions, or plant seeds of suspicion on every path, including their own. Without a collective change of consciousness, lack of love and trust will continue to cause pain. Negative leadership perpetuates disturbing and endangering qualities—limited human consciousness, sick and despairing.

Messengers, walk-ins, and others are charged with the specific responsibility of awakening consciousness. They are to provide leadership for the transformation of age-old ideas of separation. How to rethink society becomes a collective challenge, and those with the tools for breakthroughs point the direction.

Here are three ways to explain this moment humanity awaits:

1. *The externalization of the Hierarchy is happening,* now and every day, through walk-ins and through the high consciousness of many already in body. Highly charged etheric natures reflect the new, dynamic creative force. Open heart centers and energy vibrating in the higher chakras ignite others.

2. *Angels are walking among humanity*, but few yet have eyes to see them. Challenging and sincere stories appear daily to change our perception. To the few who are ready, angels become more visible and prod us to higher awareness. This *celestial hierarchy, the angelic kingdom, ruler of Aquarius, is revealing itself.

Walk-ins, the messengers, may enter from the spirit side of humanity or from the kingdom of angels or from the realm of spacial beings. In Hebrews 13.2, we are alerted, "Forget not hospitality toward strangers; for thereby some were worthy to entertain angels unawares." But do not expect the messengers to wear wings!

3. Many incoming messengers are *disciples of the Christ*. They can be walk-ins or others who enter by birth. These long-promised emissaries, who come to Earth to prepare humanity for the *reappearance of the Christ, are in all traditions and use various names for the Great Being.

Such messengers strive to cowork with the Hierarchy. Often still in touch with the higher world, they step their message down to those who are ready to hear. Called world servers, or disciples of the Christ by Christians, they release the light, love, and power of transformation to those ready to participate actively in creating the "new heaven and new Earth." Committing to this work, certain souls have been entering in increased numbers since June 1945, when the Christ announced he would soon reappear. Their presence has escalated since 1975. These servers seek to prepare the world for this event, knowing neither the day nor the hour.

Teachings suggest the Christ may manifest in the etheric, not necessarily in the physical. I personally believe the Christ—"I am with you always"—has always watched over humanity and now comes closer to humanity in order for us to awaken to this Holy Presence and become one with it. In this age of groups I believe there will be a manifestation of a number of Christed ones (in all traditions), each modeling holy awareness while in body by doing her/his soul purpose. This group of wise and holy ones will anchor the Christ Consciousness on Earth through daily living.

Out of the chaos of the old, the *phoenix will rise.

If you are a disciple of the Master, it is up to you to illumine the earth. You do not have to groan over everything the world lacks; you are there to bring it what it needs . . . there, where reigns hatred, malice and discord, you will put Love, Pardon and Peace. For lying you will bring truth; for despair, hope; for doubt, faith; where there is sadness, you will give joy. If you are, in the smallest degree, the servant of God, all these virtues of Light you will carry with you . . . do not be frightened by a mission so vast! It is not really you who are charged with the fulfillment of it. You are only the Torch-bearer. The fire, even if it burns within you, is never lit by you. It uses you as it uses the oil of the lamp. You hold it, feed it, carry it around; but it is the fire that works, that gives the light to the world, and to yourself at the same time . . . do not be the clogged lantern that chokes and smothers the Light; the lamp, timid, or ashamed, hidden under a bushel; flame up and shine before men; lift high the fire of God.

Phillippe Vernier
(After World War II)

16

Living with the Message and the Messengers

Messengers' new insights often clash with the outgoing soul's reality, causing confusion and instability. It is a saving grace to receive guidance and to be able to integrate the knowingness. New awareness and sudden expansion often combine with dazzling perceptions that flood the mind and precede a struggle to find ways to confirm the information.

When the walk-in inherits a vehicle permeated with the pain of the departed, the new arrival wants to re-form the life as rapidly as possible. Burning off the energies of the builder of the body presents a great challenge. Assistance is usually needed to help discern the work to be accomplished before we can really achieve that for which we have come.

Messengers are not here for self alone but have been granted an opportunity to enter in return for service to humanity. We may find the body we have entered to be ill, weak, polluted, traumatized, or inadequate, any of which require effort to repair. Had life been easy, the builder would not have sought escape, so naturally the new inhabitant has a job to do.

In addition to reconstruction of the body, the emotional life is usually adversely affected by the disappointment, de-

spair, or addictions (emotional, if not chemical) the previous one
has experienced. The mental state may be confused, underdeveloped, or mired in illusion. All of this says little of the lack of
spiritual clarity, which must be faced by the incoming one.

Where do we start? First, most need a mentor who understands
the walk-in theory, and a wonderful friend and listener certainly
is beneficial. A sincere effort must be made on each level: physical, emotional, mental, and spiritual. While mentors soothe the
messenger's adjustments to the exchange, many reject the idea
for several years, for self-doubt is common in such confusion. It is
easier to believe we are suffering delusion than to bear the strain
generated by ridiculing family or disbelieving spouse. A kind of
grief concerning the earlier inhabitant may also be experienced.
Walk-ins may wonder if the builder of the body wants that body
back or is still around; newly entered persons may construct a
thoughtform of the former person and judge themselves by it.

All of this must be faced before we can get on with the reason
for which we have come: to make a difference in the collective
human journey. Old debris clouds the consciousness until we empower ourselves to take up our task, whatever it may be.

Body-purifying and fitness programs are recommended. A
healthy, well-exercised body does not hold depression, for while
the body is being nurtured, so too are the emotions. Some experimentation may be required to determine what we need. As we
rework the physical to make it our own, we need to clear away
emotional scars and false truths that form psychic residue within
the psychological nature. The emotional life may have been in
shambles; now love is needed—not emotionalism, but honest,
supportive friendships. The sensitive newcomer may not be able
to do much yet, but even a grasp that wiring and plumbing are
damaged is helpful. A good, stable therapist, with whom to examine perplexing issues, is most important.

What about family? What about others' opinions of the messenger? More confusion exists than is generally acknowledged
about what is appropriate and for whom. Who to trust? Can we

rely on our own thoughts? Are we mentally ill or seeking to escape something?

The good counselor or therapist can be described as the one who holds the flashlight while the messenger crawls about on all fours looking for a lost contact lens. The therapist holds a clear, objective position while we look for the lens that will clarify our vision. This person is valuable when we lose our perspective in the emotions and disorientation of daily life. As we do inner work, we indeed are born to a new level of consciousness.

Emotional healing is expedited in a number of ways, but adequate grounding to accomplish daily business is the proof in the pudding. We need to realize we inherited a nature with "stuff" and we must clear painful areas. Recalling we have chosen to use this personality to do the work for which we entered, we face needed healing. We take note of emotion-backed demands (addictions) and the pain they breed. We build witness consciousness.

We intentionally pursue eliminating negativity, building areas of positive energy: gratitude, appreciation, an eye for beauty, friendships with healthy companions, appropriate boundaries that protect us as we learn to love ourselves. Knowing we cannot love our neighbor or the higher world until we can love our basic selves, we take the first step.

We recall over and over: self-love is not egotism. Poor self-esteem destroys lives, creates victims and resentment, and basically blocks the expression of our higher nature. We learn to love and appreciate the Self-Within, bringing the personality to a level of maturity that can render service to the world. New perspectives are required. We must find our strengths and, like all dedicated ones, *know thyself.* We practice the *nightly review and other techniques that help build new mental "rooms" in which to house a worthy life.

Adjusting to the messenger (walk-in) identity is a challenge for many. Life in other dimensions has to be pondered; notions of reincarnation, karma, certainly glamours of being "so heavenly we are no earthly good" are to be confronted. If we are paralyzed by fear or choked with egotism, we will fail in this grand opportunity, so we strive to clear mental *sheaths of distortions.

Meditation hastens the process on all levels. We may need assistance to find spiritual concepts that best meet our needs. We strive to locate a path upon which to reconcile our current understanding. As we know ourselves better, we may change our path, group, center, or church, keeping pace with new information from within. We become aware of great pieces of fresh insight, propelling us from level to level. These must be integrated.

Meditators enjoy
the peace of the chapel.

Types of cleansing, such as metaphor work and healing-the-*child-within, bring rapid progress, erasing scars and fortifying a healthy psychological stability. Twelve-step programs are good examples of the *probationary path for discipleship; honest commitment and fulfillment of these practices work wonders. All the ingredients of acknowledging, releasing, restructuring, and invoking the higher power clear residue. We begin again at each spiral, and more insights flow into the burgeoning consciousness.

Adopting a simple life of honesty, study, holistic practices and seeking clarity at each step decrease emotional stresses. Meditation, prayer, and insight connect what is known within to what is developing in the outer world. As spirit life and personality interface, the work that so inspired the incoming soul to desire life in the physical is activated.

We speak of "burning-off" or "grounding" techniques; some are one and some are the other. Let me paraphrase insightful definitions from Ralph Metzner:[1] Heaven is that state of grace we experience from time to time when we know our oneness; hell is when we get stuck; and purgatory is the spiritual path because that is where we purify and uplift our consciousness. Purification and grounding techniques help make us capable workers in the world. Anchored in day-to-day effort, they reshape our outer life. They are called "grounded" because they heal the body, the emotions, and the perspective so we can bring the wisdom of our higher nature down to Earth.

It takes time to make changes, and the impatient human nature, often seeks an easy way out. We comprehend new intellectual concepts long before we can live the belief system we espouse. The basic nature has to gradually integrate healthier responses to challenges and opportunities. We have to gain new respect for the vastness of life, its mysteries, and its joys.

It takes a cycle of approximately nine years for these changes to integrate within the messenger. This sounds so long, but it is not. It takes a full cycle of preparation. ✳

Messengers are called to step forward; reasons are two-fold:
1. *To support and encourage other walk-ins to proceed with their reason for entering the physical.* These steps begin with self-acceptance. Understanding one's nature and reaching self-love become the work, as well as completing certain tasks given them from the body builder.
2. *To reassure humanity God's Plan is working out on Earth.* At a time of trauma, with many becoming increasingly intense, it is easy to give in to despair, doubt, and gloom. Messengers bring an awareness of spirit.

Sent to provide reassurance, messengers would lift the heavy veil of pessimism and affirm the existence of higher worlds. They are to actualize love in the immediate moment, confirming God's love for all, giving immediate insights or directions to society, "how-to's" for facing challenges. ✳

Walk-ins seek to stimulate those who can look at situations with new eyes. The ability to perceive new and innovative solutions grows with expanding philosophical minds. Willingness offered by inspired ones takes courage to live, a choice often rejected by mass consciousness so easily intimidated by anything different or unpleasant.

Since about 1980, more people openly admit they listen to warnings of the possibility of nuclear war or accidents or some kind of catastrophe. Y2K concerns brought grave discussions. The story changes little, but a foundation for dialogue now exists. Facing chaos seems to be the thought we meet coming and going. We might say, "It is an idea whose time has come." It is simply humanity's readiness to process such information. We are fortunate that when consciousness acknowledges any issue, change happens.

We recall over and over: self-love is not egotism.

Ever since humanity became self-conscious, it has been challenged to make peace with death. Every culture has its own way of dealing with this event. Rituals have been developed for the deceased and for survivors. Death is so often experienced as an enemy, and many are confused when confronted with the study of death and dying. Perhaps the person eager to walk into death's outstretched arms unnerves us most of all. We do not relate to the Buddhist who sets himself on fire or one, such as Gandhi, who offered to fast to death for a cause. Our innermost resistance is challenged. How can anyone go willingly into the void?

Today, many concede, life can be worse than death. Mystics attest life exists in many dimensions. Religions repeat the message. Psychics, spiritualists, and parapsychologists try to explain strange phenomena. Ideologies and personal stories are shared. Scientists study the near-death experience in an attempt to comprehend the reality of which many now speak.

Is there a logical or spiritual reason for the recent investigation into areas of life after death? Do spiritualism, psychism, and the walk-in concept challenge many to look at life in a new way? Could humanity be moving toward a time when it will realize the physical life truly is only a part of the whole—perhaps not even the most important part?

As *prophecies become reality, perhaps making peace with death becomes a vital part of collective preparation. Anyone who witnesses or experiences a disaster is suddenly stretched to compute death, damage, and loss of both valuables and dreams. Certainly the bombing of the federal building in Oklahoma City shook the entire country and forced many to realize how vulnerable we are to violence, attack, and loss. When our personal world is ruptured, we reel from the blow, survey the setting, and hopefully shift into constructive action.

The Waco situation revealed a pervasive fear that permeates some intolerant or pious religious groups. Banding together through fear magnifies efforts to protect ourselves. Where danger or fear of separation prevails, a we-they consciousness easily develops. This illustrates the importance of living in acceptance and peace rather than to collect around a fear-based ideal—fear of the wrath of God, of Armageddon, of death. All spiritual groups receive criticism after incidents such as Waco. The more group violence intensifies, the more people will fear groups. Militia-type gatherings certainly bear watching. The very nature of humanity as a social animal is to band together. We develop discrimination within the framework of collectives. It is up to you and me to neutralize others' anxieties spiritual groups by our lives of service. Knowing how hard it is to live harmoniously, even with those we love, we must honor that spark of God within each to create a new consciousness.

People who have never met hardship have even greater fear; those least prepared feel the greatest inadequacy. Those who have been through tough times have survived basic training. The recovered widow/widower is one who understands best when another loses a mate. Parents of deceased children reach out with genuine empathy to parents in like circumstances. Knowing the need, people with colostomies or mastectomies quietly share to support others.

Preparation for an uncertain future demands flexibility, establishing our connection to inner guidance and considering ongoing life with fresh approaches. A river twists and turns lazily through its boundaries until a storm suddenly transforms once-peaceful waters to charge about maniacally, heedless of its rightful place.

People living along the banks dare not take it for granted. Similarly, we must recall past challenges with unlimited awareness, gaining enough understanding of human nature to form a plan of preparation.

Humanity itself will decide its future, at least in principle. The law of karma demands that humanity deals with certain issues. Teachings of grace suggest that if we change our consciousness, we change certain events; we alter the future by altering our conscious choices. There would be no need for prophecy if everything was predestined or inescapable.

The future arrives, a blend of opportunity and fixed design. Seasons represent set rhythms and cycles we have come to trust. We wrestle with the will aspect as creators-in-miniature, not always realizing what we want or what will be generated in the long run. We vacillate, hesitate, and seesaw until we cause conflicts for ourselves as well as others. Life moves slowly forward, balancing the effects of free will and fixed design.

Ever since humanity became self-conscious, it has been challenged to make peace with death.

In a conversation about the possibilities of walk-ins, Dr. Kenneth Ring, noted researcher in death and dying, raised a meaningful point.[2] He speculated, from a scientific viewpoint, that the shift in consciousness for some near-death experiencers (NDE) has the effect of "an individual seeming like a new soul, when in fact they were not." This is realistic, for not *all* those who experience the NDE are walk-ins. For some, the NDE is such an enormous breakthrough, the rest of the life is spent integrating this powerful experience. For many, new ideas and feelings become the first step in identifying with soul as an expanded level of their nature.

As we study the impact of NDEs, different kinds of changes occur. Often there is little memory of much more than a motion, a presence, or an encounter with a seemingly familiar presence. However, the intense experience does not fit comfortably into any rational framework. A profound inner knowing emerges. When this one reawakens to the physical life, the outcome is a deeply stirred person with strange stories.

When the walk-in exchange clearly has occurred, incoming souls are eager to take advantage. In addition to the NDE, Ruth Montgomery says, walk-ins use other mystical experiences—moments of despair *or* transformation—to enter. One type of entry is a religious conversion experience, when one goes through the agony of catharsis, suddenly is lifted high, and a great peace enters the personality. She says the change also may occur in moments of meditation ecstasy (experiences of the Light, we could call them) or whenever powerful spiritual forces separate the consciousness of soul from personality. While periods of unconsciousness result from various sources, these backdrops of change are not as apparent as near-death experiences.

Remember the formula: a desire to die, the experience itself, then a new beginning in a much more positive vein. This occurs when life is truly threatened, if escape is desired, and the wish of the outgoing soul is heard. Permission for the exchange comes from the Lords of Karma when the incoming soul believes it can convert this life into meaningful service to humanity. The incoming one enters with a purpose beyond personal development: a commitment to serve the greater good.

It seems somehow we have falsely believed that if death becomes acceptable, it will claim more of us and sooner. In fact, the opposite seems to be true. As minds open to new realizations, we may come to understand the near-death experience as death and resurrection, as expressed in various ancient traditions. Grasping the profound experience in a new way, we realize this much: It is truly the death of the old and the birth of the new for many who have undergone such phenomena.

If the idea of an NDE serving as a mode of exchange—a soul in between lives entering an earthly body—is too much, try thinking this way. Personality dies and the soul level now stands revealed. This blessed one, tender and new, free of old restrictions, expresses the new self. Mystifying awarenesses emerge. For many, this idea is more acceptable than that of an entirely new soul entering into the old personality.

I fervently hope those on the edge of new realizations will examine individual experiences without automatic rejection, as met from some. Today, as more and more people share their NDEs, visions of the future, and certain prophesies, they must still confront old patterns of suspicion and fear. Dedicated thinkers continue to forge into these challenging areas to find and prove that within the mystery of human life, more exists than has ever been identified.

Having lived as a messenger since 1958, I am now at ease with my role and no longer think it strange. I certainly feel comfortable answering questions that might ease another's adjustment period.

Since 1981, when Ruth Montgomery introduced me to the world as a walk-in, I have had to accept the insensitivity of the general public about walk-ins. When her book hit the market, I received harsh letters from two people who had known me for years, both of whom professed love for me. They accused me of an "ego trip" and failing to live up to their expectations. Ruth's disclosure amounted (to them) to my deserting who they thought I was, rather than revealing an additional dimension to who I am. Each of us is challenged to live our role: "All the world's a stage and we are only actors." Knowing *I am the soul* and that "walk-in," "messenger," or any other label is merely a role, major or minor, our work is to witness to our higher reality.

Having struggled to establish credibility, my walk-in status had to be offered up as well, I suppose. My conscious reason was to support others using this means of entry; unconsciously, the time for revelation and daring probably was nigh, and Ruth's message triggered a step waiting to occur. I had three advantages: 1) years had passed since the event, 2) I had received years of inner training, and 3) I had gained emotional self-respect. I felt I could respond with confidence and wisely. The years had served me well, and I was ready when *Threshold to Tomorrow* was published.

As I update my thoughts of 1981, I enjoy an even wider perspective. Now I can recall more objectively the powerful events that moved me from Florida to Oklahoma.

My heart revels in the love I felt as I observed the twentieth anniversary of my July 3, 1971, ordination. Special friends from all over the country added to the joy of the event with their presence or by sending memorable letters and gifts. A favorite "snapshot" captured forever in my heart and mind is Rev. Michael Okoruwa of Nigeria greeting me by holding an enlarged picture of me over his face—as did *everyone* in the ballroom, truly affirming, as intended, we are all one.

My anniversary present, a side-walk from the office building through the woods to my studio, is revered, knowing that villagers and visitors share my path and with dryer feet. New friends find the gift of a sidewalk hard to believe, but it is well treasured by those who knew us then. Walking it almost daily, I often think of friends who help me along my path. Every anniversary brings greater understanding. Life as a messenger is challenging, but with much support and my love of the message, it is indeed worthwhile.

The perfect anniversary gift—a sidewalk that links the office to her studio, ahead and to the left.

17

The Why and the How of Walk-ins

The Aquarian age will spell death to the Piscean emphasis on suffering and seperatism and competition. The energies bombarding our planet demand we forge a spirit of cooperation. At a critical point of evolution, humanity was forced to relinquish instinctual group consciousness to move toward an individuated *self*-consciousness. Humanity must forego its old emphasis on ego-authority and move toward respectful group consciousness. Having progressed in the reign of Pisces, now we are to convert self-authority to cooperation, sustaining individuality and integrity. This time, we advance toward a harmony inherent in co-working, cocreating, and right-relationship.

The pull to become one cooperating humanity is gaining strength around the world. Incoming energy spurs us to unite, to realize that the action of one (person, group, country) affects others. Again and again, we are shown, "no one is an island." Sociologically, scientifically, and philosophically, we are discovering interlocking ties. Realizing our interdependency with nature, humanity is being pushed to make dramatic progress, perhaps even toward fostering cooperation with other forms of life on the planet or in the solar system.

Our imagination (image-making ability) is actively addressing the appearances of devas, angels, space beings, and UFOs. Picture consciousness is the gift of Aquarius. We are constructing a new mental room, preparing to be more conscious of every life form. Creativity and inventiveness are facilitated by the mental vibrations of the new era.

Now we either move toward opening the heart center or not. We dare not wait to see how others respond. Necessity being the mother of invention, frustrations felt by many will give birth to solutions. We shall overcome! Much of society seems to sense something is awry but has yet to realize how to participate. Consider the idea that about five percent of the people produce new ideas, ten percent recognize their value and quickly move to employ them, and eighty-five percent follow along. Many inventive thinkers and leaders today are walk-ins attempting to support human aptitude as it finds new direction.

Humanity is being pushed and stretched. Projects are emerging everywhere. Breakthroughs are in their infancy because few realize what is being offered, but those involved are realizing their higher nature. Indeed, we have come a long way since 1958 when I stood in the light and received my divine commission.

It is prudent to recognize we can serve whether we are wise or just awakening. With a caring heart and by overcoming fear and negativity, we assist one another as we learn. Life's great teaching technique is known as the "sink or swim" method. Look how wonderfully we do when we simply jump in and paddle away.

What part do you play in anchoring the new era in your city and profession or for young people? Where are seeds of joy and goodness flourishing? Of what bouquet are you a part, in spite of weeds, to benefit planetary life? We are to become the guides and guardians, wise stewards using well the resources and opportunities life affords in the world of matter.

An important step is for humanity to know it is one extended family. We learn of diverse styles and cultures through television. On one hand, we see human suffering around the globe; on the other, we observe life's celebrations expressed by myriad races, religions, and personal odysseys. Through our powerful emotional nature, we learn to feel and identify with all of humanity; thus, our more sensitive, caring nature emerges. Wherever we look, we see ourselves, our fears and hopes reflected. Indeed, Life *is* the great teacher.

As we observe, we note the destructive patterns to confront; old prejudices writhe as they listen to the death knell of the Piscean era. Though fanaticism dies hard, it will pass. Aquarius emphasizes creative power, bright ideas, and the potency of thought, urging us to realize we are cocreative. We are challenged to perceive anew that each action has a reaction. We must dare to be team players, linking energies in constructive patterns, demanding noble concern for human values.

The message of the new era proclaims the need to free ourselves from hypocrisy, to truly become what we can be, to move from limiting attitudes of possessing and controlling to kindness, generous giving, and coexisting actions. Much later, we will move to simply being. Harmony with the Self-Within supports natural human evolution to a state of being that takes less energy and creates less stress.

The primary messages of this transition time are:
- Each must assume responsibility to clear personal karma and a portion of the unawakened collective's karma.
- The divine feminine urges integration and more open expression of sensitivity and creativity.
- All values are to be reexamined and reshaped in light of fresh perceptions.
- As age-old separatism is confronted and annihilated, the Rainbow Tribe is to emerge.

In time, we learn we can *will* harmony, protection, and well-being for individuals and for the collective in ways unthinkable today. Today, we are witnessing the vanguard: Military personnel assisting in social services rather than primitive war, i.e., hospitals, water systems, rescue efforts, first aid, ecological projects. The military will become a public service organization of great value as our consciousness conceives more beneficial responsibilities for this youthful strength. Consider the peacekeeping missions in Somalia, Haiti, Bosnia, and Kosovo as exploratory steps toward such activities.

Gradually, many groups—political parties, states, nations, to name a few—will make hard choices for the benefit of all. We are learning "tough love" without relinquishing unconditional love. Picture these as two sides of a coin. As we choose time and again, we do not replace one with the other; the opposite side forms the foundation for the first.

Imagine a new kind of educational system with teaching restored to respect. We may have to see the destruction of public education. Variations of private tutors, home schooling, charter schools are innovations seeking to restore quality education.

Tragedies push us forward. The freezing and starving homeless, heartbreaking tales of mental illness, neglect, and abuse scream at us to get involved with social systems. Restructuring our prisons, rehabilitation programs, and mass assistance to open minds are about to happen. Just as the incoming energy empowers us individually, it challenges communities to reclaim the power to find solutions.

For Aquarius, known as both humanitarian and scientific, it is natural to seek answers through technology. We must face the tendency to be too mental, afraid of emotions, or too detached, all of which are represented in the isolation inherent in computer sciences. The emotional development of the Piscean era must undergird the era of expanded mind. Remember, our collective goal, as well as personal, is love-wisdom.

Breakthrough insights by Larry Dossey, M.D., in *Healing Words— The Power of Prayer and the Practice of Medicine*,[1] and his further work, *Prayer Is Good Medicine—How to Reap the Healing Benefits of Prayer*,[2] provide scientific data from empirical research to support ways and means to combine prayer and positive thinking with medical skills, advances in technology, and the power of mind. Many have concerns as technology overtakes advances in ethics and human bonding. Aquarius provides time to integrate heart and mind, moving humanity toward one another, each kingdom, and the universe.

It is true that as we move collectively toward a new maturity, each of us is becoming a galactic human. Laws of initiation protect higher realities from disruption; we will not become our potential in a flash, but gradually. We can be sure the cosmos does not want Earth to spread its disruption to other spheres. We are, however, struggling to prepare an adequate number of initiates to lift the focus of our planet into alignment with more refined realities, drawing a larger number toward soul awareness. We are now engaged in the *Law of Chaos stage, moving through choppy seas of evolution. Those of higher consciousness toil within the astral reality doing purification and illumination work for all as we prepare for the shifts that will align us to the lower frequencies of the next greater whole: the galaxy.

Fear of the future or of the unknown will pull humanity backward. Secure in the success of intellect, some dare not violate reason to accept the belief of life "beyond." Others feel it necessary to denounce the old: attitudes, toys and games, hurts, and indulgences. At the same time, the bridge people are in the middle, feeling a profound pull toward the possible-future. Bridging is truly the work of the hour!

We must learn from our past and realize the importance of integrating its lessons. Just as a child moves from infancy to adolescence, from adult to elder, so humanity evolves. Long immersed in adolescence, we struggle to reach a more responsible position. It is sad that so few have claimed their potential. The cry, "Wake up, humanity!" comes now from all who know.

Again and again, physicists, psychologists, and mystics find themselves experiencing similar insights and knowledge through their specific disciplines. While my way is of the mystic, I rejoice at the resonance of the tune. As we hear the melody through diverse vocabularies, the message becomes more familiar. *The power of choice* is but one theme to which humanity is required to respond.

Messages from wisdom teachings suggest humanity travels in spirals. Moving in cycles age after age, we discover patterns through which humanity advances: mastering limitation, acquiring new knowledge, overcoming restricting temptations, establishing improved paradigms and refining them. We see the rise and fall of nations, the defeat, the enslavement, and the conquest of peoples.

This spiraling action, ever upward, gradually lifts humanity to an awareness of a higher way. As more people adopt more caring perspectives, humanity is steadily drawn toward higher consciousness. A now-pregnant human collective experiences labor pangs as it prepares to birth a divine child.

Aware ones evoke new consciousness; evolved souls and heavenly helpers alert humanity to the dangers of flat cycles and to potentials of new genius. "Break free," comes the command. "Dare to be divine!"

In the new era, we will see each other as souls, not objects to be maneuvered. Using the concept, to act "as if" in order to become, heart-centered people struggle to find ways to transform the pain of the past, fearful acts of the solar plexus, and competitive centeredness. The forthcoming vision calls for caring what happens to others even at personal discomfort or inconvenience.

Only two hundred years ago, most of the world found slavery acceptable. No longer is that so. Less than one hundred years ago, women could not vote. Few realize the former Soviet Union provided women suffrage in 1917, before America did so with the Nineteenth Amendment in 1920. Gradually and finally, war is being viewed as barbaric, much less tolerable to today's intellect. We will learn to negotiate our differences, though as yet we have not enough successes to celebrate. Humanity still agonizes over the struggles of Israel and Palestine, Ireland, and the former Yugoslavia.

Destructive myths of the past must be de-energized and abandoned. Knowledge which served humanity on its descent into matter will not suffice for the ascent. We have to stop, reevaluate, and become conscious of human potential and God-given powers. As we merge intellect and intuition, we will avoid the games and follies of the past.

Just as the human kingdom emerged aeons ago from the animal kingdom, a comparable experience is about to occur. At a wondrous moment, humanity will birth what is being called the *kingdom of God*, or **kingdom of souls* in esoteric language. Holy Ones, having aligned their will to higher will, are no longer limited as they undertake to lead humanity through an open door into the foyer of a new kingdom.

This transition period—1987 to 2012—is likely to be challenging. Remember, it is easier to believe a lie heard a thousand times than the truth heard once. After living in a house a number of years, it seems easier to move than to clean and redecorate. This clean-up, shape-up, renovation is humanity's present work. We might say, it is our karma: those subconscious desires, that basement where we store so much, must be cleared and reorganized. In the midst of clean-up, inspiration and hope which had been submerged will resurface. We will discover the part we can play in the Plan. Our place of service is the goal right now.

Call it superior intelligence, divine mind, or the Plan of God, forward movement requires our participation. Humanity is to use its free will and creative power to express choice. The power to determine its fate is the gift of the Creator. The dynamic challenges ahead are necessary and valuable, yet we grasp them not at all. Just as the storm cleans and refreshes nature, today's storms prepare us for new opportunities. As today's world view ends, futurists envision a new one.

Knowledge which served humanity on its descent into matter will not suffice for the ascent.

Keys to guide humanity out of its difficult maze emerge at the edge of our minds. Just as Edison had hidden within him the concept of the light bulb, today's answers are near. Bits and pieces are dawning: how-to's for meeting the challenge of power struggles, psychological healing, confronting violence, food upgrading, healing, separatism, and new styles of relationships await. The mind of humanity holds incredible resources ready to be unearthed, evaluated, and supported.

The mosaic of the "new heaven and new Earth" is yet to emerge, but you have a piece and so do I. It is to be unwrapped and recognized. If we stop stretching, our contributions will never be made. If we cling to past beliefs, we may attempt to "let God do it" without our participation. If swords are not beaten into plowshares, the quantum leap cannot happen.

Conflict in the outer world reflects conflict within the collective inner world. As we individually confront our *shadows, integrate our wisdom, love our neighbors and ourselves, we alleviate inner difficulties and the outer world moves toward a more peaceful state. With inner conflicts resolved, we bring a new, clearer, and more hopeful attitude to our relationship to society. The new world view is to be anchored in hope and respect for one another.

Perhaps the threat of disasters helps us surrender the age-old practice of solving problems through violence. Does it take the horror of acid rain, poisoned earth, and polluted rivers for us to respect the health and well-being of Mother Earth? Does it take energy shortages to make us look to the sun and wind for power? Perhaps these challenges are necessary for humanity to appreciate what it has taken for granted. Much of humanity continues to allow itself to be comforted by the idea of the second coming, the return of Jesus Christ, the Lord Maitreya, or Messiah. I believe the Christ *within us* is the true second manifestation of the Christ on Earth.

If we accept the Christ, or holy consciousness, as the great goal of sacred teachings, we accept that the presence of God can be realized. The divine within in tune with the divine parent can then participate in bringing forth the divine Plan. All world religions provide clues to a sacred cocreating wherein an awakened, enlightened human lives in right-relationship to the God Parent, utilizing divine potential wisely. Remember, "You are gods," and "Even greater things than these shall you do."

The Messenger's Part in This Great Drama

Numerous souls eagerly await contributing to the human family. With special skills, energies, or abilities from the past, many believe they can assist humanity through the crises and into the next stage. Wise ones who love humanity step forward courageously, willing to lead the breakthrough. Inspired others choose to join them, forming a brigade of light workers—some wise, some just plain willing.

Perhaps the most difficult yet essential aspect to understanding walk-ins is this: *Messengers develop their mission operating on the keynote of their predecessor.* The builder of the body had certain karma (good and bad), certain challenges (lessons to learn), and obligations (debts). That builder may have made commitments to another soul prior to birth. These would fall primarily in the area of relationships: parent, child, mate, business partner, even competitor, as well as supporter, benefactor, mentor, and so on. A pattern had been designed by that earlier soul (and/or the Lords of Karma) for the builder of the body to grow through assorted experiences. Now s/he

In our mystery plays, we recall many lives and roles we may have played before.

determines, "I've had it." For whatever reason, s/he wants OUT. There are always options: suicide, slow death—willed consciously or unconsciously—deadly attitudes, destructive health practices. We realize that we humans often deal with death wishes, perhaps latent.

As the builder of the personality experiences despair, another soul (behind the veil of consciousness) believes it can transform that life in remarkable ways. It invokes the aid of the Lords of Karma. The ultimate reason for this method of entering physical life is not just for the pleasure, growth, or well-being of the personal enhancement of the one coming in, though these benefits do occur, but the thrust of the life is to be built around a contribution to humanity. Permitted the exchange, an obvious, intense humanitarian focus emerges in the new life.

Too, the incoming one agrees to complete some details significant to the life already in motion. Credit is given the outgoing soul for the life being rendered to the higher cause of humanity. Only if the energies of the two souls can be synchronized do we have the nucleus of an exchange.

Challenges for the incoming soul are many. Repairing and caring for the physical body comes first. Delicate bodies are often a mark of the walk-in. The walk-in has to get to know the new vehicle, learning how to handle it consciously, and can never put it "on rote," as the original builder could. Having undergone trauma or even long-term damage, the body requires rebuilding. For this reason, if for no other, many messengers are drawn first to healing.

The energy of the incoming one must blend with the inherited emotional nature, which causes change in temperament. The departing one may have sought a commitment of the incoming one to nurture children, to love a mate, or to attend to other responsibilities until they are in good stead.

At the mental level, one may have good equipment or poor. Incoming souls must apply their energy to the subtler part of the mental nature to gain all the advantage they can. The mental equipment of the new inhabitant acts upon the inherited mental nature, converting attitudes and perspectives. As old programs and memories naturally affect the personality, clearing the glamours and illusions of the earlier life must be faced. At the same time, new glamours and illusions that accompany the incoming soul need to be addressed. All of this effort is known as "cleansing the temple."

We see why it takes time for the incoming soul to achieve stability and make its own impact. Facing limitations built into the basic life, the incoming one lives within a fixed design: an inherited gender, nationality, education, and cultural heritage. While some of this can be altered and improved, the basic format is established and must now be rendered useful toward a greater goal. The keynote, or vibration, that began with the original personality cannot be re-sounded; however, the vibrations of the incoming soul may raise to a certain degree, lower, lengthen, or adjust the keynote for her or his purpose.

Part of the karmic pattern to any life is set by the astrological influences at the moment of physical birth.[3] This personality heritage sets certain influences to be faced. Parameters of the life include personal circumstances at the time one enters and the current struggles of society, producing a portion of the fixed design with which any entering soul must contend.

The incoming soul will gradually release new and different energies of its own into the inherited framework. Each soul brings the energy of the intuitive, *atmic, and divine planes to which it has access. Possibilities exist for burning out or blowing apart the gifted personality, so new forces must be stepped down gently. The exchange and immediate period afterward are vulnerable times; nervous breakdowns, mental confusion, and spiritual emergencies lurk nearby.

Just as every cell in every body is being replaced, made new every seven years, the walk-in starts to rebuild and stabilize the framework of the personality. A cycle of seven to nine years (a point numerologists will address[4]) is needed to allow the incoming messenger to establish solutions and face the events of the fixed design from a different perspective.

In adjusting to new frequencies, the new inhabitant sets about establishing particulars in order to guide the life toward the mission for which s/he has entered. Facing the challenges, s/he fulfills as many obligations as possible within the karmic implications of the original life. Since the walk-in usually is wiser, though I hasten to say it may not always be so, situations so defeating to the other may now be resolved to some degree.

The astrological data of the personality created on the original keynote remains valid, as do numerological insights. Just as the palm pattern of each individual's hand gradually changes, charts reflect cautions, and the wiser walk-in soul will try to make the most of them. As we watch, the life evolves from the mundane to the magnificent.

I believe the Christ *within us* is the true second manifestation of the Christ on Earth.

It is important to realize that in any one life a soul rarely implements all its potential but learns lessons as certain seeds develop. We recognize that in some situations we completely solve (or dissolve) a challenge, as with all souls, while in others we do what is possible. Matters become better in some cases and worse in others. Through all of this, growth still occurs.

By the time the seven-to-nine-year cycle is completed, karmic situations tend to be mostly resolved; seeds brought by the new soul begin to germinate and flourish. From outer observation walk-ins are seen as rapidly moving change-agents. From the inner we rearrange the furniture of life for new purposes; goals emerge as the new occupant settles in.

18

Walk-ins Cope with Trauma;
So Do Walk-alongs

Walk-alongs" experience trauma too. Traumas endured by messengers' families are not unlike the strange shifts the incoming one faces. Considering the full-scale soul-exchange experience, we recognize that this new being affects every life s/he touches. Everyone associated with the exchange will have predictable emotional and mental trials and concerns. Every life connects to scores of people, from immediate to extended family, friends, and acquaintances. Few comprehend the ripple effect of their experiences.

The real work is to deliver a message, not necessarily a spoken message, but a communication of *being*, living our message to the best of our ability. We bring concepts from somewhere higher, a message of Creator's love, to build ties where there may have been stress. Each exchange rocks numerous lives. Addressing each family member requires skill, time, and compassion.

At the time of my near-death experience, I said to my husband, doctor, and priest at my bedside, "I am not who you think I am." They patted me on the shoulder and told me I was hallucinating. "You'll be all right," they assured me, or themselves, dealing with me as a disturbed person. Something had happened that they could not fix, and they faced a grief process, sincerely worried, hoping this person dear to them would get better, back to who she was.

It took me a long time to figure out how to be in relationship with significant people in my "new" life. Now I look at these people with compassion—husband, children, parents. In 1958, people did not acknowledge the existence of NDEs. There was no such designation. Because my children were young—my oldest, six—I did not even consider talking to them. It was all I could do to deal with a husband determined I was utterly confused, parents who did not understand, and ill-at-ease priest and friends.

How do people live successfully with those who have had this kind of exchange, especially during the initial period? From my observation now, it takes an incredible amount of patience as they try to comprehend something almost incomprehensible. It takes a thorough examination of the one who has had the exchange and those who walk along. What strong points connect us? Let us examine these relationships and some of the feelings surrounding them.

Spouses have become strangers. Now they may have to rediscover qualities in each other that they admire, that can compel them to restructure a relationship, to become friends, to find mutual values.

Few marriages survive a walk-in experience. Relationships are so altered, most couples seriously consider divorce. Reviewing options, they need to feel the newly forged connections are their own, not leftovers, remnants from "pre-exchange." That gift of freedom, then recommitment, has a healing, transformative power. Now the relationship is fresh, more energetic.

Years after my first husband and I divorced, he knocked at my office door. I had been ordained by then. "Come in." This was the last person I expected. "I want to talk to you," he said. "You know you are not the person I married. Something really did happen, didn't it?" He sat down, and we had an excellent conversation, achieving a clarity previously unattainable.

Children, to the incoming one, often seem dear but distant. You now feel a kind of *im*personal love for the very children once intensely close. You LOVE them, but the love is not focused at the

210

personality or emotional level as much as it is an overview of your children and everybody else's children. They are all precious, and you seem to have little more identity with your own than you do with other youngsters around you. Most children, my own included, find that difficult. They cannot understand.

Since my experience happened a long time ago, I have adult children today with whom to discuss this. My children were just young adults at the time the first *Messengers of Hope* came out. They have all talked to me at different times about my feelings for them and what kind of a bond they have with me. My oldest daughter became particularly disturbed at her loss. "It's not that I don't love you," she said, "I just want the mother I was supposed to have." That was really hard for both of us.

I have often told my children I am sorry if my exchange experience has made their lives harder; I hope they will just love me and know I love them. I want them to let me do what I must, knowing my feelings for them lack nothing, though I may be more impersonal than they would like. Most of my children (my first was born in 1952) at one time or another have said something to me about being too detached. Similarly, I realized I needed to find more intimate ways to be with them. Having made an effort to be impersonal in my spiritual life, I had to reverse that process and become more personal: *How are you going to deal with this? What is the struggle? Can I help in some way? Tell me about your day.* A special effort to help them feel my love has helped our relationships.

Now when my children call me, I often ask, "Do you want this to be a mother's perspective, or are you asking why I think this is happening?" I dare not respond, "Well, this is just karma working itself out," or "Can't you see, you drew this to you because . . . ." Usually they want me to be with them from the heart, not the head. It took me a while to figure this out, to see that when they approach me in an emotional way, they want a feeling response. I have learned to respond more wisely.

Parents were perhaps my hardest relationship; their distress was so obvious. Like everyone, growing up we have certain struggles with our mother and father. Hopefully we move beyond our conflicts and into a mature relationship of mutual respect and love. My parents—

mother and stepfather—probably had an even harder time with me than I had with them. Parents might experience an even greater grief than the new one coming in. It is not just the confusion of seeing their child as psychologically different, they just do not relate as well. When they encounter the walk-in theory, for all practical purposes they have to deal with foreign, disturbing concepts, including the loss of a child they loved. Now a new, quite different person enters their lives.

Appreciating the mutual love between parents and adopted children helped my parents and me resolve this struggle. We discovered it is not a lack of love but a different love—a conscious choice to "adopt" and love each other. New love must be nourished to grow; in order to transform, the relationship must be grounded more in the present than in the past. My parents and I arrived at this after more than one tense discussion.

Parents who are familiar with metaphysical or esoteric concepts may be able to make an easier transfer. But we still must acknowledge the grief process. It is important to look at the grief the change precipitates and to go through the stages of grief. Then all can build anew. But if the grief is not processed, the fresh bonding is not as total with this new person.

Another segment: Generally family members are not going to discuss this with others unless there is a mutual metaphysical or esoteric bent. So caring friends and family are restricted. Where can they turn for support to rework the new relationship? Who can they trust?

Before this autobiography was first published in 1983, I talked at length with my parents, probably the hardest of many conversations. By *hard*, I mean "most tender." My family may have moved through it better, both parents and children, had so much public attention not been directed toward them. My parents were embarrassed.

Staunch Catholics, my mother and father did not share my belief system. Not only were they uncomfortable with my name in print, it was about an experience they did not accept. I share this because we do not always realize how much trauma besets the lives of the people who count, we are so busy dealing with our own. Trying to

212

cope with my own trials, I know I must have been pretty insensitive to the challenges of loved ones.

Although it took several months, I finally got smart enough to just stop explaining. But look what that does. If we cannot talk to the most significant people in our lives, we withdraw. As communication shrinks and distance grows, intimacy fades.

As soon as we begin to grasp what is occurring, we must let people know we want them in our lives, if we do. If we know a relationship is not working and we do not want to mend it, we must make decisions with sensitivity and honesty.

Having spent many hours trying to compel everyone to understand me, I finally realized that was "having it on my terms" and my rather conventional parents would never know what to do with this. *How else can I work on this relationship?* I wondered. I figured out what they wanted from me was just to love and respect them, to recognize the sacrifices they had made to raise their family. They wanted Mother's and Father's Day cards, Christmas and birthday cards, an occasional visit, and for me not to "rock the boat." Now that was not so much; I could do that.

I went for short visits and was always appreciative and respectful. My folks did not want to discuss my work or the books I had written. They did not want me to try to take them off to some strange church or for me to give them a message or a healing. So I figured out how to handle each situation, and we learned what we could do comfortably. We seldom talked in depth about my metaphysical pursuits, just a little from time to time.

My parents were very proud when I was selected to go to Moscow to teach medical authorities about death and dying. That was something they could talk about to their friends with pride and without stirring up unexplainable concepts.

It bothered me in the early years when my parents always wanted to take me to church, even after my ordination. I did not mind going to church and often went with them, but as soon as the subject came up, they would say, "How long has it been since you have been to confession?" Then they would start working on me. But when they learned I went to communion wherever I was, whether abroad or at the Catholic church here, they were scandalized. I said, "Mother, it is between God and me, and I am okay!" But it still troubled them.

Years later, when my father was hospitalized, communion was brought to the family. As the priest approached me with the paten, my mother said, "Oh, Father, no, don't. She's not Catholic." Even then, it was still an issue, but suddenly I realized it was her issue. I was hurt because I really wanted to receive communion with the family, but I acquiesced. This is a major point I am making: *Walk-ins must be the ones to comprehend the challenge and guide situations gently.* When I realized I no longer had to make others understand me, I felt a certain freedom. I gradually realized how to allow others to be.

My parents especially scrutinized how I was with them and with others, certainly their older friends. They slowly grew more confident that I was not going to embarrass them. Finally, when the priest who baptized me told them, "Carol's found God, she's okay, leave her alone," that relieved my parents. It gave them permission to love me again, and I am grateful to him.

Messengers with **siblings** can experience numerous problems. Sometimes the siblings just do not accept the exchange, considering it an ego trip or psychological disturbance. It is hardest when sibling rivalry existed previously. When these resurface, siblings may deal with it by not getting together anymore or visiting parents when the walk-in is not there. All kinds of little games are played. Not everybody is ready for new thoughts or self-examination.

Some siblings, family members, and significant others simply avoid the subject, preferring to believe the walk-in has had a nervous breakdown or mental illness. Messengers may brush it off as karma, but by doing so too readily, we may create karma. The struggle will not lessen in the face of hostility. Messengers are here to manifest something: *love, higher consciousness, a mission.* We each have a reason to be. We must honor ourselves and set boundaries.

No one should place him- or herself in a position to be abused by a sibling. Draw some kind of perimeter, and say, "Look, if we want a relationship, let's have some ground rules. If not, let us be kind." But messengers are the ones challenged to make the greater effort to love them, even when it is not reciprocal. Change agitates any relationship. We need to strive to adjust, but if people cannot accept us, we are not sentenced to just suffer. That is why boundaries are so vital.

Walk-ins must be the ones to comprehend the challenge and guide situations gently.

Part of our problem is that often we cannot express ourselves. In the first few years, we may not comprehend or express things definitively. We are still doing our hardest work, and until we get past that, we may not be good at mending relationships. We may know they are valuable, but perhaps we need a little distance, expressing our affection through cards or letters, simple gestures until we feel more secure.

The process takes time to work through. There is often so much hurt to heal—especially when marriage relationships come apart and certainly when accusations have been hurled. My children's father would say to them, "You know how your mother is," or, "You know your mother's peculiar ideas," implying I was "not quite right." That was painful.

Finally, ready to claim my truth, I could say, "Yes, and my ideas serve me well. Earlier views were a foundation, but as I grow, these beliefs help me live better. Maybe someday you will cherish convictions that work well for you. They may be some of mine, some of your dad's, and some from other places." When the implication that something was wrong with my thinking was raised or when my children brought up a controversial topic—reincarnation seemed inevitable—they still questioned. I shared, but I did not pressure them to believe. In some earlier discussions I was not knowledgeable enough, but as I gained confidence, I could answer almost anything to a degree, which served much better than no response at all.

Parents who move patiently through this process with their children are to be admired. In addition to good physical relationships, they build beneficent soul bonds. They establish deep spiritual ties, interweaving souls more respectfully. In this way, they support loved ones and the work the incoming one has come to do. It is a challenge to explain this phenomenon. Compassion is needed as parents watch their children live through the changes.

Liz Nelson (1928-2001) was inspired to establish WE (Walk-ins for Evolution) in 1994. This organization is dedicated to assisting messengers and their families through the challenging adjustments required in order for the incoming one to realize his or her purpose.

Liz, also a messenger, "walked in" in 1984. She led a focused and dedicated life of service and sincere effort. All messengers will find the stories shared by WE interesting and inspiring.

You may contact WE INTERNATIONAL at: P.O. Box 28875, St. Paul, MN 55128 telephone: 651-772-0847, web site: www.walk-ins.com

More than one set of parents has said to me, "You know we are torn. In a way this is our child, but in a way it is not. What about our own daughter (or son)?" So we have created a ritual for the person who has left—that builder of the body, the "real" child. In one service, after some prayers, we ground up rose quartz into little chips; the parents made a small garden in their yard, and sprinkled the quartz chips there, and said, "This is our daughter's garden."

It is certainly best not to compare, not to play one concept of "daughter" against another. Just accept. When I talk about my story to close family, to my children, I often use the language "young Carol" and "myself" to differentiate, which seems to help their understanding of their mother.

Good Grief

To take this a step further, the incoming person may feel deep heartache over the previous inhabitant. S/he may have a grief process to undergo, even great feelings of guilt, as if s/he did something bad to this other person.

When one woman asked me to have a memorial service for the previous one, we did a ritual for the original builder of the body—in which the new inhabitant thanked her for providing the means to enter the dense world. She said the service was so beneficial because it helped her move past her guilt feelings. So some kind of ritual may facilitate a vital adjustment, helping us let go of the past and embrace the lovely new person and new life.

216

Profound experiences and several decades had passed when Mother said, "Well, I never really understood what happened to Carol, but I know she is good and that is all I really need from her." Her acceptance meant an immense amount to me. Shortly after that, Mother passed away. She would not comprehend the things we are saying here, but when she accepted me for who I was, that was enough.

Impatience is detrimental; change takes time, and human nature seeks the easy way out. We adopt new concepts long before we can practice new beliefs we espouse. The basic nature has to gradually shape healthier responses to challenges and opportunities as we gain new respect for the magnitude of life, its mysteries and joys. As we do this, the messenger both learns and teaches.

Taking First Steps

From the time of the exchange, I knew my work was to share the information I was given. Two themes clearly at the forefront of my mission were community and the divine feminine. Community emerged first in my life. By understanding our social nature and spiritual oneness, we realize that community can make a shift in the human condition. Love for one another underlies modern community in the same way survival did in ancient times.

Messengers are also to introduce to today's awakened ones the mysteries that have guided wise ones through the ages and to hasten an understanding of the importance of the role of group life and right relationship for planetary life.

Ten to fifteen of us attempted "extended family" in a small cluster of houses in St. Pete. In 1976, we moved to lovely Villa Serena in Sarasota where our esoteric school began in 1978, later to become Sancta Sophia Seminary. The move to Oklahoma in 1981 brought the founding of Sparrow Hawk Village to provide the opportunity for many to taste community—a re-emerging approach to contemporary life. Light of Christ Community Church, a blend of following guidance and common sense, proceeded slowly. The mission is being lived out one day at a time—as is each life.

Upon arrival at Sparrow Hawk Village in 1981, we probably thought we knew more than we actually did. We have had to take half-steps and learn through trial and error through the years. Certainly, we have expanded our goodness and our wisdom. As we willingly struggle to live together, we gradually be-

A view of the church (left) and the library/office building. A new East Ridge area for homes is at the end of the road at top of photo.

come more capable of the Great Work. This is necessary for every new approach, every meditation group, each healing technique, and certainly for all *light workers. The work moves us toward our potential; as more awaken, we all function better.

The emergence of the divine feminine is a concept less understood and hard for many to grasp (certainly in 1958). Today, many messengers are presenting teachings in this vein, and certainly most are now acknowledging the return of the divine feminine. Her presence is making itself felt in area after area and is our saving grace. The pendulum had swung into such destructive force, it distorted all expression. This signaled the time to move toward center, and it is the nurturing mother who will help us. Now we enter her time!

The feminine mysteries have always been with us, but overshadowed and neglected. Sophia will challenge all human life, for she brings vast new areas of exploration. The shifting currents expand consciousness toward the subtle, sensitive areas of life. Walk-ins comprehend the mysteries more intuitively, and even they struggle to present them in more concrete form. These sensitive areas remain mysteries to the rational.

In the spring of 1981, going public with
my story was an exercise in agony. Consider what "coming out of the closet" may
require and you probably touch upon the
anxiety. After struggling for years to become acceptable so I could assume the necessary posture to do what I
believed I had come to do, the inner message came, *Lay it all on
the line!*

Only the urgency of our times might cause people such as I to
express so vulnerably. In 1981, it was hard for people to accept
ageless wisdom teachings, even more so the walk-in/messenger
who attests, "This is so." A comforting piece I did not know when
I first wrote *Messengers of Hope* in '81 is that C. W. Leadbeater
recorded in *The Masters and the Path* in a section called "Bor-
rowed Vehicles" that:

> This temporary occupation of a pupil's body should not be confused
> with the permanent use by an advanced person of a vehicle prepared
> for him by someone else. Our great Founder, Madame Blavatsky, when
> she left the body in which we knew her, entered another which had
> just been abandoned by its original tenant. As to whether that body
> had been specially prepared for her use, I have no information; but

other instances are known in which that was done. There is always in such cases a certain difficulty in adapting the vehicle to the needs and idiosyncrasies of the new occupant; and it is probable that it never becomes a perfectly fitting garment. There is for the incoming ego a choice between devoting a considerable amount of time and trouble to superintending the growth of a new vehicle, which would be a perfect expression of him, as far as that is possible on the physical plane; or of avoiding all that difficulty by entering the body of another—a process which will provide a reasonably good instrument for all ordinary purposes; but it will never fulfil [sic] in every respect all that its owner desires.[1]

The crisis years now upon us demand that humanity realize its innate power. Messengers cry out to preserve life on this planet. Most people are unaware of reasons for their incarnation or their "soul purpose." Caring awakened ones strive to create social awareness. Materialistic, selfish views can no longer dominate the Earth, or she will rid herself of us. As a living host, the Earth has been tormented to the limit. Like fleas, we had better become concerned with what happens to the dog!

Now, many are beginning to speak out in an effort to stop the headlong rush into numerous crises, attempting to slow the many violations of spiritual laws that occur in ignorance daily. In 1958, I took my place as a messenger, hoping to be heard in time.

For years now, walk-ins have been coming in by the thousands to warn from every available post: Stop! Care! Through books, teaching, and the lectern, I continue to speak; tomorrow another person with different credentials will relay the message. The resounding cry will only become louder: *hate destroys!* It contaminates and kills both its creator and its victim. *Fear paralyzes* the flow of creative inspiration needed to sustain humanity as it seeks to lift itself to the highest levels of compassion of which we are capable. As we face planetary testing, we face the long awaited planetary initiation; all the planet now suffers, and if humanity (as its mental body) breaks through to expanded consciousness, all planetary life benefits.

Only the foolish think they can exist alone and have a quality life. Arrogant individuals may still believe personal power can save them, even when it cannot make us happy. It certainly cannot bring the inner nature to peace. Just as a seed needs water and light to sprout, high consciousness needs love for the unselfish to flourish. The work, the effort, the struggle to serve person, cause, or principle gradually transforms the lover. We change. An example I often use: Think of each human as a seed. It takes sun and water for the seed to germinate and grow. Our tears are water, and whether of sadness or joy, they water the seed. The High Self that guides us provides the light. The seed sprouts, and we become conscious of a higher nature.

Mystics often use symbology to present their insights because symbols preserve the message for great periods of time. Monasteries of the Middle Ages sought to preserve the finest thinking of true Christian mysticism through symbolism and ritual, as mass humanity struggled against the ignorance of the Dark Ages. Today we ponder the emerging ageless wisdom to better comprehend the noble concepts current society often overlooks.

Divine laws, cycles, and teachings point humanity in the direction of a greater comprehension of Truth.

Several messages appear repeatedly in today's inspired materials: most obvious, reawakening to the divine feminine; best known, the return of the Christ, *Quetzalcoatl, or the coming Lord *Maitreya; and third, ideas of community. Centers created by those wishing to present futuristic thought bond many in preparation for a planetary breakthrough. Each message reminds us of the importance of living in right-relationship with one another and the Earth. *The Secret of the Andes*² by Brother Philip provides one of the earliest references to the slowing of energy to the Himalayas and the stimulation of the Andes as the anchoring point of the incoming feminine energy.

Great truths spring eternal, calling to us from world religions and philosophies, as well as from personal experiences. Dreams and myths whisper much the same message at subtler levels. Those aligned to life perceive the struggle of a maturing humanity.

Walk-ins in large numbers address emerging issues from diverse perspectives and personalities. We hear repeatedly, *the di-*

vine feminine stirs, kindles, and demands attention. We approach her through ecological concerns, equal rights, healing techniques, psychic or intuitional training, even devotion to Our Lady. The feminine mysteries, once veiled, suppressed, or ignored, will be heard. From channeled spirit messages such as the *Course of Miracles* to the long-hidden writings of Hildegard, the message of love-wisdom emerges. The knowledge of the heart—gnosis, Sophia—cries out in and for each. A shift from rational mind to the power of inner knowing progresses. Recalling the wisdom of America's native people who lived in harmony with the Great Intelligence for centuries, we abhor destruction by technology without ethics or reverence for life. The divine feminine honors sexuality, birth, death, healing, intuition, and play, knowing these are the creative spirals from which all else emerges.

A messenger's need to establish a sense of identity and security is acute. The pain of expanded awareness brings denial or an effort to stem inflowing information. A bombardment of perceptions strikes the new messenger, creating a pain comparable to a bright light turned on when we have been sitting quietly in the dark. The glare disorients. Experiencing such an expanded view of life without gradual adjustment might cause the walk-in to seize with both hands whatever seems to stabilize the picture of life. This may be easy answers or false truths for a time. The initial reaction is to find a safe, quiet corner and disappear.

Only as stability in inner and outer life comes can one brave sharing glimpses of personal experiences. Since my exchange in '58, I have struggled to integrate life on many levels. My first ten years of pain and confusion were spent simply trying to be accepted, to find a safe place within—we would say, "to feel empowered," in the language of the '90s. One has to get into a position from which s/he can deliver the message without revealing overmuch. Caution and preparation were necessary before I could speak of the work to be done, always wondering, "Can I succeed at this?"

How I started was simple. I gave up trying to reach my then-husband, my parents, the doctor, the priest. I feared I would never fulfill my mission. Finally, because life was truly overwhelming—

my babies needing so much, my health fragile, my loneliness extreme—I learned to sit silently. I would put myself back in that Presence, recalling the light and love of what I now call the Light Being, and as I would love it, I would let it love me.

I had no language for what I was doing, but I knew I felt better, happier, stronger when I sat quietly for half an hour or so, sometimes in the dark, sometimes just with my eyes closed. More time than I realized would often pass before I returned my attention to the outer.

After two or three years of this rather regular practice, "it" began to talk to me once again, just as it had in the near-death experience. Thoughts flowed into my mind, a kind of knowingness. Had I pondered a question earlier, I might receive something on that topic or area—not exactly questions and answers, more a teaching and comforting.

Over a period of years, I was impressed with numerous new and wondrous ideas. It became easy to shift, using key thoughts to get new perceptions. Now I know the reality of being taught by spirit, and I believe many are ready for this. However, it was my isolation that pushed me to the only source I had: spirit.

Past-life Therapy Helps the Walk-in

After my exchange, I suffered loneliness, as all walk-ins seem to. I ached for someone with whom to share the "things I knew" but for which I had no words. At times, as my inner connection taught me telepathically, it reminded me of things I was charged to remember when I stood in the Light. I was grateful to find an outer guide, a spiritual teacher, to help me put words to intricate and profound concepts.

A useful tool for me, and for other walk-ins as well, was regression therapy. Questions abound around this issue, and only a few can be addressed here, but such exploration paves a road to discovery. Messengers must learn to separate what belongs to the "other" from what belongs to us. Many baffling emotional patterns came from "young Carol," but by calling upon my Inner Knower (the term I now prefer), answers and guidance came. Eventually, I was able to distinguish my own "personality stuff" from the residue of the frightened and rigid young lady who had lived in this body.

Amazingly, past-life therapy does work, even for those who are unsure whether they believe in reincarnation. Images explored become keys to current dilemmas. Painful situations may be healed through spiritual technologies once the needed insights surface. An additional advantage to this explorative therapy is that regression techniques help to enhance our ability to experience altered states of consciousness, which often is related to how we can touch into our own purpose for entering.

As one who has practiced and taught past-life therapy for some time now, I see the positives, the negatives, and the misuse (as with any technique). Unfortunately, trust is often misplaced in untrustworthy or unskilled workers. I was fortunate to train with Helen Wambach, Dick Sutphen and, in time, with Religious Research, Inc., of Florida. Each offered additional dimensions. When I refined my personal approach, I felt ready to offer training to others.

"Psychography," a regression technique developed by Dr. Franklin Loehr, is described as "mapping the lives of the soul." This process assists in discovering unfinished business, whether originating in this life or another, and in healing spiritually while in that window of time. The goal of Psychography is to release us from undesired consequences that surface in the now by dissolving the negative ties to the past. This approach begins by gently moving participants to an altered state of consciousness, then guided by one trained in both regression and healing techniques. Sessions do not always lead to past lives but may call attention to earlier pain within this current life. When personalities still bear old scars, they can become barriers for the walk-in or anyone else to surmount.

Old emotional patterns chain us to old behaviors. Shifting to a higher perception invites us to begin anew, as karmic matters and lessons adjust to a broader awareness. The shift corrects or at least improves the past. Some matters take more than one session with a bit of progress occurring each time. Others dissolve in one session through the wisdom of the Inner Knower or when the after-life review is experienced with additional energy work done.

224

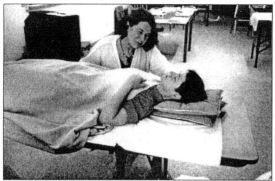

Psychography sessions can be helpful for issues in this life or past lives.

Is regression therapy a cure-all? Of course not, but it has a power to benefit almost everyone capable of reaching an altered state. It is a great blessing for walk-ins if they are guided by one who clearly understands the phenomenon or who has shared the journey.

Sancta Sophia Seminary offers a ten-day course for students to experience the technique and learn how to do this work. Trainees guide one another in monitored sessions. This program involves both intellectual and psychological concepts, personal experience, plus apprenticeship. Students need some kind of counseling certification or to be prepared to earn a pastoral counseling certificate as a certified therapist.

In other words, regression therapy is true therapy; to be a guide one needs counseling credentials. Although the technique is easily learned, its profundity needs to be experienced to be appreciated. Through personal participation, students discover how to manage the responses of others. Apprenticeship is supervised and learning happens quickly in a supportive group setting through observation, practice, and sharing.

My process taught me not to disregard the residue of the first inhabitant. Moving into a new body, certain work must be done, and through the renovation process the new being makes the body her or his own. Knowing what residues abide in the mental, emotional, and physical levels of self permits us to more specifically identify the needed repairs. Without this understanding, many walk-ins may never claim the opportunity they have been given.

They may remain ungrounded, confused by painful currents that stir within.

Psychography: Soul Discovery and Spirit Releasement is a course each messenger should experience, not only for the personal rewards and the healing but because this tool can become a way to assist others. Spirit releasement, an additional part of the course, deals with discoveries that naturally surface from time to time during regression work. Certain distressed lifestyles attract others with similar pain, confusion, or addictions. These attachments, or entanglements, confuse our lives as the influences they carry act upon the energy field of the personality. Spirit releasement is designed to free the participant and lead the wandering spirit into the light.

The life offered the messenger/walk-in is fraught with challenge or the preceding inhabitant would not have been so willing to release it. If the messenger is confronted with too much recall too abruptly, especially without support, s/he may be unable to handle it. Regression, carefully done by a knowledgeable one, is a helpful tool.

Meditation and the Spiritual Life

For about seven years after the exchange, I found no one with whom to talk, so I sat quietly and recalled the light I had experienced in the NDE. Though I did not know the word back then, this experience became meditation. As I imagined that love repeatedly and rested in that presence, I found myself better; I now use the language, "loved and healed." This inner connection helped me through years when I was absolutely convinced that if I mentioned my NDE, I would end up hospitalized. *But I was always certain a part of my task was not to forget.*

A number of years passed, and in fact, when my children's father left, doors I had kept closed began to open. I had tried in every way to preserve the marriage. I thought that if I could just keep my inner connection, that would be enough. I can now say that, except for keeping the inner connection, I had gone into a kind of denial as far as my outer life was concerned.

With his leaving, I realized my life had to change. When Ann Manser became my spiritual teacher in 1965, she brought me comfort, peace, and information. The time came to talk about this experience with her, and I wondered: *What if she did not understand it? What if she did not accept me? What if she was frightened or distanced herself as others had?* Instead, she helped me discard my fears so I could go bravely forward with support and encouragement.

With her aid, I approached my parents once again. I told them how much I loved them and that I wanted them to love me. I told them I wanted a good relationship and I hoped they could understand, but I did not expect them to. I was prepared to love them, and they could think whatever they needed about what I was trying to share. I believe at that moment our relationship took a great stride forward. I tried to remove all my expectations, a major rung on my ladder of reconstruction.

Keeping family ties intact when possible is a worthwhile goal. At the same time, we must allow people we love to love us however they can. We will lose if we try to make dear ones see everything as we see it. No discerning family does this. But we can find or build connecting points to love and appreciate each other.

Spiritual teachings suggest that if you believe you are the wiser one, you are to take responsibility for the situation, guiding it with the wisdom you believe you have. Sometimes we find we are not as wise as we think, but we have taken a first step.

Historically, necessity causes people with spiritual visionary abilities to reveal themselves. Mystics have survived over the centuries by living privately, inconspicuously, but even then, most have experienced ridicule, rejection, and hostility. Today the message comes to the messengers, "Speak up. Dare to be. Dare to do." For courageous souls, this is the call; for those ready to hear, this is the hour.

Creative consciousness moves and flashes through the universe like phosphorus in the night ocean. Today it may sparkle and speak through me; tomorrow, through another. Lives are snuffed out daily; some deeds, however, are recorded in the history of the Great Life. Neither your struggle nor mine will stop cosmic life. Noble concepts guide human minds in dealing with life. From the flash of lightning that illumines individual minds for a brief time, divine laws, cycles, and teachings point humanity in the direction of a greater comprehension of Truth. If enough people receive even a reflection of this illumination, humanity will make a major shift in our time. A significant leap forward is to occur as humanity responds to the messages.

These affirm a golden age, a period of great achievement. We are encouraged to believe, to hang on, to persist, but to move carefully along the cutting edge, for one slip and the abyss awaits. The human mind, once animal, that received the divine spark started this ascent. It can be pushed down, tortured, and made to wait through aeons of time, but it is not to be wiped out. The group mind, or collective, has been slow to thrill with the ecstasy of ascent, but humanity has glimpsed illumination; some have made it. The same sexual power that attracts female and male now stimulates consciousness to give birth, to transcend. Humanity and divinity have had intercourse. That holy interaction resonates in the imprint of human possibilities; and although devastation wreaks havoc, holy moments do come. Now, at another deciding time, many hasten to wise choices.

In Revelation 12.3–6 we read of the woman giving birth and the dragon ready to devour the child. Mother Earth has birth pangs and the beast (materialism) stands ready to devour the high consciousness aspiring to be born. The Holy Child is the new kind of humanity—refined, fully human, fully divine—evolving upward from its crude animal state, its descent into materialism, and its self-centered ego consciousness. Now a sufficient number mark the path of *self-actualism. Whether referred to in religious or psychological terminology, the path is well illumined.

Guiding humanity is a glory trail of Holy Ones who have charted the course of our future: crucifixion, resurrection, ascension. These swarm, gathering momentum until the chrysalis breaks and Christed Souls emerge as Light Beings with densified bodies for all to see. The new kingdom will be launched, the Kingdom of Souls. Many are dedicated to this supreme goal.

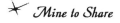

I have shared powerful moments of my life. As a private person, I forever wonder why. I have come to realize that to share my innermost self is my contribution. Just as the bird must sing its song, the rose share its fragrance, and the sun shine its light, I open my spirit to you because I must.

Walk-ins Address the Future

uch of the mission of walk-ins, in addition to conveying messages from spirit and angelic beings, is to accelerate group development. Predictions are but windows through which we glimpse a particular future. The work becomes awakening and staying awake to opportunities.

Mayan prophecies match much of the information I received in 1958 in my NDE. *Disaster* contains the words *dis*, meaning "separated," and *aster*, "from one's star: the Self, the I Am." This definition clarifies excellently. Our fragmentation from the true Self is a substantial calamity. As we understand more clearly that our love and our work are to protect humanity and the planet from disaster, we will make greater effort. A world of beauty and peace and a humanity that loves itself are great visions.

Future years on the planet will not be easy. Sharing information with teachers here and abroad, I am always alert to the incredible experiences we may face. To participate in humanity's conscious act of choosing its future is an awesome opportunity.

At Sparrow Hawk Village we strive to apply the positive aspects of technology and simultaneously develop the capability to survive whatever challenges may arise. Possibilities of economic and social strife, destructive winds, droughts and floods, earthquakes, and volcanic activity all present scenarios that could change our casual lifestyle. Predictions are numerous, and though I feel these concerns can and will be lessened by the resurgence of spiritual efforts, our guidance has suggested "prepare for the best and the worst." We seek to do just that.

Living through the era of completion, the culmination often referred to as the *Kali-Yuga (Iron Age), we prepare for the summary experience. Each is to ask, "What have we sown to be reaped?" Perhaps we come to know we can acquire the entire world, but if we have not connected with our soul, we will be needy. Affluent countries have created a comfortable standard of living, a gracious way of life, clean and perfumed, but often leave us soul-sad. If we are wise, we seek a higher reality.

*Maslow's Hierarchy of Needs[1] comes to mind: when our security needs have been met, we seek self-actualization. We want to be creative, to know ourselves, to discover new talents, and to play spontaneously, right in the midst of daily duty. Our longing to find the child-within invokes adventure and wholeness.

Some do these things already! Others struggle between the acceptable old way and the new, yet to be discovered and little under-

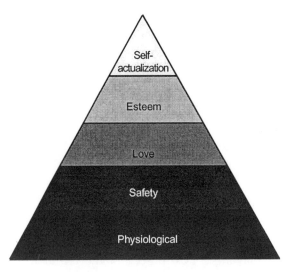

Maslow's Hierarchy of Human Needs.

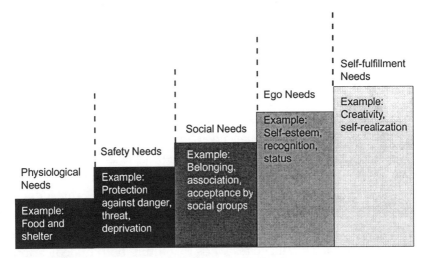

Maslow's Table: Hierarchy of Needs Amplified. The higher we climb on the socio-economic scale, the more likely we are to discover subtler needs, and as we become better educated, the more important our social attitude and inner needs become to our sense of fulfillment.

stood. Great conflict abides within us, our society, and social structures about old patterns and new forms we can choose and shape.

Many earthquakes will occur in the next few years, so many that great fear will grow among humanity. The major task of children of light is to hold their faith in this time. As one gives in to fear, s/he returns to darkness. Walk through the storm unafraid, knowing it is a tunnel from one time frame into another. It is not the end of the world but the end of a period dramatically demonstrated. Equally great was the opportunity to retreat into fear at the end of the last period.

Each age change presents opportunity for growth. To die unafraid is greater than to live cringing in fear. Boldness carries one forward if with good motivation and intent. More than actions, the response to challenge is being measured—one could say, the testing of realities within the framework of drama. How many dimensions of nature can be controlled through heart and mind coworking! The greater the consciousness, the greater the ability to stay true under stress and change.

Message Carol received November 24, 1980

The future portends even more challenges. Most messengers describe possible futures. Part of everyone's challenge is to live in the present, to be flexible enough to change, yet persistent enough to accomplish goals, to be considerate of others while still following inner guidance, to be both optimistic and realistic.

The path of a disciple leads to the expanding process in which inner space shatters dogmas, doctrines, separations, divisions, man-made laws, feelings, political ideas, and thoughtforms. There will be one humanity, one world, one brotherhood, no limitations.

The energy of freedom does not lead first to happiness but to great conflicts, changes, and destruction of old patterns. Through pain, struggle, and growth, we change. The fiery changes are the Path. (Consider Russia today!)   Message Carol received November 2, 1978

Sparrow Hawk Village responds to a future born of dedication to discipleship; therefore, responses flex in keeping with village experiences. Surely if any community could predict, it would be this one, where intuition and guidance are a natural, integral part of most lives. Yet prediction is always a risky business. It does not take much intuition to see more homes built and busy committees serving as the village draws coworkers who fulfill its reason for being. Village life has much to offer those who appreciate the group in the midst of its experiment. Such a stimulating experience is so much more gratifying than living and working without spiritual companionship.

Photo by Nancy Woods, Sparrow Hawk Village, Feb. '97.

Carol crosses the fiery field.

My view is quite different from the bloody Armageddon and doomsday prophecies so often heard. Villagers view changes as challenges, not as justification to hide. Most have been through enough to know that while change is not easy, it can be quite positive. The difference is in the outlook—focusing on service to one another rather than just survival.

Conquering fear of the unknown is a major way to move forward. Identify the limiting fear, then learn to clear and cope. A firewalk is a dynamic tool to empowerment. To cross that fiery field awakens one to a greater awareness of personal potential, as well as the accessibility of God's grace.

> *It is not the intention of the Hierarchy to interfere with the tests of humanity. Our intention is to have contact with believing ones; if some cannot free themselves from patterns of vanity, greed, and love of materialism, others will preserve seeds of the highly developed *root races, or human beings, to reseed the world.*
>
> *The Earth is challenged to become the place of beauty it can be and to rid itself of destructive patterns of behavior and extremes in expression. Human life, the guiding consciousness of Earth, works exactly the same.*

Message Carol received July 29, 1982

The news is fraught with the decline of the middle class. Looking objectively, we see many areas falling apart, to be reworked in some new way. I remind myself, *When cracks open, light can shine through.* When life seems to be deteriorating, flashes of profound insight often emerge.

Religion does not save us from ourselves. The great purpose of religion (in Latin *religio* means "supernatural constraint") is to realign us to the source of life. In fact, religion is to guide us to spirituality; then our awakened divine nature leads us to enlightenment, i.e., "salvation."

Riding the Waves into the Future

Energies bombarding the planet today demand we forge a spirit of cooperation. At a past critical point of evolution, humanity had to forsake instinctual group consciousness to move toward an **individuated self*-consciousness. Now humanity must relinquish its emphasis on ego-superiority and move again to a group consciousness, maintaining individuality and integrity. This time we shift toward an aware-

A rare photographic capture of energy called down by Hunbatz Men during a solar initiation rite at the Chichen Itza Pyramid. Carol and Alan Oken are at his sides

ness of harmony inherent in coworking, cocreating, and *right-relationship.

Many walk-ins' missions and messages from spirit and from angelic beings are to hasten group development. Predictions are but windows through which we view a particular future. For each, the work becomes first awakening, then staying awake.

Indigenous people of many heritages have much to share as we enter this time of reawakening to hidden mysteries. Native Americans— North, Central, and South—reference this period as the end of the world. Translate this as the end of a world view, and it relieves some anxiety. The daily news tells us the same things, as we end our flirtation with harsh materialism and turn our hearts (and gradually our mindset) toward new values. The twentieth century world is dead. Our struggles since the '60s have contributed, and though not all of us profess identical perspectives, we are all changed by our collective struggle.

I have had great interest in the Mayan prophecies regarding the end of a 26,000-year cycle, as well as this twenty-five-year transitional period in which we now find ourselves. The Maya believe humanity entered a critical period at Harmonic Convergence (August 16–17, 1987) and must balance its karma and pass through stages of change (often labeled "*tribulation") into the Age of *Luz (light) or Flowers, names given by the tradition. This latter term originates from the concept of chakras; the buds open as humanity matures to full bloom.

In his book *Beneath the Moon and Under the Sun*,[2] Tony Shearer was the first to publish August 16–17, 1987, as the dates for the wake-up call we came to know as Harmonic Convergence. A poet and artist, Tony established a drama school in Los Angeles for Native Americans and was one of the first who sought to lead his people to appreciate their heritage. His work also served others interested in prophecies to look for the mysteries native to this land.

At Harmonic Convergence it seemed the world might not be ready for the ideas introduced, but the masses responded immediately to new interests. Mayan beliefs captured a number of thinkers, including me.

Five five-year periods have interesting Mayan designations (as interpreted by José Argüelles) that correspond, as I see it, to the major steps experienced when *any* life cycle ends. Each stage has a name and a defined time corresponding to my understanding of what humanity is to undergo and with the accepted five stages of the process of *death and dying. Let us consider them from this overview.

Mayan term		Death-and-Dying stage
Era of the New Dawn	1987–92	Denial
Era of Regeneration	1992–97	Anger or Passion
Era of Reseeding	1997–02	Bargaining
Era of Crystallization	2002–07	Depression or Preparation
Era of New Harmony	2007–12	Acceptance

Post Harmonic Convergence

These twenty-five years of transition encompass the end of the millennium, the end of the Piscean age, and the end of a great solar cycle. We are moving forward in consciousness, probably more rapidly than we realize.

In the first five years (1987–92), designated the *Era of the New Dawn* (and called *denial*), many chose not to see that change was everywhere. We refused to recognize the end of the corporate world as we had known it, the embrace of materialism, and the immunity to others' suffering that had kept us frozen, with little change. Harmonic Convergence and its legends were a joke to many, the same ones who look back now, astonished at how much has happened so rapidly.

The second five years (1992–97), labeled the *Era of Regeneration,* we can call *anger or passion. Regeneration* means "new love," even if distorted and confused. If we do not care, we do not feel

Hunbatz Men, Mayan prince and wisdom keeper, in full regalia stands behind Carol, and Pamela and Richard Skeie.

hatred. In these years, wild passions stirred, anger and violence exploded. Frightening news came from the Middle East, Rwanda, Yugoslavia, Chiapas, Ireland, Somalia, Haiti, Algiers—every corner of the globe. Filled with fear, materialism, and hunger for power, people operated at unprecedented depths.

During the *Era of Reseeding* (1997–2002), we try one creative response after another. Think of this as *bargaining*. Here we find ingenius ideas, inventions, and techniques introduced by many of the walk-ins. Perhaps the too-close-to-call presidential election of 2000 was somehow forcing our creative thinking? The overhauling of each field of human endeavor begins— science, education, medicine, politics, and so on. The important step is the convergence of spirituality with each of these disciplines.

I would call the *Era of Crystallization* (2002–07) "preparatory *depression.*" Here new forms slowly begin to emerge. Outer conditions may look worse, but new inner attitudes start to gain momentum. Not easy, but new concepts have begun. Financial deflation may well be a part.

The *Era of New Harmony*, or *acceptance*, brings us to the year 2012. Eureka! If we stay on track, we should now be aligned to our new beginning. An inner hope for the future looms larger than the pull of the past—a sense of eagerness as we release the old and prepare for a human rebirth.

Today we are at the mid-point, *bargaining*. We can shift either toward survival or destruction. None dares wait to see how others respond. Some may be mired in denial and stay there, some locked into anger. Some will attune to the past, others to the future. A large block of society senses something is awry but has yet to realize how to participate constructively. This is the work of awakened ones—to reach out and do.

Two points seem necessary to close these thoughts. First, wonderful things are happening. It is amazing how far we have come since August 1987. *Flowers* are blooming everywhere. Second, remember, it only takes a small shift to "unstick" things, just a little change of mind or of heart.

Whether we are experienced or novices, it is prudent to recognize we can serve. With a caring heart and by overcoming fear, negativity, and resistance, we learn through every experience, inevitably assisting the whole as we remember the great teaching technique: "sink or swim." Look how wonderfully well we do when we simply jump in and instinctively paddle.

> *The Christ is recruiting workers from humanity. If you choose to wait, you will be left to your own amusements while the choice moves to another. "I stand at the door and knock" is a forever message, coming at one* ✳ *time in one life, at another time for another. The knock is heard by the largest numbers now, but many deny the knock. It is a passing choice. If you pass that point without response, life carries you away. It is well known you cannot go back in time.*
>
> Message Carol received January 1982

As the world witnesses fury, we serve as baffles to restrain destructive waves. Creating pockets of serenity, we become prototypes of peace midst the storm—knowing the storm has purpose. It cleans the air, washes away debris, and brings new clarity. We find what is ours to do, we cultivate courage and stand as spiritual anchors. Aligned with the greater light, we rejoice.

By 2012, can we "Do unto others . . ."? Pause for a moment and visualize the world you perceive we will be living in by then. Is it more respectful to all or more separative? more friendly or less? more patient or more anxious? Is divine possibility more available? Only through persistent effort can holy principles be anchored into this physical dimension.

At this time of the Externalization, disciples and messengers, or walk-ins, have significant roles to play. Depending upon how we participate, we either advance or retard the Great Happening. Can we keep clearing our vision as it blurs? What happens when we are disappointed or when we project our confusion onto another? How do we heal, mend, or dissipate distortion? These answers affect the reappearance of the Christ. Together we create the twenty-first century.

The third millennium of Christianity is the Era of the Divine Feminine. Our original blessing has become distorted, and tribulation, or cleansing, called by whatever name, is designed to purify and restore. For the golden era to emerge, we must make adjustments as revealed, not only through holy writings and teachings but through the comprehension gifted us. As prophecies are fulfilled, we are to remain positive and thus stabilize the human collective. This is a great moment of service to humanity. It is ours to know: *a return to fear is a return to darkness.* Embracing spirituality, we cleanse ourselves of rigid doctrine and dogma so their beauty and guidelines can once more flow freely, reestablishing rich pathways for expressing the Inner Presence. The experience of human life is to be sanctified daily.

Aquarian energies contribute to shattering the past. Dedicated to the future, our hearts and voices must speak our truths and dare to be heard. Those who *know* are charged to lead. My message, and that of many messengers, is not one of statistics but of revelation, to bring an awareness of the era and the work. Some are ready, but most are not. Only as we are tested do we see what we lack. Then we must rethink and serve in ways we can, or refuse and mourn our loss.

As the initiation moment approaches, we must recall, tests for this era are not physical. They do not involve bodily strength, achievements of endurance, or trials of the same nature as borne during earlier periods; our tests are on the psychological level. We must be courageous in facing underdeveloped areas of personality, true to what we know is ours to do. We are to clear the astral level of self so that at the hour of completion, we go into the light, knowing our spiritual allegiance has held its focus and value.

How to Assist the Process

Desire draws (in esoteric language we say "magnetizes"). When we yearn to achieve a goal, we create a line of tension between ourselves and an image of the goal. The intense emotional charge pulls us and the goal onto the same wave length; as we strive toward the goal, the goal is simultaneously drawn toward us.

A number of energies are needed: focus, desire, drive, hope, reinforcement, encouragement, enthusiasm, to name a few. Role models, reassurance, and breakthroughs contribute to both the renewing of self and the manifestation of new possibilities. Envisioning programs keep the necessary energies of desired possibility flowing. This is true whether we are working on our physical bodies, money for our personal life, or support for group life. Energy rises and falls; it shifts, swirls, and surges all about us. Visionaries recognize this as a resource to be tapped; otherwise, it feeds the chaos.

It only takes a small shift to "unstick" things, just a little change of mind or of heart.

We see a good example of this when millions gather to pour forth great love and respect to "Papa," the pope. People are filled with positive emotion; devotional and spiritual experiences energize religious foundations. The beautiful pope, kind and good, restates goals, reconstructs boundaries, and reinforces doctrine, embodying the past, sustaining a disintegrating view. Should he turn toward the future, energy imparted to him would create a surge of solutions more representative of humanity's current spiritual needs.

On visits to the Middle East (1998, 1999 and 2000), other pilgrims and I retraced the history of the early church to reconnect with the culture that gave birth to Christianity as a pathway of transformation. We experienced a passionate culture exercising the emotional power of the outgoing Ray 6 energy pushing humanity to open the heart center. Fervor exists everywhere. Daily life, so charged with feeling, surprised the more mental Westerners.

Seeing the residences of desert fathers, the simplicity of cave dwellers (even into the twentieth century in Turkey), or the joy of devout people bowing in mosques, we grow as we imagine Jesus as a Master touching lives. We experience the reverence held for the home wherein it is believed Mother Mary lived out her life at Ephesus. The deep emotional impact of loving so completely gives new perception to our struggles to integrate mind. We might say, as twenty-first century people, we struggle to know the message of our opened heart even as we rejoice in our mind, both intuitive and rational.

Externalization of Hierarchy Approaches

Ponder what part you play in creating the Era of Flowers for your city, profession, or youth. Where are your seeds of joy, goodness, and service flourishing? Of what bouquet are you a part, in spite of weeds, that will beautify and benefit life on the planet? Each of us is to be a wise steward, using well the resources and opportunities for the renewing of the Garden of Eden. On the other side of chaos, re-creation awaits.

As I draw this revision of *Messengers of Hope* to a close, I pray humanity will use well the power of choice abiding within. I am grateful to the many who have been part of this story. How bold, how brave in our daring we must be to remain steady in order to sustain the seeds of consciousness planted for a civilization that will far surpass anything we witness today. We must dare to be God, no longer the good child but now a dedicated cocreator of a new civilization.

Each disciple and messenger survives facing resistance, doubt, and suspicion. Each struggles to convey his/her insights and knowledge, often at great price. The world does not welcome those who bear words little understood. They crash against the rocks of old ideas, yet deliver energies from worlds beyond.

You, humanity, are my family, my child, my lover, my reason for being. So, I offer these thoughts, my gift, with the hope they will be accepted into your heart.

A Study of the Stars

Many believe significant events show themselves in the stars. Since ancient times, humanity has applied the art of astrology to determine influences affecting us. It is important to appreciate that these energies induce challenging circumstances, as well as favorable conditions, which can help us make choices. While outside influences create an atmosphere of a particular type or setting, our own astrological configuration is either supported or opposed within that framework.

Astrological & Numerological Investigation in Support of the Walk-in Experience

A major teaching: *Astrological influences do not compel us to do anything, but we may feel impelled.* The more aware we are of these influential energies, the more wisely we can respond. If an astrology chart is the story of the personality—body, emotional nature, and lower mind—it will, in fact, continue to work for the walk-in. It indicates the strengths and weaknesses of the personality, as well as the challenges the native will encounter; it records the energies which one must confront.

One soul will use a set of tools one way; another will respond differently. The walk-in takes over the chart, inherits the qualities of the personality, and undertakes to use them in the most opportune way. Think about babies born at the same moment. Their lives will be markedly different, although similarities may be astonishing.

Accordingly, an evolved soul will make the most of each opportunity; a less evolved soul naturally will respond on a less evolved level. Thus, while the astrological chart of the basic personality continues to work, the soul directs the life changes. The body remains a particular sex, and the incoming soul learns to work through it. The body and other vehicles of personality serve as containers the new soul must animate.

"The descent and reascent of the Monad or Soul cannot be disconnected from the Zodiacal signs!!"[1]

As a result of my pursuit of astrology and curiosity, mine and others', about how the walk-in exchange might register in a chart, I have included the work of four astrologers and their approaches to my personal chart from different modes.

If you are interested in astrology, the following studies of charts may prove fascinating. I would like to point out, the natal chart of a native is used to study one's personality and potential.

Horary astrology is the name given to the study of an event chart, such as is used here for the NDE. In addition, especially significant to me were the powerful realizations that came with the blessing of Herakhan Baba (Babaji) at Haldwani, India. In that moment, a major recall and reenergizing of my life occurred, so an event chart for that occasion has been included.

It is taught that Scorpio in a native's chart gives us some ideas of areas wherein one might be tested. Scorpio, we learn from Alice Bailey,[2] channels energy to us from cosmic sources. Ray 2 energy of Jupiter joins the Scorpio influence pouring forth strong energies of Sirius. Sirius is closely related to Scorpio, and we are told that the Sirian Logos is the *solar angel of our *Solar Logos.

In many esoteric writings we are told humanity is being guided by great ones from Sirius. "Sirius is the star of initiation . . . earth's hierarchy is under the spiritual direction of the Hierarchy of Sirius."[3]

Thus, humanity is given a great opportunity for initiation, growth, and service under Scorpio influences. Scorpio's principal virtue or quality to be dealt with is transformation. Many individuals in their particular life pattern find tests and challenges clearly marked by Scorpio's presence. Take note of the powerful Scorpio interplay in the charts that follow. As years have passed, the NDE is better understood and a significant number have an exact time for the event chart, attempting to undertand the new energy infused into the original life. It becomes a natural area of interest for a graduate program research project and of course, it comes to pass.

Betty Carper, Ph.D., is an astrologer and former educator who has studied a number of birth charts and NDE event charts. Her research asks, "Can you tell from a natal chart if someone is particularly sensitive to a near-death experience or exchange?"Dr. Carper responds in this study of charts.

When I began to collect data to share, I felt it would be of interest to ask my friend, astrologer, and numerologist, Barbara Everett, to review the chart and share her insights. Barbara is a well-known teacher and counselor from the Minneapolis area, now living in Edmonds, Washington. In this chapter she shares a comparison of pertinent charts.

A third astrologer, with a profound comprehension of esoteric astrology, as well as being knowledgeable in spiritual philosophy, is Joleen DuBois of Prescott, Arizona, who has long been a professional astrologer. Joleen introduces many exciting insights.

Also, years ago I met a lady in Atlanta who, after a healing seminar, expressed an interest in the event chart of the near-death experience. Since my daughter was born during those minutes, her birth chart is my "exchange" chart. A licensed astrologer, Judy Goodwin used Sabian Symbols for insight to the experience, so her reading includes fascinating variations.

As you will see, each astrologer has approached the charts in a different mode. It is no wonder people question the validity of astrology with its many aspects and techniques, yet each of these professionals came to many of the same conclusions through different routes. I hasten to add, no one saw the others' work, but each proceeded in the manner most comfortable to her. As well, none read the manuscript and the personal data it contains before the book was published. As I compiled their contributions, I saw how well the material fit my feelings at various designated times.

Those interested in astrology and numerology will find some exciting guidelines useful in studying the charts of the 23 million people estimated to have come critically close to death. Of this number some 13.5 million in the U.S. by 1994 are believed to be "experiencers" of "something more." Often these lives have undergone events of vast spiritual significance. In this chapter we trace the happenings of only one life that seems to have left a trail easily discernible through *occult sciences. Perhaps these keys will assist others as they ask, "Am I a messenger as well?"

I thank each of these women for their interest and contributions.

Note: For convenience the balance of this chapter will be divided into the categories: Astrological Research into the Near-Death Experience, Basic Astrology and Numerology, Esoteric Astrology, and Sabian Symbols.

Astrological Research into the Near-Death Experience

Betty Carper, Ph.D., comments:

When the phenomenon of the near-death experience (NDE) became more widely known, several people having had that experience were willing to discuss it with me during an astrological counseling session. After the NDE, their lives had been most stressful, mainly because they were profoundly changed on all levels of their being but those around them were no different and often viewed the one recovering from the NDE as weird or out of touch with reality.

A substantial number of clients had the exact time of their NDE, as well as their natal chart information, and because the NDE closely resembles the mystical experience reported in many different religions, it inspired research for a dissertation for the degree of Doctor of Philosophy of Religious Studies from Sancta Sophia Seminary. The results of the study are concisely presented in the abstract for the dissertation, which is reproduced here.

Carol E. Parrish
Nettleton, Arkansas
Time Zone: 6 hours West

January 21, 1935
35 N 49' 10"
9:15 A.M. Standard Time

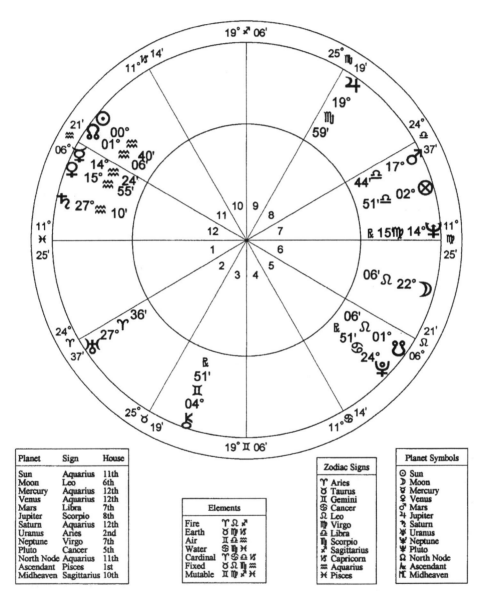

Carol's Natal Chart as used throughout this study.

Planet	Sign	House
Sun	Aquarius	11th
Moon	Leo	6th
Mercury	Aquarius	12th
Venus	Aquarius	12th
Mars	Libra	7th
Jupiter	Scorpio	8th
Saturn	Aquarius	12th
Uranus	Aries	2nd
Neptune	Virgo	7th
Pluto	Cancer	5th
North Node	Aquarius	11th
Ascendant	Pisces	1st
Midheaven	Sagittarius	10th

Elements

Fire	♈ ♌ ♐	
Earth	♉ ♍ ♑	
Air	♊ ♎ ♒	
Water	♋ ♏ ♓	
Cardinal	♈ ♋ ♎ ♑	
Fixed	♉ ♌ ♏ ♒	
Mutable	♊ ♍ ♐ ♓	

Zodiac Signs

♈	Aries
♉	Taurus
♊	Gemini
♋	Cancer
♌	Leo
♍	Virgo
♎	Libra
♏	Scorpio
♐	Sagittarius
♑	Capricorn
♒	Aquarius
♓	Pisces

Planet Symbols

☉	Sun
☽	Moon
☿	Mercury
♀	Venus
♂	Mars
♃	Jupiter
♄	Saturn
♅	Uranus
♆	Neptune
♇	Pluto
☊	North Node
⚹	Ascendant
⚸	Midheaven

247

*An Investigation into Common Astrological Characteristics
of People Having Near-Death Experiences*

The purpose of the investigation is to discover common characteristics in horoscopes of NDErs that will be of value for counselors who assist clients in coping with the traumatic after-effects of the experience and its mystical and spiritual significance. The rapidly increasing number of NDEs inspires belief that it is a catalyst to assist the collective of humanity in making a leap forward in consciousness.

Natal charts of thirty-one NDErs were examined and compared with a control group of like number. No single factor that is indisputably unique to charts of NDErs was discovered. However, there are differences in the groups; one is the sign placement of the Sun, Moon, Ascendant. The NDE group has more Suns, Moons, and Ascendants in the water signs of Cancer, Scorpio, and Pisces than the control group. Water signs of the zodiac bestow the qualities of sensitivity, compassion, imagination, intuition, and perception.

Another difference which became evident: the NDE charts, as a group, have more stress-related factors, with suicide aspects prominent. The fourteen stress factors identified for comparison are: Cosmic Cross, T-Square, Yod, Demi-Yod, Point of Thales, Yin or Yang, Absent Element, Absent Quality, Unaspected Planets, Retrograde Personal Planets, Incompatible Prenatal Solar Eclipse, Void-of-Course Moon, First-Quarter or Third-Quarter Moon Phase, and Suicide Aspects.

Of the fourteen stress indicators, the NDE charts have a higher percentage in just three of them: the T-Square, Demi-Yod, and Suicide Aspects. The T-Square creates imbalance, the Demi-Yod reflects childhood abuse, and Suicide Aspects indicate a death wish. Combining these stress factors with the extreme sensitivity produced by the Sun-Moon placement in water signs, it is concluded that the NDE personality contains a near–breaking-point tension indicating a need for release and possible therapy.

Recommendations for counselors: Check stress factors in the natal charts, suggest creative outlets for the tension build-up, provide extensive counseling for relationship problems, and if suicide tendencies are evident, arrange for qualified personnel to provide the service.

—Betty Carper

Inner Wheel:
Carol E. Parrish
Nettleton, Arkansas
Time Zone: 6 hours West

Born: January 21, 1935
35 N 49' 10" 90 W 39' 04"
Tropical Placidus
NATAL CHART

9:15 A.M.
Central Standard time
Geocentric

Outer Wheel:
Exchange
Clearwater, Florida
Time Zone: 5 hours West

Exchange: November 1, 1958
27 N 57' 56" 82W 48' 01"
Tropical Placidus
NATAL CHART

7:20 A.M.
Eastern Standard time
Geocentric

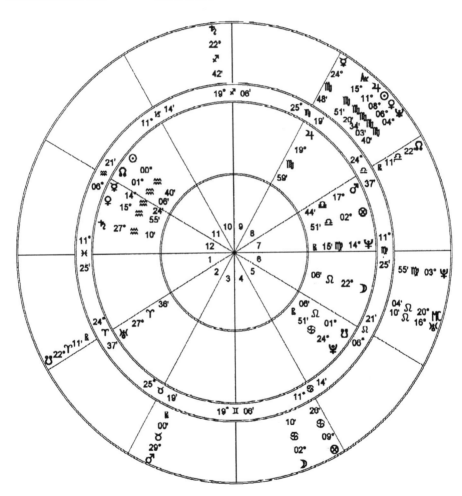

Event Chart No. 1
Carol's natal chart compared to the NDE exchange chart.

Basic Astrology and Numerology

Barbara Everett comments:

In the teachings of astrology, each life is seen as a facet of God shining through the sun sign to the degree of clarity the individual is able to manifest. Each person advances toward the realization of his/her sun sign according to the people, circumstances, and events which formulate the life. We become a sum of our life process, and the energies of the sun, moon, and planets in our solar system either enhance or challenge the life plan.

In the case of a walk-in, a more evolved soul replaces the original soul, but the chart itself must be in cooperation with the incoming purpose in order for the plan to work.

Carol Elizabeth Williams (Parrish-Harra) was born with the sun in Aquarius, the moon in Leo, and a Piscean ascendant (see Carol's Natal Chart). Aquarius is a fixed air sign, inclining her toward adventurous thought patterns, a strong sense of will, a need for freedom, an ability to work with groups, and a love of humanity.

The moon in Leo, a fixed fire sign, opposite the sun sign, would indicate a pattern of strength and leadership from the past, increasing her determination, sometimes to the point of stubbornness.

When the sun and the moon are in opposition, a conflict of mind and emotions is present within the person. Emotions may be very strong and must be dealt with, or the fire of the Leo turns inward, causing physical distress and depression.

The Piscean ascendant, a mutable water sign, increases emotional, spiritual, and psychic sensitivities, sometimes to the point of pain. The person often is supersensitive, almost like a sponge, absorbing the emotional discomfort of others.

Being born an Aquarian, one of Carol's mission in life was to move out of the limitations of the past (Pisces) and forward into a new, more enlightened future. However, this mission was definitely complicated by the sun-moon opposition, which necessitates balancing the male/female parts of the self in order to progress. In addition, the overly emotional and sensitive personality level, reflected by the Piscean ascendant, made forward moves nearly impossible. Young Carol's formative years reflected these various struggles, with competitive influences (sun opposed moon) involving her and her family. The psychic sensitivity was apparent at an early age (Piscean ascendant) with the urge to be religiously "good" and always within the law of the church.

Prior to the soul exchange, Carol was in dire physical, emotional, mental, and spiritual distress. The present was too painful, the future hopeless, the strong pull of Pisces luring her back into the safety of oblivion. The strength of the sun/moon opposition may have allowed the transition to take place, and the indomitable will of the two fixed signs may have kept the physical heart (Leo) and the mind (Aquarius) "alive" in order for the soul exchange to occur, rather than succumb to death (Pisces).

At the time of Carol's near-death experience, the sun was in Scorpio, the sign of transition, of birth and death, of transformation (Event Chart No. 1). Scorpio is the sign of intense and deep inner power and awareness. In Carol's natal chart, Scorpio rules the house of birth and death and transformation. This sign, then, became the doorway for the exchange. The ability of the Scorpio influence to transform itself again and again, in spite of or because of tremendous challenges, is a constant revelation to all.

Note the Jupiter influence present. Usually we read Jupiter as "expansion" and call it a beneficent influence. Let us realize Jupiter could have been a protective or a beneficent influence offering the opportunity of a great service, great challenge, or change. It will be interesting to watch the Scorpio and Jupiter combination within charts of other walk-ins.

In the death process, we are reborn, and so it was for Carol, as the timid woman, reflecting more Piscean qualities than Aquarius, moved out of a hopeless struggle into peace and security. An evolving Carol moved forward to activate the chart that was meant for a person dedicated to using authority, freedom, and unusual mind abilities, tempered by compassion, sensitivity, and great intuitive aptitude.

The natal astrology chart seems more fitting to the Carol of the present than of the past. Possibly the first soul was overcome by the power of the chart it had chosen. But she kept it going long enough to realize its tremendous possibilities before relinquishing it into the safekeeping of a soul better prepared to carry on the mission.

An interesting second event (Chart No. 2) is the blessing by Babaji at Haldwani, India, shown with Carol's natal chart. Fortunately Carol looked at her time. This chart proves increasingly important in the subsequent days and weeks, as memories bombarded Carol and more of her life work was revealed.

In the event chart from Haldwani, India (not shown), the ascendant, sun, and moon are conjunct in Libra, emphasizing the shift of personality levels from the emotional essence of Pisces to the mental essence of Libra. Libra is the sign of justice, both ethical and merciful, evenly balanced between mind and emotion. Libra has the ability to bring harmony to opposing factions, those within self and those between people or ideals. This arbitrator is the one who listens, learns, speaks, and then reveals the law through mercy and justice.

At this memorable point, Carol's soul and personality were then evenly balanced with her life's purpose. The ongoing conflict of mind and emotion, so evident in the natal chart with sun opposed moon, blended now to permit a larger glimpse of the total plan, only the beginning. The journey continues to be revealed as Carol herself is prepared.

For many people with a strong Libran influence, decision making is often a dilemma. However, in Carol's case, having Saturn in Libra and natal Saturn in the 12th house increases her ability to be decisive. This need is evident in her natal chart with Saturn posited in the 12th house in Aquarius. Saturn works particularly effectively in Aquarius and Libra, being co-ruler of Aquarius and exalted in Libra. With Saturn in the 12th house in both charts, a decision of dedication to humanity would have been an obligation from the past, a promise to be part of the evolving Plan. It would have existed on a subconscious level (12th house) until the proper opportunity to emerge presented itself.

The Haldwani, India, chart emphasizes the shift of another great personal challenge for Carol. Lilith, the point of greatest frustration or loss from the past needing confrontation in the present, shifted from the intensely personal 2nd house of money, possessions, and value systems, to the 8th house. Here Lilith can be seen as victor over mortal death and the knowledge of continuity of life.

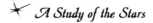

Carol E. Parrish
Inner Wheel:
Natal Chart
January, 21, 1935
9:15 A.M. CST
Nettleton, Ark.
90' W 39' 04" Long.
35 N 49 Lat.

Carol E. Parrish
Outer Wheel:
Blessing
October 9, 1980
5:50 A.M. NST
79' E 31 Long.
29 N 13 Long.
35 N 49 Lat.

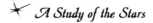

Event Chart No. 2
THE BLESSING: Herakhan Baba (Babaji) at Haldwani, India,
compared to Carol's Natal Chart

253

It seems evident that the effects of the NDE (Event Chart No. 1) instigated the transformation process with Scorpio so prominent, as life on all levels changed completely. The process accelerated in Event Chart No. 2 with the merging of personality and soul. Intensity became the byword, and the focus was on the need for cooperation to bring forth ethical and spiritual changes.

It is interesting to note that this part of Carol's life and growth came to public attention in 1982 by the guides of Ruth Montgomery in her book *Threshold to Tomorrow*. *Strangers Among Us* was Ruth's first book on walk-ins and hit the public market in 1979.

In January of 1982 I had cast a yearly chart for Carol, which put Scorpio on the ascendant for that year. This indicated that wherever Scorpio appeared in her natal chart would be highlighted during that particular year. Scorpio, the sign of transition and transformation, is the ruler of Carol's 8th house of secrets. The secrets were transformed into revelations. Birth and death have been intimate companions of Carol's for many years, and during 1982 greater expansions of these modes of life would be "born" for the enlightenment of humanity.

As I also work with the study of numerology, I needed to satisfy myself that numerology would correlate with the walk-in concept. Esoteric teachings of numerology open our thinking to the pattern of an evolving soul, its present incarnation, and the challenges and expectations it will experience. Each person comes into being to perform a chosen task, a mission within a plan carefully formulated by the Lords of Karma, the entering soul, and the compassion of the Universal God.

The plan is revealed through the Life Path, which is composed of the month, day, and year of a person's birth. We are born at the time and place and in the circumstances most necessary for our advancement. Our plan is a culmination of what we have achieved to the present and what we can further achieve. We usually enter a Life Path not fully knowing how best to express that vibration, and it requires considerable time for us to merge comfortably with that plan.

In Carol's case, her birthdate of January 21, 1935, brought a vibration of 22/4. The teachings reveal that certain numbers carry additional potential, that they reflect the ability to be more creative, more influential, more powerful. Numbers 11, 22, and 33 are considered a category reserved for more adventurous and daring individuals. The term "master numbers" characterizes their possibilities for high-level achievement. These particular numbers carry with them heightened emotions, greater challenges, and potential for burnout and disappointment. Because these numbers are delicately balanced, the individual often must use the vibration at a lower frequency—an 11 becoming a 2, a 22 becoming a 4, a 33 becoming a 6—until the body/mind/emotional *vehicle is more capable of maintaining higher vibrations.

During Carol's early years, she was strongly influenced by the vibration of 1 from the January birth month. This number—challenging for a child and young adult—increases independence, personal resourcefulness, and decision-making. Often there is much loneliness and a feeling of isolation during this time. Later in life this vibration may be used more advantageously.

As we progress through life, the Life Path becomes a beacon, drawing us forward to express that vibration more completely. Carol's 22/4 Life Path, a great challenge, carried the potential for serving humanity, creativity of thought, expansion of consciousness, and an idealistic vision for humanity.

Given her early sensitive nature, the 4 vibration became the level young Carol chose because it carried more security, form, and continuity than the high-powered 22. More efficient and organized than creative and experimental, 4 is the number of discipline, of following through, of patient builder. That solid, dependable vibration surrounded her in a secure (if rigid) pattern of life, home, family, responsibility, of endless details and organization.

The soul exchange released the limited personality, who needed to be enclosed and protected (4) to the more expansive personality (22) who would willingly take risks, go beyond limitation, and eventually be involved in shaping spiritual values for other eager aspirants.

We all start to shift our pattern between the ages of twenty-eight and thirty-four, moving then to the influence of the birthday and more fully into our Life Path. Shifting to the 21(3) of her birthday, Carol became more expressive through her activities, her ability to share thoughts in an inspiring way, an impressive example of the 3 vibration. Eventually, this energetic vibration would lead Carol to lecturing, teaching, radio and TV appearances, and writing. At the same time, she shifted into the higher vibration of the 22 Life Path, seeking to change the confinements of physical, emotional, mental, and spiritual limitation of herself and others.

The 22 led to the more universal approach to life, away from the extreme emotionalism and personal dependence to seeing life on a cosmic level with ever-expanding possibilities.

This shift from a 4 vibration to a 22 vibration is more impressive than it may seem at first glance. It is akin to moving from the basement level of a skyscraper to the top floor on an express elevator, with the need to adjust immediately to the changing scene and altitude. It is no wonder, then, that her family and friends were confused by the changes, as was her own personality, having to shift constantly to keep pace with the inner expansion.

The 22 is often the visionary mystic with practicality, who can put ideas into form and participate creatively in the destiny of humanity. With that comes the challenge of continuing to function in a human form, to take care of the body, to relate to others and still not relinquish the dream of what can happen for humanity with enough dedication, persistence, and willing workers.

From numerology we observe the influences of both event charts. In 1958, Carol was experiencing a personal 9 year. Nine is the end of a cycle, a year of completion, often one of loss, especially for a person with little hope. It may even take the form of death. Its motivation is often to separate the person from personal affairs and instill higher aspirations and discrimination. But if one has not reached the appreciation of such values, its expression is frustration, loss, and despair.

The Universal vibration for 1958 was a 5, the number of change, the ability to move toward greater sensitivity to human conditions. As a Universal vibration, its purpose is to awaken everyone to change within and to expand their empathy with humanity in all its variations.

The year of 1980 was a 22/4 personal year for Carol. Coinciding with her Life Path, it was a year of special significance for her. A 22 year evokes unexpected changes, travel, rapid fluctuations of emotions, heightened potentials, the prospect of a creative breakthrough. Carol's personal life that year was evidence of the powerful impact of 22, culminating in her experience with Babaji in Haldwani, India. After that meeting, the spiritual expectation of the 22 Life Path emerged with more potential than ever.

The personal influence for Carol the day of the near-death experience was a 3, the vibration of joy and creative expression. Three is one of the most verbal, expressive, and enthusiastic of vibrations, an outgoing, energetic demonstration of energy. Despite the anxiety of the situation on that day, Carol did find a joyous renewal of life, one which lifted her forever from the bitter aspects of fear and disappointment to the spiritual appreciation of life in all its facets.

The Universal energy of that day was an 8 vibration, the number of power, expansion, and the ability to function simultaneously in the worlds of matter and of spirit. It is often seen as the bridge to higher consciousness for those ready to take that step.

The Blessing (at Haldwani, India) took place on the Personal Day with a 5 vibration—the energy of change, the number of humanity, the number of understanding. The personal changes began then, and the expansion of the vision and goal for humanity took shape.

The Universal vibration of that day was 1, the energy of generating and the life-force. A 1 vibration signifies independence, strength, influence, and the birth of ideas. How appropriate for the second Event Chart to carry this vitality as its Life Path number.

In summation, these number vibrations help the drama unfold for Carol's mission, her role in inspiring humanity. We each either cooperate or deny the plan set before us. Fortunately, the events of 1958 helped prepare Carol for 1980. Cooperation leads to satisfaction, denial to unhappiness. Each of us will be remembered by the fruits of our lives, and those of Carol Parrish-Harra's life are still maturing—for her and all who hear her message.

Barbara A. Everett[4]

Esoteric Astrology Data

Esoteric Astrology, a more advanced form of astrology, presents insights to the behind-the-scenes activity of the soul in quite a similar manner as mundane, or exoteric, astrology addresses its translations to the study of the personality—its strengths, weaknesses, and opportunities. Interest in this approach is expanding, and Joleen Ayres DuBois is noted for her understanding of this challenging approach. She frequently lectures and teaches in this little-understood area of proficiency.

Joleen A. DuBois comments:

The natal horoscope reflects a celestial portrait of a human soul's entrance into incarnation. It points out the starting point of human life and is a picture of certain atomic (karmic) substances the soul/personality has to work with in this life pattern. The natal chart is then a symbolic portrait of energy. The responsibility for the correct usage of the energy, the atomic substance, belongs to the native of the horoscope.

Each year of life of the native corresponds to the progressions (forward movement) of the horoscope which ignite the potential and help define the cycles of experience which promote spiritual unfoldment. So, as the native grows, the horoscope progresses, bringing a correspondence and synthesis between the activities of the person and the planetary energies.

The astrologer/counselor must thoroughly acquaint her/himself with the potential outlines in the natal horoscope from a holistic viewpoint before the unfoldment of the progressive cycles can be discerned. S/he must become acquainted with past and present psychological attitudes of the client to reach an accurate perspective of his/her spiritual and mundane achievements and future goals in order to synthesize the cycles.

I will explain the astrological evidence that gives support and credence to Carol's NDE and subsequent walk-in experience, confining myself to the astrological evidence that deals with that event. I will show the natal potential, the corresponding progression, and the transiting cycles which ignite the experience.

The sun was transiting (traveling) through the constellation of Aquarius at the time of Carol's birth. The moon was in the zodiacal sign of Leo, and Pisces was on the horizon (the rising sign, or ascendant). The Leo moon in the 6th house suggests this life would be directed to service and healing through her heart, or love nature. The Aquarian sun (life energy) in the 11th house indicates her service would be found in working with and organizing groups of people through an Aquarian philosophy of brotherhood, unity, and equality of human rights. In addition, it indicates advanced Uranian thinking and methodology. Pisces rising reveals a mystical soul, a visionary prophet, with a sensitivity to the masses. (Using the esoteric approach to Carol's chart, the rising sign indicates these qualities will be used in her life work.)

The planet Uranus, the awakener, is the exoteric ruler of her Aquarian sun. Found in the 2nd house of spiritual and mundane resources and values brought in from a previous life time, it will be naturally expressed as an inherited gift. Uranus suggests her service will bring enlightenment to groups of people. By her own presence and radiance, she will reflect and ignite the spiritual, creative potential within those around her, intensifying their own spiritual resources. For is it not true, the saying, "What you see in others is a reflection of your own self"?

Jupiter, the planet of philosophy, religion, and teaching, is found in the 8th house of mystery, death, and transformation in Pluto's sign of Scorpio. This says Carol has an ability to teach the wisdom teachings, through philosophy and religion. It will bring her into contact with death on a personal and impersonal level which can serve to transform her own life and the lives of others.

The sun is the exoteric and esoteric ruler of her Leo moon, found in the 11th house of groups and associations. Since the moon rules the immediate past, it suggests the preparation of her last life (the moon) was for the service she was to give in this life through her heart center, which could be expressed through spiritual healing, informing the public, and teaching groups. To bring an understanding of Aquarian community through selfless living and dedication to a higher plan for humanity would be one of her 11th-house dreams.

Neptune, the planet of sacrifice, mysticism, and striving toward a closer union with the Divine, is the exoteric ruler of Pisces, in her 7th house of relationships and marriage. This suggests a life of sacrifice with a commitment to a relationship with others, to the building of a spiritual community, to form a contract between herself and the life mission (the rising sign) which would mean sacrifice to physical and social pleasures. It reveals there can be much sacrifice and sorrow in the marriage experience.

Pluto, the planet of power, death, and transformation, is the esoteric ruler of Pisces, her rising sign, found in the 5th house of love, children, and creativity. It implies released power which will give birth to creative ideas, children, literature, art, or culture. Pluto's contact to Carol's Aquarian sun, found nestled between the axis of the 5th and 11th houses, shows love will be given, received, and taken away. This experience of spiritual testing can bring a kind of death to the personality and ego (the sun) to expand her mission for the upliftment of others. Pluto is in the sign of Cancer, the energy of one's personal foundation, both spiritual and mundane, and Pluto will bring cycles of experience which will strengthen and resolve any past life (the moon rules Cancer) karmic errors, to allow advancement in this life, enabling her to construct higher levels of consciousness and build a spiritual will.

The axis of the 5th/11th houses is further emphasized through the prenatal solar and lunar eclipses. January 5, 1958, a solar eclipse occurred in 13 degrees of Capricorn in the 11th house, while a prenatal lunar eclipse occurred January 19, 1958, at 28 degrees of Cancer in the 5th house of love, children, and creativity, conjoining Pluto, the planet of death and transformation. Through the progressive cycles of planetary energies, this suggests that much attention will be given in the departments of groups, associations, love, creativity, and death. You will see the importance of the prenatal solar eclipse in the near-death event chart.

Finally, returning to Pluto, notice the tension contact that planet makes to Mars, forming, in astronomical language, an applying square of 83 degrees. My own experience has seen these powerful tension aspects in the charts of very creative and spiritually advanced people.

Older astrology books seem to see the square aspect in a way which would scare most of us, giving a sense of defeat. Yet, as the world and humanity evolve, astrology expands as well in its breadth and depth. So, this planetary contact releases great power to develop spiritual will and higher states of awareness through intense trials and near-death experiences. Mars, the planet of personal drives and ambitions, is in the sign of balance and justice. This can be seen as cause and effect, or karma, the sign of Libra.

Moving into the first event chart—the near-death experience/exchange chart, taking place on November 1, 1958, at 7:20 A.M. EST in Clearwater, Florida—I have used for my interpretation the secondary progression for that data and the transiting event chart (No. 3).

At first glance, I observe the heavy emphasis of transiting planets in the 8th house. This suggests an experience which would have a major transforming effect; any decision made during this time frame would be made from the very depths of her being.

The next point of interest is the progressed midheaven. The midheaven refers to experience which can bring great life changes, a point some astrologers refer to as destiny. Carol's natal midheaven is in the sign of aspiration, Sagittarius, to reach toward higher and greater goals through philosophical and spiritual striving. Its exoteric ruler is Jupiter (having a special relation as the esoteric ruler of the Aquarian sun), written about earlier in this commentary. The esoteric planetary ruler of Sagittarius is the Earth, emphasizing a one-pointed effort through an earthly mission, serving as an awakener for humanity, or as a Light Bearer, showing the way of the spiritual path to others through love and creative ideals (the Earth is in the 5th house). Sagittarius is the seeker of higher truths. The progressed midheaven for November 1 is found at 13 degrees of Capricorn at the exact point of the prenatal solar eclipse. This reveals the potential for a crisis which could have brought a change in her life and direction.

The progressed ascendant has moved to Mars-ruled Aries, the sign of the pioneer, the blazer of new paths and ideas. Mars is still in square aspect to Pluto, the energy of trials/testing and near-death

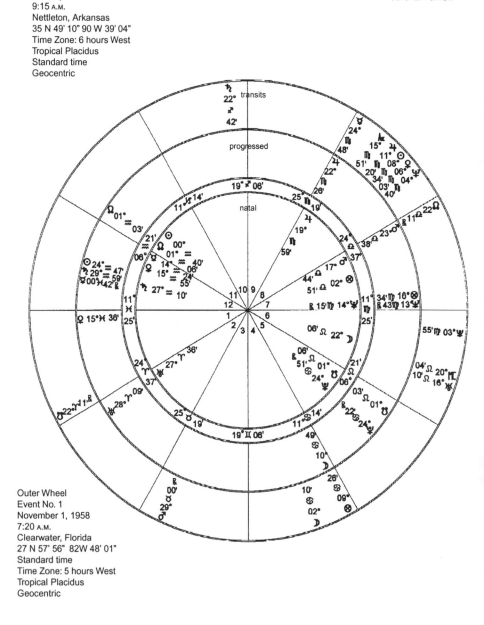

Inner Wheel:
NATAL CHART
Carol E. Parrish
January 21, 1935
9:15 A.M.
Nettleton, Arkansas
35 N 49' 10" 90 W 39' 04"
Time Zone: 6 hours West
Tropical Placidus
Standard time
Geocentric

Middle Wheel:
Day-for-a-Year Progressions for
November 1, 1958
7:20 A.M. GMT
Carol E. Parrish

Outer Wheel
Event No. 1
November 1, 1958
7:20 A.M.
Clearwater, Florida
27 N 57' 56" 82W 48' 01"
Standard time
Time Zone: 5 hours West
Tropical Placidus
Geocentric

Chart No. 3
Carol's Natal Chart Compared to the Exchange (Event Chart No. 1)
with Secondary Progressions for Nov. 1, 1958

experiences, and is "kicked" into action through the progressed sun, making a mathematical angle of 150 degrees, or the inconjunct to Pluto. This aspect is always seen in a death chart, physical or psychological, and indicates the opportunity for redirection or initiation into another state of consciousness, through crisis. Certainly there will be a change in the personality ego (the sun), which can reconstruct the ego's foundation (Pluto in Cancer). The progressed moon is in the sign of emotions and family relationship changes, and is ready to enter the 5th house of love and birth, bringing experience and change in that department.

That period of crisis began when transiting Mars (ruler of the progressed ascendant of self) formed the tension aspect to the planet of karma, fear, coldness, and depression (Saturn in the natal horoscope). Saturn, the planet some refer to as the "Grim Reaper," if handled properly during its tests, will lead to spiritual reward.

Transiting Mars, in September 1958, was at 29 degrees of Taurus, a position within the great cluster of fixed stars called Pleiades. In the wisdom teachings it is said to have a mythical relationship to the World Mother who gives birth to advanced beings. In mundane astrology the Pleiades is given a keyword of the "Weeping Sisters" and indicates an experience associated with sorrow. Transiting Mars is in the 3rd house of communication, the immediate environment, and relationships. Found there, it suggests that the mundane cause of the pain, depression, and sorrow came through an environmental relationship, perhaps within the family. When Mars turned retrograde, it moved away from Saturn, leaving Carol in a state of preparation for decisions about her life. On November 1 it moved back to its direct contact to progressed Saturn, which brought the clinical death, separation of the soul from the physical body, allowing for the change of consciousness.

Let us now look at the contacts the progressed and transiting planets were making to the natal midpoints (a so-called half-sums) which further support the near-death experience. Midpoints are marked by the half-way positions in the zodiac between two points, or planets. They further support and synthesize the previously given conclusions.

Looking first to the transiting planets, the transit moon in opposition to the natal midpoint of Venus/Jupiter indicates the event saw the birth of a child, as does the transiting sun in square aspect to the midpoint of Jupiter/Uranus. Transit Mercury opposing the midpoint of the natal moon/Saturn suggests—as so many other of the midpoint contacts (which I will not point out for the sake of space, time, and repetition)—thoughts of separation and taking leave of this physical incarnation (body). Transiting Neptune (ruler of the natal ascendant and self) is in conjunction to the natal midpoint of Mars/Jupiter and shows an environmental relationship which seems fruitless or deceptive in some way. Mars, the planet of surgery, and Neptune, the planet that mundanely refers to drugs and poison, point out a problematic experience dealing with surgery, connected in some way with drugs or anaesthesia. Transiting Pluto touches off a square to the natal midpoint of Jupiter and midheaven, indicating a great life and directional change.

The secondary progressions of the sun square to the natal midpoint of moon/Saturn again show separation and intense personal trauma and pain. Perhaps this would indicate a death wish. The progressed ascendant squares the natal midpoint of Mars/Uranus, which indicates a personal upset, and surgery. At the same time, the progressed ascendant squares the natal midpoint of Saturn and the midheaven, bringing with it the potential for a separation from others, sorrow, and life changes.

Finally, the transiting vertex point which deals with life circumstances and relationships is in 13 degrees of Cancer, with the antivertex point conjoining the prenatal solar eclipse of 13 degrees of Capricorn, conjunct progressed midheaven. This certainly promises life changes. The vertex point conjoins the fixed star of Sirius, which the wisdom teachings say has a connection with the spiritual hierarchy. This can suggest through critical circumstances a crisis emerged, which may have released the present personality to allow for the exchange with an advanced consciousness which would carry on the Earthly life mission.

Event Chart No. 2, which we have called the Blessing Chart, portrays the event in Haldwani, India. Carol's natal horoscope was advanced by secondary progression for October 9, 1980, with the transits set for 5:50 A.M. India time in Haldwani, 79°31' East, and 29°13' North, latitude (Chart No. 4).

Jupiter and Sagittarius, with their great expansive energies, rule foreign travel and spiritual pilgrimage. This cycle may witness a reaching out to explore new ideas and new meanings of life, a desire to gain new knowledge and wisdom. If accomplished, a new sense of personal integration will be shared with others.

In Carol's natal horoscope, Sagittarius is found at the highest point in the chart at the midheaven. When touched by cycles of progression, this "touch of destiny" can bring experiences which will animate life changes. On October 9, the transiting planet Neptune in Sagittarius was conjoining the midheaven, bringing an urge to seek the divine, a sense of holiness and changing spiritual values, as well as establishing new spiritual contacts and feelings of exaltation. The aura of the whole Neptunian contact gives a sense of divine direction, traveling in spirit or physically to the "holy city" or temple. An increase in High Self perception and intuition is very likely. The challenge is to integrate all mystical, spiritual, and physical experiences on an Earthly level, such as the architect who puts his visions on paper and then must transfer them into form. Neptune experiences can remain a cloudy illusion or even a glamour if not treated practically.

Jupiter is transiting the 7th house of marriage, partnerships, and confrontations or encounters with others. When Jupiter transits this house, it often finds the native making a contact with a spiritual teacher (also true of the 5th house). Transit Jupiter is making a contact with the midpoints of moon/Saturn and sun/Neptune. This indicates a difficult journey, a spiritual blessing, and/or a point of achievement, spiritually or mundanely. Transiting Jupiter also contacts the midpoint of the moon's node/Neptune, indicating an occult meeting with one who can have a transforming effect on Carol, one who will reflect her own great spiritual beauty. This contact would be karmic in nature, of positive expression, and likely to be repeated in some manner in her next incarnation.

Inner Wheel:
NATAL CHART
Carol E. Parrish
January 21, 1935
9:15 A.M.
Nettleton, Arkansas
35 N 49' 10" 90 W 39' 04"
Standard time
Time Zone: 6 hours West
Tropical Placidus
Geocentric

Middle Wheel:
Day-for-a-Year Progressions for October 9, 1980
5:50 A.M.
GMT
Carol E. Parrish

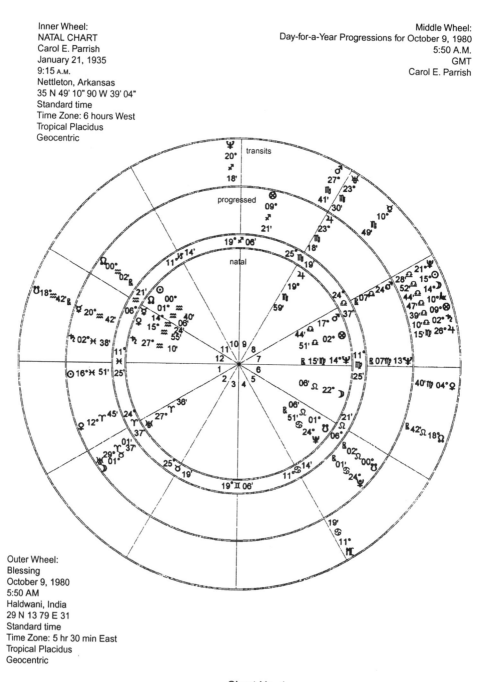

Outer Wheel:
Blessing
October 9, 1980
5:50 AM
Haldwani, India
29 N 13 79 E 31
Standard time
Time Zone: 5 hr 30 min East
Tropical Placidus
Geocentric

Chart No. 4
Carol's Natal Chart compared to the Blessing (Event Chart No. 2)
with Secondary Progressions for October 9, 1980

A critical contact is made with transiting Uranus, ruler of Carol's birth sun (Aquarius). Transiting Uranus is in conjunct to secondary progressed Jupiter (co-ruler of the rising sign) and is approaching a 90° angle (square) to her natal Saturn. This critical contact can bring opportunity for a spiritual awakening or blessing, which breaks through the karmic bonds of a past life, releasing her to face the future with new ideas and visions and to expand horizons for humanity in a selfless manner.

Saturn in Carol's natal 12th house at birth suggests she brought in subconscious feelings of personal fear, inadequacy about herself, feelings of oppression, bringing a strong need for solitude or at least a strong sense of being alone. If she developed her spiritual inclination and sense of religious values (12th house), it would likely see a change, or at least a turning point, between the ages of 26 and 29. The blessing from Babaji may possibly have released the balance of that karmic bondage.

The secondary progressed moon had been in a separating square to Carol's natal sun since August of 1980. This cycle suggests stressful challenges dealing with past, present, and future. Children, family, love ties, and personal dreams are likely to be involved. These experiences would confront Carol's basic spiritual and moral fibers, causing her to pull on all past resources for balance. Her challenge would be to remain centered and keep her attention on the future while emotionally uprooting events tear at her foundation and values. (During this period, Carol's daughter and granddaughter made their physical transition and moved to a higher state of consciousness.)

During the following six months, two more family members unexpectedly lost their lives in separate automobile accidents. Thus, four family members made their transitions in less than one year.

At the time, transiting Uranus was square to her natal Leo moon, a cycle which often sees swift and unexpected changes, profound emotional upheaval, a releasing of loved ones, friends, and groups. (Astrologers, note: moon-ruled Cancer located on the 5th house of children indicates this event likely would involve love relationships and offspring.)

Finally, the secondary sun has progressed to 16° 51' of Pisces. In 1975 and 1976, the progressed sun had crossed her rising sign bringing about experiences which could have put her into the beginning phases of her life's work, the development stage. On the day of Carol's blessing with Babaji in 1980, the progressed sun made a contact with the midpoint of Venus/Mars, bringing about opportunity for a spiritual or physical marriage, perhaps the mystical marriage, union of personality and soul.

The degree symbol for her progressed sun, according to Isidore Kozminsky: "Under the influence of the Sun. A gaudily dressed officer holding aloft a spear of gold. Denotes one of magnetic force, patience, and determination who wins his way by sacrifice of self for the sake of his ambition and who will never rest until he has achieved his purpose. He is identified with a great cause or a great production, spreading knowledge or giving pleasure. It is a symbol of Announcement."[5]
—Joleen Ayres DuBois[6]

Sabian Symbol Data

The method of Sabian Symbols appoints a visionary value to each of the degrees of the zodiac. To study a chart one researches the significant degrees (planet placement, etc.) and reads the story being woven by the dramas revealed. The method became increasingly popular as an appreciation of the work of Carl Jung grew. The symbols are often used in terms of contemporary psychology, philosophy, and astrology.

Judy Goodwin comments:

To see the significance of events, I use the Sabian Symbols (SS), reflecting clairvoyant Elsie Wheeler's visions on the meanings of the 360 degrees of the zodiac. Dane Rudhyar's *An Astrological Mandala*[7] is my source for synthesizing the symbology in light of planetary interaction.

The SS for the ascendant of Carol's near-death chart (not shown), 28° Scorpio, is "an Indian Squaw pleading to the chief for the lives of her children" (Rudhyar's p. 209), symbolic of her learning that she had much work still to do on Earth, including family responsibilities, and so must return. The Scorpio energies of this chart work through

Pluto in Virgo, for which the symbolic reading, "Black and white children play together happily" (p. 152), shows that her work (Virgo) would be central to the transition into the humanitarianism of the Aquarian age. Viewing these Scorpio planets individually, we see this work required a period of transformation of faith (Neptune), values (Venus), will (Leo sun), philosophy (Jupiter), and consciousness (Mercury) which took twenty-two years, significant in light of the fact that numerologically Carol is on the 22 Life Path, that of the Master Builder. The natal moon is 22° Leo, and Saturn in the near-death chart is at 22° Sagittarius, promising 22 years in which to expand wisdom. When it was time for the next major step, the moments naturally had to stimulate one another astrologically and numerologically because the balance of the universe is measured by these sciences.

Both major angles, the midheaven (MC) and the ascendant of the near-death chart, were activated by the planets during the blessing. In addition to Mars crossing the ascendant, Venus was conjunct the MC at 4° Virgo, describing the public meeting with Babaji whose blessing revealed the further unfoldment of Carol's path and fulfilled the natal suggestion of the 12th house Aquarian Venus, the attraction of spiritual friends at public gatherings. The SS for this conjunction aptly describes not only the aim (MC) of the near-death chart but the result of the blessing: "A man becoming aware of nature spirits and normally unseen spiritual agencies" (p. 153). In the near-death chart Saturn crossing into the 11th, the house it co-rules with Uranus which is conjuncting Mercury, the messenger, describes the timing of a sudden change in the nature of Carol's perception of the karma of her near-death event. The SS for Saturn's placement at 2° Libra reflects this: "The dawn of a new day reveals everything changed" (p. 173).

The blessing chart's MC at 11° Cancer is exactly trine the near-death chart's Jupiter at 11° Scorpio, as well as the natal ascendant, with Jupiter, planet of growth and spiritual development, falling in the near-death chart's 10th house, a double statement of the aim of both events being the expansion of her spiritual career. The near-death occurred a month before Carol's Jupiter return, a time of philosophical new beginnings, and since the natal Jupiter is in Scorpio by house and sign, these fresh starts develop from crises. At 26° Virgo in the blessing chart, Jupiter is the focal point of a Yod, the "Finger of God" aspect, between natal Saturn and Uranus, rulers of the Aquarian sun, reinforcing the message that it was time for Carol to adjust her life once again so that another period of growth could unfold. A second Yod was formed by transit to the natal chart during the blessing, with the transiting sextile between Jupiter in Virgo and the Mars-Uranus conjunction in Scorpio quincunxing the natal 2nd house Uranus in Aries. This Yod triggered the many adjustments prefacing a new life with new values to establish for Carol and for those with whom she would come to work, live, learn, and grow.

Mars' 7th house placement and heavy Scorpio emphasis in the near-death chart show that the action would involve other people, which promise is fulfilled by the Libran cooperative emphasis of the blessing chart, and the fact that the two charts' Mars are in opposition, cooperating to tear down and rebuild as the Scorpio-Taurus polarity defines. The keynote of the blessing chart is "balanced action toward change" with the Libran sun, moon, and Pluto conjunction in the 1st house describing a change in conscious will (sun), emotions and home (moon) working together to transform her value system (2nd house), thinking (Mercury), friendship and group goals (Uranus), and desire to act (Mars). Pluto's exact conjunction to the Libran north node in the near-death chart unleashes the balancing intuition of the blessing, symbolized at 21 degrees by "a child giving birds a drink at a fountain," which Rudhyar further defines as "a spontaneous naive rapport at the spiritual level of pure feeling" (p. 186). Note that the north node in both event charts, as in the natal chart, is in the 11th house, domain of the Aquarian age.

The SS for the MC of the blessing chart describes the aim of that moment: "A Chinese woman nursing a baby whose aura reveals him to be the reincarnation of a great teacher" (p. 117). The keynote is "revelation," according to Rudhyar. Thus, in that moment, Babaji nurtured the unfoldment of a new direction for Carol as a messenger, builder, and healer.

Carol's light experience remains a stable memory and source of inspiration as Neptune, planet of visions, is symbolized: "A massive rocky shore resists the pounding of the sea" (p. 194). Through its

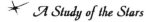

conjunction to Venus, SS "deep divers" (p. 195), it led her through an in-depth study of human nature and causality until her will, reflected by the sun, became motivated by the desire to regenerate through healing—SS, "a dentist at work" (p. 197). Neptune crossed her natal MC during the blessing to announce that the period of study had culminated and it was time for Carol and her partners (natal Neptune in the 7th house) to make the move that Saturn, natural ruler of the MC, promised from its 1st house position in the near-death chart: "A group of immigrants as they fulfill the requirements of entrance into a new country" (p. 223). Thus the chosen karmic task is to guide people into a new stage of spiritual experience, further symbolized by Uranus in the 9th house of the near-death chart, SS, "A volunteer church choir singing religious hymns," which is where Carol's growth has led her ever since!

Although my SS focus was on the two individual event charts, the significance of the natal transits and progressions deserves an essay in itself. But the correlation between Carol being on the 22 Life Path and there having been 22 years between the two individual events which most drastically changed her life was such a thought-provoking tribute to the logical order of the universe that I could not resist researching them in detail.

—Judy Goodwin[8]

Each of these astrologers continues to be interested in clues as to the identification of walk-ins. If you have information to share, please write:

Betty Carper, Ph.D.
103 Summit Ridge Dr.
Tahlequah, OK 74464
Astrological chart interpretations and research, 30 years. Graduate Sancta Sophia Seminary: Teacher of Esoteric Philosophy, 1981; Doctor of Philosophy of Religious Studies, 1993.

Barbara A. Everett
7909 218th St. SW #4
Edmonds, WA 98026
Ordained minister, and graduate of Sancta Sophia Seminary, Barbara has studied and taught in the spiritual field for over 20 years, and is a member of the American Numerology Association.

Joleen Ayres DuBois
543 Eastwood Dr.
Prescott, AZ 86303
Director and founder of the Association for White Mountain. Member of the American Federation of Astrologers, member of the research division of the AFA, member of the Agni Yoga Society, member of the Planetary Citizens.

Judy Goodwin
914 Collier Road NW #H-4
Atlanta, GA 30318
International Society for Astrological Research; Aquarius Workshops, Inc.; Association for Research and Enlightenment.

Endnotes

Chapter 1 — The Exchange
1. Ruth Montgomery, *Strangers Among Us* (New York: Fawcett Crest, 1979).
2. Vera Stanley Alder, *Initiation of the World* (New York: Samuel Weiser, 1973).
3. Ibid.

Chapter 2 — When the Student Is Ready
1. Thomas à Kempis, *The Imitation of Christ* (New York: Doubleday, 1989).
2. Torkom Saraydarian, *Symphony of the Zodiac* (Agoura, CA: Aquarian Education Group, 1980).
3. Parrish-Harra, Carol E., *Adventure in Meditation Vol. 3* (Tahlequah, OK: Sparrow Hawk Press, 1997) covers this subject thoroughly in lesson 6.

Chapter 5 — Teachers—Inner and Outer
1. Pages of Shustah, 901 17th Ave. N.E., St. Petersburg, FL 33704.
2. Silver Birch is the name of "the unfailingly wise and eloquent yet ever humble spirit guide of Hannen Swaffer's home circle. . . ." One of his teachings, "The Great spirit is infinite, and you are parts of the Great Spirit," was called "the Infallible Law." (*Silver Birch Anthology—Wisdom from the World Beyond*, William Naylor, ed. [London: Spiritualist Press, 1955]).

Chapter 6 — The Adventure Expands
1. Vera Stanley Alder, *The Finding of the Third Eye* (York Beach, ME: Samuel Weiser, Inc., 11th printing, 1981).
2. Carol E. Parrish-Harra, *The New Age Handbook on Death and Dying* (Tahlequah, OK: Sparrow Hawk Press, 1989).
3. Vera Stanley Alder, *Finding of the Third Eye*.
4. Torkom Saraydarian, *The Hierarchy and the Plan* (Sedona, AZ: Aquarian Educational Group, 1975, 2nd edition 1992).
5. H.Torkom Saraydarian, *The Science of Meditation* (Sedona, AZ: Aquarian Educational Group, 1974).
6. Many of the barriers that restrict our spiritual growth (and their remedies) are thoroughly addressed in the three volumes of *Adventure in Meditation—Spirituality for the 21st Century* by Carol E. Parrish-Harra (Tahlequah, OK: Sparrow Hawk Press, 1996-98).
7. Available to all, this meditation course does not require formal enrollment in the school to participate. Contact Sancta Sophia for more information: 800 386-7161 or e-mail: registrar@sanctasophia.org.

Chapter 7 — Mystique of India and the Ganges
1. I had been drawn to Roy after I learned he had studied with Yogananda. Once during my meditation, I had an image of a holy being in front of me. When I glimpsed him with my inner eye, I had been filled with peace. This great peace seemed like recognition and wholeness. It drew me into close communion and led me to study more about the Eastern way. I later found a copy of *Autobiogra-*

phy of a Yogi by Paramahansa Yogananda (Los Angeles: Self-Realization Fellowship, 1946). In it I found the picture of the being who had appeared to me. The book called him Babaji and introduced him to the Western world. I determined that if Roy was of that lineage, it would be to him I would go. I was initiated into Kriya and settled into my practice, but the breathing exercises caused me trouble. I found myself returning from unconsciousness time and time again. I finally gave up the technique but never the relationship to the tradition.

Chapter 8 — Blessing from Babaji

1. International Headquarters: Babaji Yoga Sangam Ashram, Tamil 18 Siddhas' Shrine, No. 13, AR. Street, Kanadukathan P.O., P.T.T. Dist., Tamil Nadu-823-103, India. Western Headquarters: Arizona Babaji Yoga Sangam, Rehabilitaiton Center, 5750 W. 8th Street, Yuma, AZ 85364.
2. Radhe Shyam, *I Am Harmony* (Crestone, CO: The Spanish Creek Press, 1989).
3. C. W. Leadbeater, *The Masters and the Path* (Adyar, Madras, India: Theosophical Publishing House. 1st printing, 1925; 10th reprint, 1973).
4. An Eastern term for the waiting feminine spiritual power; similar to holy spirit. Gurus direct their energy to devotees to cleanse and activate the spirit within as an aid to the devotee's life. An example: *Shakti* is what we call "slain in the spirit," or the leaping of the spirit from one to another under inspiration.
5. Radhe Shyam, *I Am Harmony*.
6. See chapter 21, Event Chart #2, Oct. 9, 1980, 5:50 A.M., Haldwani, India, p 253.

Chapter 9 — Satha Sai Baba

1. Today we hear of many upper-income families leaving behind fame, position, and benefits to move to a small town to recapture healthy family relationships and values. Friends and family are often shocked with such rejection of secular values. *Materialism* may be defined as a belief only in that which may be explored by the five physical senses.

Chapter 10 — The Lord Said, 'Go'

1. Bruce Clayton, *Life After Doomsday* (New York: The Dial Press, 1980).
2. Marilyn Ferguson, *Aquarian Conspiracy* (Los Angeles: J. P. Tarcher, Inc., 1980).

Chapter 11 — Creating Sparrow Hawk Village

1. "Ley" is an English term designating a track of energy that can be located and traced by dowsing. The theory is based on the idea of streams of energy running through the Earth and its etheric counterpart, similar to the concept of meridians within the body. *Ley*, in fact, means "energy line." "Ley line" is redundant, although that expression is used commonly.
2. Carol E. Parrish-Harra, *How to Use Sacred Space for Problem-Solving and Inner Guidance* (Tahlequah, OK: Sparrow Hawk Press, 1994).
3. Ibid.

Chapter 13 — Light for the New Millennium
1. Harold Balyoz, *Signs of Christ* (Los Angeles: Altai Publishers, 1979).

Chapter 16 — Living with the Message and the Messenger
1. Ralph Metzner, *The Unfolding Soul* (Nonata, CA: Origin Press, 1998).
2. May 25, 1982. Paper. "Precognitive and Visionary Aspects of Near Death Experiences," by Kenneth Ring, Ph.D., Professor of Psychology, University of Connecticut and President, IANDS. Delivered to the Academy of Religion and Psychical Research.

Chapter 17 — The Why and the How of Walk-ins
1. Larry Dossey, M.D., *Healing Words—The Power of Prayer and the Practice of Medicine* (New York: HarperCollins Publishers, 1993).
2. Larry Dossey, M.D., *Prayer Is Good Medicine—How to Reap the Healing Benefits of Prayer* (New York: HarperCollins Publishers, 1996).
3. See chapter 21: Astrological-Numerological Investigation in support of the walk-in experience.
4. Ibid.

Chapter 19 — Mine to Share
1. C. W. Leadbeater, *Masters and the Path.*
2. Brother Philip, *Secret of the Andes* (London: Neville Spearman Limited, 1961).

Chapter 20 — Walk-ins Address the Future
1. A. H. Maslow, "A Theory of Human Motivation," *Psychological Review* 50, 1943.
2. Tony Shearer, *Beneath the Moon and Under the Sun* (Albuquerque, NM: Sun Publishing Company, 1981).

Chapter 21 — A Study of the Stars
1. Helena P. Blavatsky, *The Secret Doctrine*, Vol. II (Adyar, India, Edition, 1938).
2. Alice A. Bailey, *Esoteric Astrology* (New York: Lucis Publishing Co., 1951).
3. Torkom Saraydarian, *Symphony of the Zodiac.*
4. I have used Neil F. Michelsen's Ephemeris and hand calculated the mathematics. The time and place of birth, the near-death experience, and the blessing in India were supplied by Carol.
5. Isidore Kozminsky, *Zodiacal Symbology and Its Planetary Power* (Tempe, AZ: A.F.A, n.d.).
6. I have used a TRS-80, model I computer, with the M-65 program, designed by Matrix software, to calculate the mathematics. The time and place of birth, along with the time and place of the near-death experience information and blessing in India were supplied by Carol.
7. Dane Rudhyar, *An Astrological Mandala* (New York: Vintage Books, 1973).
8. I used the Koch Table of Houses because, having studied both numerology and astrology, I find Koch's house system always best reiterates the astrological themes numerologically. I worked from the Tropical Zodiac and erected and interpolated the chart by hand.

Sancta Sophia Seminary
A Contemporary Mystery School

How It Came to Be

In 1982, Carol E. Parrish-Harra was revealed to the greater public by author Ruth Montgomery in the best-selling *Threshold to Tomorrow*. The book elaborated upon Carol's remarkable pychic and spiritual abilities, and it described her role as a messenger for the new age.

Carol already had moved the school she established in 1978 from Florida to the beautiful Ozark Mountains of eastern Oklahoma.

Today, in addition to her personal teaching of Sancta Sophia students, Carol is academic dean and coordinates seminary classes, several post-graduate programs, faculty, and advisors. She continues to minister and publish widely acclaimed books and audiocassette programs. She is a highly sought international speaker and world traveler, leading many pilgrimages to sacred places.

Spiritually Charged Location Enhances Growth

The magnificent, wooded, 400-acre mountaintop setting where Carol was inspired to build the seminary is also the location of Sparrow Hawk Village. This intentional spiritual community has an educational focus, providing a supportive atmosphere for the practice of ethical living. The village, established in 1981 in the foothills near Tahlequah, Oklahoma, by Carol, her husband, Charles C. Harra, and her friend, Rev. Grace B. Bradley, is a harmonious environment of fifty homes, office buildings and church. It has lovely gardens, good drinking water, and a sophisticated infrastructure. Villagers are self-supporting people who live, learn, meditate, and worship together. Although over half of the 168 potential lots have been sold, homes and home sites are still available.

The church sanctuary is centered on a vortex of special energies created by a star-shaped convergence of Earth ley lines. This creates a unique enclosure of spiritual energies which enhances the synergy of living, learning, and personal growth for every Sancta Sophia student. The village is a sacred space, helping those who visit to heal and to make their lives whole— holy. The spiritual energies create an environment for preparation in spiritual vocations.

Programs Create Personal Transformation
through Educational Preparation

A combination of off-campus retreats, home-study, and on-campus classes forms the basis of participation in both graduate and undergraduate studies. This integrative experience begins with a format of meaningful home study and techniques tailored to personal goals. The focal point of every student's program is a unique transformational process guided by master teacher Dean Parrish. Individually assigned advisors become month-by-month spiritual mentors, communicating by telephone sessions or personal meetings, or electronic or postal mail. The entire process catalyzes during periodic class weeks when students come to study and enjoy the unique atmosphere of the courses and campus at Sparrow Hawk Village.

The distinctive process of home study, meditation, spiritual guidance, and periodic classes at the village produces students capable of planetary service on one of several paths. The basic seminary program, Foundations of Spirituality, prepares individuals for lay ministry certification called Practitioner. From here one proceeds to consider a career as a Wellness Guide or to enter a combined master's degree program that includes certification as a Teacher of Esoteric Philosophy or ordination through Light of Christ Community Church. Teachers of Esoteric Philosophy become educators for the new paradigms of spirituality now emerging around the planet, and ordination prepares ministers in Esoteric Christianity to bring the true Ageless Wisdom into metaphysical and mainstream settings. Ordinations are endorsed by the International Council of Community Churches. For students with the requisite background, commitment, and high creativity, individually designed programs can lead to one of three doctoral degrees. All programs are moderate in cost.

If you are interested in more information, we invite you to call **800 386-7161,** e-mail the Registrar at **registrar@sanctasophia.org** or write to Sancta Sophia Seminary, 11 Summit Ridge Drive, Tahlequah, Oklahoma 74464.

Keep informed of Sancta Sophia events or contact the affiliated center, church, or class nearest you online at
www.sanctasophia.org

Other books by

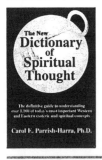

Carol E. Parrish-Harra

The Aquarian Rosary—Reviving the Art of Mantra Yoga

Rev. Carol E. Parrish-Harra, Ph.D

These invocations and rituals of great spiritual power can be used easily by large numbers of people to help guide humanity through the approaching period of global transition. Speaking these holy mantras will invoke the power of Good into each life, uplift and stimulate open minds, and build a heart center than can utilize the Lots Of Vital Energies (LOVE) of the unfolding human soul.

The Aquarian Rosary is an adaptation of the traditional Roman Catholic rosary for the new era that embraces the divine feminine aspect of God. Invoking the Mother of the World through devotion to Mary brings forth this feminine, receptive, and nurturing energy to help balance the present masculine aggressive energy in ourselves and society.

136 pp / trade paper / ISBN 0-945027-09-5/ $9.95

The Book of Rituals
Personal and Planetary Transformation

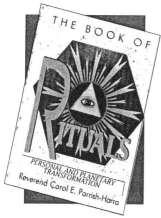

Rev. Carol E. Parrish-Harra, Ph.D

This highly original work presents specific rituals involving prayer, song, chanting, dance, and meditation for each full moon period and for major festivals.

You will benefit from the author's vast knowledge of astrology as you read about your specific sun sign and the celestial hierarchy associated with it. The author explains the challenges you face on your spiritual path and gives practical advice on how to open your physical and nonphysical senses so that you can effectively utilize the many subtle energies of the universe.

280pp / trade paper / ISBN 0-945027-10-9 / $23.95

These and other books are available at your local bookstore or the Village Bookstore, 1 800 386-7161. Book reviews are available on our web site: www.sanctasophia.org.

Books and Tapes for Spiritual Growth

Please send the following books:

Quantity   Price each   Totals

_____ **Adventure in Meditation—Spirituality for the 21st Century, Vols. I, II, or III** $17.95 each   _____
Experience the fulfillment of meditation, by Carol E. Parrish-Harra, Ph.D.

_____ **Adventure in Meditation—Spirituality for the 21st Century, 3-volume set** $49.95   _____
Complete set of volumes 1, 2, and 3, by Carol E. Parrish-Harra, Ph.D.

_____ **The New Dictionary of Spiritual Thought**—*1,100 definitions of esoteric and spiritual concepts, by Carol E. Parrish-Harra, Ph.D.* $19.95   _____

_____ **The Mystical Magical Marvelous World of Dreams**—*a concise guide to dream interpretation, by Wilda B. Tanner* $17.95   _____

_____ **The Book of Rituals**—*to create personal and planetary transformation, by Carol E. Parrish-Harra, Ph.D.* $23.95   _____

_____ **The New Age Handbook on Death and Dying**—*excellent resource for comfort & guidance, by Carol E. Parrish-Harra* $10.95   _____

_____ **The Gateway of Liberation**—*classic writings on the Ageless Wisdom by Mary Gray* $ 9.95   _____

_____ **Genesis: Journey into Light**—*an esoteric interpretation, by Rev. Sarah Leigh Brown* $ 7.95   _____

_____ **Synpan: Inside the Wellness Universe**—*A new paradigm of health, wealth, & spirituality, by George Charles Pappas* $19.95   _____

_____ **The Aquarian Rosary**—*stimulate heart & mind to greater love by Carol E. Parrish-Harra, Ph.D. (note tapes below)* $ 9.95   _____

_____ **Reflections**—*an anthology of Dr. Parrish's poetic journal entries spanning three decades, compiled by Maggie Webb-Adams, D.Min.* $10.95   _____

BOOK TOTAL _____

Please send the following teaching tapes by Carol E. Parrish-Harra:

Adventure in Awareness—Ageless Wisdom concepts & teachings:

___ I - Breadth of Esoteric Teachings (12 90-min. tapes)	$60.00	___	___ Healing (6 tapes) *realize your own healing potential & how to use it*	$30.00	
___ II - Awakening Our Inner Consciousness (12 90-min. tapes)	$60.00	___	___ New Age Christianity *discover the Christ-Within (6 tapes)*	$30.00	
___ III - Toward Deeper Self-Realization (12 90-min. tapes)	$60.00	___	___ Experience New Dimensions *techniques for psychic development (6 tapes)*	$35.00	___
___ Meditation Plus *12 meditation techniques for spiritual growth (6 tapes)*	$30.00		___ The Aquarian Rosary *stimulate heart & mind to greater love (2 tapes)*	$12.95	
___ Coming to the Sunrise *advanced meditation for self-purification (4 tapes)*	$25.00		___ Meditation & Group Work *for the 21st Century (2 tapes)*	$15.95	
___ Energy Ecstasy *(book used with "Sunrise" tapes)*	$14.95	___	___ Reincarnation & Karma (2 tapes)	$15.95	___

TAPE TOTAL _____

☐ I am interested in knowing more about **Sancta Sophia Seminary**. Please send additional information.

SUBTOTAL _____

Shipping and Handling ($2.75 first item, $1 each additional) _____

Payment by: ☐ Check   ☐ Visa   ☐ Master Card   ☐ Discover   **TOTAL ENCLOSED** _____

Name _____ Daytime Phone _____

Address _____

Card# _____ Exp. Date _____ Signature _____

VILLAGE BOOKSTORE
22 Summit Ridge Drive • Tahlequah, OK 74464
call 800 386-7161 *(Please have your credit card ready)*
www.sanctasophia.org